LEARNING
HOW TO LEARN

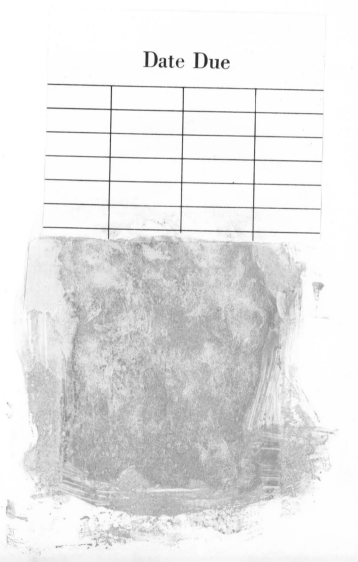

LEARNING
HOW TO LEARN

The English Primary School
and American Education

Robert J. Fisher

EASTERN MICHIGAN UNIVERSITY

Harcourt Brace Jovanovich, Inc.

New York   Chicago   San Francisco   Atlanta

PHOTOGRAPH CREDITS

Chapter 1: Courtesy of the Devon County Council, Exeter, England
Chapter 3: *The Times*, London
Chapter 5: Martin S. Cohen
Chapter 6: Courtesy of the Central Office of Information/British Information
Services
Chapter 8: *The Times*, London
Chapter 10: *The Times*, London
Chapter 12: Martin S. Cohen

Library of Congress Catalog Card Number: 72-78021
ISBN: 0-15-550396-0

Printed in the United States of America

To R O B I N *and* D A V I D, *who learned
about learning in English primary schools.*

Preface

The following conversation was overheard in the senior common room at Berkshire College of Education near Reading, England:

"The Americans have invented a name for us. We advocate *open* education. We are opening the schools, and our children are free from unnecessary restraints."

"So that is what we have been about these past several years?"

"Yes, we are engaged in a great experiment. Our children are learning to be free because our schools are open wide."

"If the teachers, too, are free and openly accessible, why do we work so hard? All we need do is open the doors and the children should be able to come and go as they please."

"It is a good thing that we have such close links with the Americans. Otherwise we might never find out what we are doing."

With good-natured irony, the last remark was directed toward me, then spending the first of two years at the college. This book developed from contacts and visits made during those two years. It is a reflection of the insights gained from teaching classes for prospective primary teachers, accompanying prospective teachers into classrooms for related school experience, supervising practice teachers, holding tutorials, and taking part in college social life. In addition, it incorporates the reflections generated during approximately one hundred interviews with English college and university lecturers, chief education officers, primary school advisers, English college students, and American exchange students and professors.

Although this book does not claim to contribute a great deal to original cross-cultural research, it does reflect cross-cultural analysis. The impressions may be subjective, but the references point to the available scholarship in the professional literature. Anecdotal descriptions of particular situations are avoided; instead, generalizations are drawn from a variety of sources. Comments and comparisons have been confirmed by a dozen English colleagues who have read chapters with care, not only eliminating as too flippant a number of American witticisms and colloquial expressions, but also suggesting more profound changes in tone, emphasis, and factual treatment. Whatever balance the book retains is due to the critical influence of these friends and colleagues.

For commenting on sections of the book I would like to thank Fannie Shaftel of Stanford University and the following members of the Berkshire College Education Department: Monica Baldwin, Norman Morris, Alan Paisey, Sheila Quarrell, Mike Reading, Ann Reilly, Audrey Wait, Les H. Weeks, and Keith Willis. My thanks go too to Bill Baldwin of the Berkshire College Mathematics Department; to Martin S. Cohen of the Pennsylvania Advancement School; to Geoff Ivimey of the London Institute of Education; to Frank Plimmer, head teacher of the Great Hollands Junior School, Bracknell; and to Tony Rawlings, president of the Berkshire College Student Union. I am greatly indebted to Sheila Hopton, who served as my secretary for two years and typed innumerable revisions of the manuscript. Finally, I would like to thank the principal, James Porter, and the rest of the staff and student body of Berkshire College of Education, who, through the exchange program with Eastern Michigan University, have since 1968 patiently withstood the impertinence of American exchange students and professors.

Robert J. Fisher

Contents

Contents xi

1

American Failures and English Successes

Generations of Americans have clung to the belief that the value of education is self-evident. The more educated the populace, the sooner intolerance and poverty will be reduced. The more years a person remains at school, the better his life chances. The more money voted to finance public schools, the better the local community. But positivism is on the wane as social problems become worse; the young opt out of established traditions, and school taxes keep rising with little to show for them. As a result there is a crisis in public education, and it reflects grave doubts and fears that the nation lacks the will or the capacity to extricate itself from international and domestic conflicts.

THE CRISIS IN AMERICAN EDUCATION

The turbulence of the times poses acute problems for education, of which five have become crucial.

1. Racial tensions have hastened the flight of whites to the suburbs and to private schools, leaving vast metropolitan districts largely the province of the blacks, the poor, and the alienated.

1

2. Bureaucratic inflexibility stifles initiative and robs creative teachers of their professional dignity. Centralized decision-making denies the independence of individual schools.

3. Hemmed in by a multitude of regulations, smothered by textbooks, guides, teaching packages, manuals, workbooks, and standardized tests, teachers lose interest in creative self-determination and settle into a more comfortable conformity.

4. The inadequate basis for school financing, pegged to assessed valuation of property and voter resistance to further tax assessments and bond issues, restricts the allocation of limited funds.

5. Teacher education has become increasingly dysfunctional. It poorly equips prospective teachers to face demands in conventional, middle-class, suburban schools; it is almost totally inappropriate for schools in central-city neighborhoods.

These problems have eroded public confidence in the power of education. School districts have come under attack from right-wing pressure groups, taxpayers' associations, and supporters of parochial schools, who resent paying taxes to support public schools that their children do not attend. Even liberal and radical parents have become disgusted with the bureaucracy, conformity, mediocrity, and political interference so often associated with city school systems.

Experienced teachers, already harassed by deteriorating conditions, are stunned by the loss of public confidence. They respond by losing interest in curriculum improvement and become overly concerned with negotiations over salaries and working conditions. The job market is tightening as budgets are cut and increasing numbers of college graduates compete for openings. Meanwhile, many intelligent university students have abandoned the prospect of teaching as a challenging career, or they have joined the growing movement for radical, independent education.

There is no simple formula to "save" the public schools—from their enemies or well-intentioned former friends, from the tired professionals or the interfering laymen, or from the alienated who have written them off as hopeless. And one predominant consideration rules many alternatives out of the question: good education costs a good deal of money. Only government units backed by massive public expenditures can build proper buildings, purchase the necessary equipment, pay teachers any sort of decent salary, and encourage curriculum improvement on a sufficiently wide scale.

But the public schools are worth saving. They alone have a broad enough base to educate large segments of the working classes for social mobility. They continue to offer the hope for a semblance of social integration among increasingly antagonistic groups, for public schools remain among the few American institutions that endorse cultural pluralism. They have the potential to bring the young together for contacts that cut across racial, ethnic, religious, and socioeconomic distinctions. That schools today are less socially integrated than they were fifty years ago constitutes an alarming corollary of the increasing segregation of the population along racial, class, and religious lines.

The crisis has called forth a multitude of responses—increased expenditures, proposals for curriculum reform, new teaching strategies, financial incentives from government units. Despite these attempts to influence the public school system, American teachers have not changed much. Problems are becoming more acute, but nothing very different is happening in the classrooms. Observers would find it hard to identify any profound changes that have been widely instituted in American elementary schools over the past twenty years. Although schools should not be expected to tackle all the pressing concerns of American society, they should at least respond with some degree of effectiveness to persistent internal problems.

ENGLISH PRIMARY EDUCATION

In contrast to American inertia, over the past twenty years English primary schools* have changed markedly, and the rate of change appears to be accelerating. While the American public expresses frustration, doubt, and confusion, the British are expressing increasing confidence in their state primary schools. More and more middle-class parents are sending children to state-maintained or state-aided primary schools, while at the same time many independent preparatory schools may be beginning to suffer from declining enrollments (Glennerster and Wilson, 1970).

English schools have no shortage of problems. Some of the same conditions that have eroded public confidence in the Ameri-

* Primary schools in England include nursery schools (three- to five-year-olds), infant schools (five- to seven-year-olds), and junior schools (seven- to eleven-year-olds). The secondary schools serve eleven- to eighteen-year-olds.

can educational system plague English schools as well. Primary schools are provided a low level of financial support. Schools are ridden with class bias; they are slow to adapt to changing social patterns. No system of incentives or requirements impels in-service education of experienced teachers. Even so, the irritants that attenuate American confidence do not penetrate as deeply in England. School administrators in England are not as immobilized; head teachers, the equivalents of American principals, exert active leadership in the instructional program. Classroom teachers are not as discouraged; they carry out their responsibilities with self-respect. Teacher education is not as dysfunctional; colleges equip students with the skills to adapt to changing demands. The critical problems of racism, bureaucratic inflexibility, instructional conformity, and inappropriate teacher preparation that defy solution in American schools have not troubled England so intensely. Though financial support is even less adequate than in the United States, imaginative responses in England have developed in abundance.

Joseph Featherstone first intimated that English developments might intrigue Americans in a series of articles he wrote for the *New Republic* beginning in 1967 (Featherstone, 1967a, 1967b, 1967c, 1967d). This interest swelled with the astonishing popularity of Charles Silberman's report in 1970 documenting the now familiar crisis, in which he contrasted American rigidity and joylessness with English informality (Silberman, 1970). Professors and teachers have returned from England with glowing accounts (Rathbone, 1969; Barth and Rathbone, 1969; V. R. Rogers, 1970; Barth, 1969; Weber, 1971). Private schools especially organized to provide a greater degree of freedom for children (Hoffman and Tower, 1969), along with public schools at last awakening to the stagnation about them, have begun to look to England for a new model (Resnick, 1971; *Newsweek*, 1971).

This model presents at least three areas of sharp distinction from the American public school system—teacher preparation, curriculum control, and classroom freedom. The following discussion touches briefly on these differences; later chapters will develop them in detail.

Preparation for Teaching

Two years at a teacher-education institution in England have convinced this observer that the prospective elementary teacher in

America receives a decidedly inferior preparation to that provided students at Colleges of Education in England. Enrolled in a large and impersonal institution, the American receives only a smattering of vocational guidance, given at the wrong time and organized in the wrong way. Generally speaking, his courses lack challenge, rely on faulty motivation, are too segmented and too bookish, and often are largely irrelevant. Many required introductory courses are presented in mass lectures, and even the courses in the academic major seldom rise above the survey level. Because professional education courses are generally not given until the last few semesters, there are few opportunities to evaluate concepts through practice. After minimal exposure to the social and psychological foundations of education, some courses in teaching methods, and a period of student teaching that is often unrelated to what has gone before, a prospective teacher is routinely certified. Students complain that teacher education, divorced from the schools, without children, with few opportunities to test ideas in practice and few commonly agreed-on purposes, has little relevance to vocational demands.

Colleges of Education in England are much more clearly involved with vocational goals. Almost every prospective primary teacher attends a small, single-purpose institution in which the general direction and guiding aims are clear to students and staff alike. The three-year course schedules professional education from the very beginning, making possible a treatment in depth. Many opportunities to work with children are provided from the start, and at least three separate segments of full-time practice teaching are required over the three years. The tutorial method of instruction stimulates student participation and challenges powers of critical thinking. England may well shift teacher education from single-purpose to more multipurpose institutions and allow students to postpone the commitment to teaching until later in the course (Devlin, 1971; Church, 1971; Robinson, 1971; Burgess, 1971; James, 1972), but most of the characteristics of the Colleges of Education will probably be retained in the preparation of future primary school teachers (Hewett, 1970).

American students might well ask if English features cannot be replicated within subunits of American universities. At the very least they might demand that they be offered a more challenging, relevant education with frequent and realistic opportunities to apply what they are learning in school-based situations.

The beginning American teacher suffers a shock when he takes his first job. Too often he joins a school that is overly concerned with discipline, conformity, routinized instruction, competitive grading, and segmented learning. The pupils may either misbehave to test his authority or show passive disinterest to dampen his enthusiasm. If the prospective teacher is critical of prevailing school conditions, bureaucratic forces will diminish his reforming spirit. Too few American teachers believe that it is possible to beat the system, and of those who do believe it possible, too many are hesitant to try, for tenure provisions encourage caution. When he is alone in the classroom, the teacher often falls back on the only patterns he thinks he knows well—the teaching he observed when he was a student himself.

English probationary, or first-year, teachers have built their confidence in three different practice teaching locations. Throughout teaching practice they were offered specific help by classroom teachers, head teachers, and college tutors, who visited frequently and were regularly available at the college for consultation at the end of the school day.

Probationary teachers in England have a good chance of teaching at schools in which individualized learning, self-discipline, integrated content, flexible organization, concern for creativity, and independent initiative are encouraged. They are quick to recognize that teaching the class as a total group, whether from textbooks or teacher-dominated "class" discussions, is counter to developing trends.

Even though the American student may have had no direct contact with England, his imagination will be stirred by the contrasts presented in the following chapters. As he tries to visualize what teaching will be like, he need not feel disheartened by painful memories of his own schooling, by the irrelevance of most of his courses, or by the threat of what lies ahead. The prospective American teacher can come to realize that relaxed, informal schools are entirely possible, that showing respect for children need not be considered a sign of weakness, and that expressing pride in his work need not become a cue for cynical laughter.

Best of all, the beginning teacher is young enough, mobile enough, and perhaps solvent enough to visit England and see for himself. One by-product of studying the English system in a pre-

Learning How to Learn

service course is the impetus it might provide to visit English schools during June and July, when they are still open. Even more beneficial are the programs that allow American undergraduates to study abroad and participate directly in an English teacher-education institution (Fisher and Paisey, 1970).

Curriculum Control

When American teachers begin to comprehend more fully what is taken for granted by English teachers, they will demand some rather self-evident professional rights that they have been denied too long. Chief among these is the right to determine how they will direct their energies. This right is axiomatic in England, but in the United States curriculum control has yet to be turned over to those who do the teaching. Gaining control will involve a restructuring of relationships between professionals and school board members, a realignment of power within school bureaucracies, and a redefinition of the functions of the elementary school principal.

Later chapters develop comparisons more fully, but it might be well to highlight a few of the major differences between curriculum control in England and in America. In England, determination of the curriculum is delegated to the individual school; governing bodies seldom interfere, and few parents would dream of complaining to the school board or to the central administration. If parents do approach the head teacher, he does not relate to them as an appeasing public servant, fearful of arousing community dissatisfaction. School administrators at the national and local authority levels offer assistance to schools through advisory services, never through bureaucratic controls or the dictation of policies. Unlike the American elementary school principal, who, as an administrator, is too often seen by classroom teachers as a member of the enemy camp, the English head is a teacher among teachers. His preoccupation is with providing instructional leadership for the sake of the children. English classroom teachers determine their own instructional programs; they are the ones who make the ultimate decisions about what they have been hired to do with children.

Creative, imaginative, highly competent American teachers too often feel restrained by the systems in which they work. They are hampered by formal curriculum requirements, boxed in by required textbooks, abandoned by immobilized leadership, and harassed by the public. Yet American teachers are resilient; many of them flock to curriculum courses to seek more knowledge about new materials, promising methods, and recent trends. No longer so concerned merely with survival, experienced teachers can concentrate their attention on ways to improve teaching effectiveness. These teachers want to arm themselves with a convincing defense against the lock-step rigidities of graded schools.

Classroom Freedom

Creative American teachers should gain encouragement as they become familiar with current developments in English primary schools. A number of practices commonly found in England are relatively rare in the United States. These include flexible grouping practices, considerable emphasis on the creative arts, informality in room arrangements, open access to materials, high standards in the exhibition of finished work, and the central importance of pupil self-direction. English primary schools have been overcoming rigidity by, among other things, de-emphasizing textbooks, disbanding reading groups, discouraging grouping by ability, putting aside mass teaching, decreasing competition, relaxing discipline, and opening the watertight compartments of the curriculum. Schools have been reorganized to encourage greater flexibility through team teaching, open-planned buildings, and family grouping arrangements.

A good deal of attention is devoted in later chapters to the ways in which English teachers relate to others, including the children, their colleagues, and the public. Toward the children, most English teachers show more genuine respect than do many American teachers. They treat children as individuals, respect their plans and ideas, listen to them with careful attention, modify expectations while helping to raise levels of aspiration and performance gradually. With their colleagues, English teachers are inclined to work more cooperatively, sharing facilities, materials, and ideas. (In small primary schools, of course, staff members cannot avoid face-to-face contacts.) Toward the parents, English teachers do not express the hostility or fear so often overheard in American staff rooms. The school seldom becomes a battleground for conflicting community forces. Relations with the public are anchored in a clear distinction between the functions to be performed by the home and by the school.

In England it becomes possible to accomplish what American school officials find it almost inconceivable to mention. English teachers make changes without first seeking "community approval." English parents are as unfamiliar with current changes as American parents are; they are just as suspicious of the unfamiliar and can hardly be expected to heartily endorse that which they do not fully comprehend. But no public relations program has been launched to keep the parents happy. Any parent who has a question or a complaint knows that he can consult the head teacher. Heads are adept at pacifying parents individually, although they seem less secure when faced with the prospect of a large gathering; this is one reason that many remain chary of parent organizations. Nevertheless, some self-assured heads are willing to put up with P.T.A.'s, provided that the officers largely limit their business to raising extra money for the school. Despite increasing murmurs of middle-class dissatisfaction over home-school relationships (Goodacre, 1970) and strong pressures to encourage greater home-school cooperation (D.E.S., 1968; Douglas, 1970; C.A.S.E., 1970), no one is seriously suggesting that the balance be tipped in the American direction, where fear of parental disapproval blocks professional initiative.

Experienced American teachers can gather from this account that state-maintained schools need not become paralyzed by bureaucratic rigidity or fear of community backlash. English primary schools have been slowly but persistently changing over the years, with little resistance from the public and a great deal of support from governing bodies. And these changes are occurring not here and there in isolated, experimental schools, but in every conceivable locality in all parts of the country.

ON COMPARING ENGLISH AND AMERICAN SCHOOLS

Comparisons in education are always hazardous. Any observer is bound within his culture; he has great difficulty making subtle distinctions within a different tradition. Americans, waxing enthusiastic over appearances and taking slogans as serious descriptions of conditions, may easily overlook fundamental features of the English system. But despite incomplete perceptions, the cross-cultural perspective is valuable; by studying a contrasting system of education, one gains insight into one's own tradition.

Comparative education has been developing methodologies for analyzing specific problems with the cross-cultural perspective (Holmes, 1965; Kelsall and Kelsall, 1970a, 1970b; Lauwerys, 1969; E. J. King, 1966, 1970). This book is too subjective and too global to submit to the discipline of comparative education, but it remains comparative in a sense. English primary schools are described within the context of the author's long association with American elementary schools. The treatment in this book does not emphasize numerous American strengths, which should not be overlooked, despite the current fashion to condemn the shortcomings of American urban schools (Ornstein, 1971). Instead, the focus will be on England, concentrating on those aspects that have implications for the United States.

Similarities between schools inspired by the progressive education movement in the United States during the 1920's and 1930's and the state primary schools of England today come to mind. There is the same attention to individual differences, problem-solving procedures, children's interests, active investigation, project work, and integration of content. Progressive education flowered in a limited number of American university-sponsored laboratory schools, private schools, and suburban public schools serving upper-middle-class communities. These schools and English schools owe a common debt to John Dewey and other theoreticians of progressive education. One might ask if the English are simply forty years "behind" the United States and will eventually be engulfed by a content-dominated revolution (or counterrevolution). Although an English traditionalist backlash is possible, it is hardly likely. Progressive education in England is widely based in schools that serve a spectrum of social classes, it has developed slowly and steadily by modifying traditions, and it is buttressed by the experience of practicing teachers, heads, college lecturers, and government advisers.

American interest in English primary education is growing rapidly, but a few cautions must precede any detailed analysis. English schools cannot be uprooted and transplanted directly to a foreign soil, no matter how lavishly enriched the ground. And many features of English primary schools are so deeply rooted in tradition, so tightly interwoven with local educational history, so closely associated with commonly held attitudes of teachers, that transplanting them to America would not be a simple matter. Educators in the United States need not immediately establish new English-style primary schools nor need they completely reorganize existing school systems along English lines, intriguing as these possibilities appear to be. It would be more appropriate to modify English traditions and practices that suggest potential school reform in America within the American context.

In spite of economic and bureaucratic barriers, a two-way interchange of personnel is slowly increasing. Opportunities to take part in government-sponsored exchange teaching programs continue. Openings for American teachers exist in Department of Defense schools for American dependents in England. A number of summer-school courses for American teachers and undergraduates have been organized at British universities. Independent visits to schools are not difficult to arrange provided they are cleared as a matter of courtesy through Local Education Authority primary school advisers or Chief Education Officers. Teachers in England welcome Americans, and the children often encourage them to help, regarding them as additional teaching resources. Books and films about English schools whet the appetite, but the most memorable form of comparative study is not vicarious but direct experience.

2

Low-Keyed, Gradual Change

Suddenly, primary schools in England are being hailed around the world. This should come as a shock to those class-conscious Englishmen who have traditionally placed great stock in the elitist tradition of their famous independent public boarding schools. Visitors are not particularly interested in that selective tradition but seem very impressed with the nonselective, informal primary schools. Though primary education has suffered from financial neglect and lack of attention, one could almost make a case that the *lack* of concern has given professionals enough leeway to permit the slow evolution of current developments. Untroubled by interference or attention from social and educational elites, primary educators have developed the individual school as the unit of change. The modifications have generally been built on traditional practices, and the shifts have taken place sporadically and unevenly. But the net effect over the years has been cumulative as new practices gradually spread from school to school.

FUNDAMENTAL REFORM

English educators tend to be gradualists. They believe in doing things by bits and pieces. The phenomenon of English gradualism is so fascinating that one is tempted to attribute it to a national mystique. Changes, of course, result not from a stereotyped English character trait, but through innovative individuals who hold key positions in specific schools and who live in a receptive time. Current changes can be traced to writing and practices that date back more than forty years (S. Isaacs, 1930; Hadow, 1931; Schoenchen, 1940; Gardner, 1942; Nunn, 1947). These practices have recently become more widespread as changing social conditions have made them more acceptable. Factors that block educational change in the United States do not seem to be so powerful in England. Hierarchical traditions, so much stronger in England than in the United States, put the weight of authority behind proposed shifts in direction. When English educational leaders advocate changes, the rest of the profession slowly but steadily follows suit.

The current changes in English primary schools appear to represent a fundamental shift away from the past. (Some Englishmen doubt this, especially critics of the educational establishment; their criticisms will be discussed in the next chapter.) The case in support of the fundamental nature of reform can be documented from two perspectives. In open-ended interviews, English educational leaders were asked for descriptions of changes that they have sensed since the beginning of their teaching careers. This sample, representing national authorities, college lecturers, head teachers, and Local Education Authority advisers, supplied information about the postwar years. The interviews revealed a number of common agreements about the nature and direction of change. A second set of interviews made use of cross-cultural comparisons. They were conducted with college students, exchange teachers, and college lecturers who have studied or worked in America, as well as American exchange teachers, university students, and college professors who have studied or worked in England. This second set of interviews revealed common agreements about similarities and differences within the educational systems of the two countries.

English visitors to America express keen disappointment with the more formally organized elementary classrooms they are shown. This disappointment is particularly poignant among exchange lecturers from Colleges of Education who have been led to believe that American teachers might be implementing on a much wider scale the teaching strategies advocated by progressive educators over seventy years ago.

The English style of low-keyed, fundamental reform contrasts with America's flamboyant approach to proposed changes. The Americans do not lack ambition. Even the federal government can earmark millions of dollars for education when declaring a War on Poverty. The English admire American positivism, lavish spending, and technical inventiveness, which they consider to be tributes to America's perennial optimism; they are even impressed by American failures.

The factors contributing to these failures are not difficult to understand. The rigidities of the American school system, which relies so heavily on mass methods of textbook teaching and organizational subservience to bureaucratic regulations, almost defy fundamental reform. The more sweeping the intended reform, the more impervious is the resistance to it. Americans write a lot about needed changes, but these are seldom implemented, except in highly publicized model programs. But in school after school, English primary teachers are currently adopting teaching strategies that have been advocated, but seldom practiced, for decades in America. Dewey is much more widely read and discussed in England than in America (Dewey, 1934, 1938, 1959, 1961; Hollins, 1966). The subtitle of this book might well have been "John Dewey is still alive and his ideas are flourishing in England."

The English love to parody two images of American education. They poke fun at the overregimented school and at its opposite, the school determined to modernize at any cost. Schools with long lists of rules and regulations, thick teachers' handbooks filled with school board policies, and principals supervising piles of paperwork are viewed as antieducational establishments. On the other hand, schools enslaved to computers, with children wearing headsets wired into little boxes, working their way through prepackaged lessons, manipulating gadgets, and being scientifically programed, are viewed as antihuman establishments. English visitors are disappointed when they are shown schools that seem mobilized to perpetuate regimented learning or schools that set out to restructure the whole educational enterprise in the name of someone's pet theory and invariably, it seems, fitted out with very expensive hardware.

In this chapter the differences in educational reform in the

Learning How to Learn

two countries are brought out through three cross-cultural comparisons: (1) agents of change in England and the United States; (2) social conditions blocking or facilitating reform; and (3) the units of change within the two countries.

AGENTS OF CHANGE IN ENGLAND

Head Teachers

The autonomy of the head teacher—his power, authority, and status—appears to be so crucial that it warrants a separate chapter (Chapter 4). It is sufficient to note that in England the head teacher acts with genuine authority. He takes seriously the responsibility for curriculum leadership in his school.

Local Education Authority Advisers

The local governing units in England are much larger than most American school districts. The territory of England and Wales has been divided among 164 Local Education Authorities, or L.E.A.'s, formed for each major city and county, but the giant London authority has been decentralized into more than twenty separate authorities. Since most authorities encompass hundreds of schools, the Chief Education Officer in each L.E.A. delegates authority for the curriculum to the head teachers. A small advisory staff may be attached to the central office of the L.E.A. Primary school advisers and their assistants visit the schools to assess probationary teachers and to organize meetings, short courses, and conferences. A number of primary school advisers have been very active in fostering new educational practices, such as vertical or family grouping (Bristol), team teaching in open-planned buildings (Berkshire), the integrated day (Leicestershire), and environmental studies (the West Riding of Yorkshire).

College and University Lecturers

The Colleges of Education have had a virtual monopoly in the preparation of primary school teachers. Their role has been so important that a separate chapter is also devoted to them (Chapter 9). College tutors act as agents of change by popularizing current theory and methods among prospective teachers.

The Schools of Education and Area Training Organisations attached to the universities have had a minor influence on primary education, except as they coordinate the work of neighboring affiliated Colleges of Education. A number of Institutes or Schools of Education have been forming Departments of Curriculum Development and expanding provisions for in-service education. University lecturers direct most of the opportunities to take advanced degrees and diplomas in education, stimulate much of the country's educational research, and administer an increasing number of in-service courses for primary teachers and heads. The universities' chief contribution to preservice teacher education has been the one-year certificate course for university graduates entering teaching at the secondary level.

The National Government

Three sets of initials signify three aspects of the national educational effort: the H.M.I.'s, the D.E.S., and the B.B.C. Her Majesty's Inspectors (H.M.I.'s) function in a strictly independent advisory capacity (Blackie, 1971). Formerly they spent much time visiting schools, but currently they devote the greater part of their energies to organizing in-service courses and popularizing ideas emanating from the Department of Education and Science (D.E.S.), one of the ministries of the national government. Staff members of the D.E.S. have a considerable amount of influence on English education. Again, great pains are taken to exert influence informally, flexibly, and with sensitivity to local circumstance. The British Broadcasting Corporation (B.B.C.), the nonprofit radio and television network, has a near monopoly on channels of auditory mass communication. The B.B.C. does compete with a commercial television network, I.T.V., and both devote most of the daytime hours to broadcasts for schools. The standards of production of B.B.C. radio and television are extremely high, untainted by any hint of commercialism.

The Schools Council

The Schools Council represents a national effort to foster curriculum change. Despite pioneer work by the Nuffield Foundation, a philanthropic organization that has provided grants to revitalize teaching in the content fields of science and mathematics, England moved rather slowly toward widespread encouragement of curriculum reform. The essential independence of English schools needed to be preserved. The basic goal of the Schools Council is to promote curriculum development nationally without bringing to bear the power or influence of any government body. English educators tend to be highly suspicious of direct government initiative or implied interference in the curriculum of the local school.

The Schools Council has become a unique, very English institution, with no real counterpart elsewhere. It draws financial support approximately equally from the national Department of Education and Science and the Local Education Authorities. But no strings are attached to either source of revenue. The Schools Council is an independent body that distributes its budget in any way that its members see fit. It was deliberately organized with teachers in control of a majority of the votes on all policy-making boards, thereby insuring professional rather than political domination (Blackie, 1971).

Teachers are involved at every stage of the work—from the determination of policies and the selection of projects to the field testing of projects in pilot centers to the dissemination phase. The goal is to broaden the range of curriculum choices. Teachers are free to use or reject the materials. Support is offered to those who want to change, but no pressure is applied to those who are unready or unwilling. One hundred and ten projects had been authorized by 1970. Eventually, enough Schools Council programs will exist in every area of the curriculum and at each stage of pupil development to enable individual teachers to choose from among many different strategies directed at a multiplicity of objectives.

The Council insists on certain provisions for local curriculum development within those authorities that request to be included in pilot schemes. Local Education Authorities are expected not only to contribute a share of the development budget, but also to provide facilities for diffusion projects, to release those teachers who volunteer for courses, and to remunerate teachers who participate in the projects. A fundamental requirement is the establishment of Teachers' Centres (Schools Council, 1967a; Corstan, 1969) to serve the pilot schemes, the diffusion stages, and other local curriculum development efforts. The aim is to bring teachers together to share ideas and resources while developing teacher leaders.

To encourage creative approaches to widely recognized curriculum problems, the Council allocates grants for the support of project development teams. The teams are often based at universities in order to take advantage of the academic resources and research facilities. After materials have been tried out, evaluated, and refined, they are turned over to private companies for publication and distribution.

As the Schools Council expands the scope of its work, the term "curriculum" is being defined in a somewhat broader sense. There is not as much emphasis on modifying subject matter objectives or methodology. Much greater concern is being devoted to professional interaction and the development of group leadership skills. Achievements are more difficult to attain with these more ambitious goals. It is easier to develop new teaching packages than to bring about widespread commitment to new ways of working together. Although more teachers are now attending Teachers' Centres, much has yet to appear in the way of locally devised, independent curriculum work, and teacher leaders do not yet exert much leadership. The diffusion stage of the different projects, so crucial to the Council's intent, varies greatly in the degree of teacher involvement. The diffusion of content reforms has been more widespread than the attempts to influence teacher attitudes. So far the Council has failed to bring about reforms in assessment procedures at the secondary level, despite wide recognition of the limitations of current practices. Leaders of the Council have yet to look directly at either the formal or informal organization of schools, which so often blocks change. Not to deal with power, control, conflict, or structure in the traditional forms of organization means that the curriculum can only be modified, not radically changed. At the secondary level in particular, it is often school organization rather than teacher initiative that impedes reform.

COMPARABLE AGENTS OF CHANGE IN THE UNITED STATES

Elementary School Principals

The American elementary school principal performs rather different functions from those of the English head teacher. He is expected to carry out a curriculum and to enforce policy decisions laid down by a body *outside* his school, the elected Board of Education for the local school district. He is forced to act in a public relations capacity with parents and the community. The American elementary school principal could be a much more influential figure; his potential for leadership will be discussed at greater length in Chapter 4.

Curriculum Advisers

There are curriculum coordinators, consultants, and supervisors attached to American school districts and to intermediate units, such as counties, in the various states. Like their English counterparts, they are expected to act in an advisory capacity, but American teachers seldom take their advice. English advisers have no more power than Americans, yet they are able eventually to transmit their messages. Something might be learned from the fact that English advisers are satisfied to set astir low-keyed reform movements. This might be the only kind of educational reform that has a chance of taking hold in America.

University Professors

There is no longer any American counterpart to the single-purpose College of Education. The creation of American university subunits on the English pattern is one recommendation of the chapter devoted to the English colleges (Chapter 9). Preservice professional courses, offered as a kind of afterthought to a general liberal arts college education, tend to be less effective in the United States than in England. English College of Education tutors are more directly involved in professional guidance and supervision of practice teaching than are most American professors. Because American college students have had restricted opportunities to take full responsibility for classroom instruction prior to certification, they lack the confidence to resist many of the stultifying practices that they encounter in the school systems where they are first employed.

The National Government

Only recently has the federal government become deeply involved in education in the United States. It is still primarily concerned with passing out money to the states and the districts while promoting grandiose schemes through federal Education Acts in a feeble attempt to alter the educational establishment in the public schools and universities. The United States has no H.M.I.'s nor any D.E.S. staff members charged with reviewing national policy. In fact, there is virtually no national policy. America tolerates unbelievably wide discrepancies among states and school districts in relation to financing, control, *de facto* racial segregation, and economic support that is subject to regional prosperity, the local industrial tax base, and rural-urban differences. There is nothing comparable to the B.B.C. in the United States, but federal allocations to educational television channels and grants to encourage closed-circuit programing might give greater encouragement to noncommercial television.

Curriculum Reform Groups

In the United States there is no coordinated national effort comparable to the Schools Council. It is doubtful that America could devise a structure that implies a national commitment but avoids the possibility of national interference. Already, national and state-wide assessment implies interference in the curriculum of local school districts. Where state-wide testing exists, American teachers report excessive pressures to concentrate attention on the "basic" skills covered by the standardized tests.

In the United States recent initiative for curriculum reform has come from organizations representing the separate disciplines. Leadership has been supplied by university professors, with school-based personnel cooperating as junior partners. There has been no national attempt to coordinate efforts. Mathematicians, linguists, scientists, and social scientists have stimulated a host of competing projects. Within the social sciences alone the separate disciplines of anthropology, history, economics, geography, and political science have spawned many distinct programs along with a few attempts to foster interdisciplinary studies. The same is true within the natural and physical sciences, where professional organizations of specialists have initiated independent projects in biology, physics, and chemistry. Many of these projects have been aided by government funds, based in part on a sense of national priorities, through such provisions as the National Science Foundation, the National Defense Education Act, and the Education Professions Development Act. American curriculum projects in the disciplines often enjoy a higher measure of academic respectability than those

Learning How to Learn

developed in England, but sometimes the very complexity of the designs prevents them from being adopted by the schools.

Sooner or later most American curriculum reforms end up as new textbook series. These series are dressed up to resemble multi-sensory learning kits and include all kinds of expensive teaching aids and resources. At the heart of most of the packages is a printed resource resembling a textbook, which arouses the keen interest of book publishers, who competitively jockey with one another to market ever more impressive packages.

Compared with England, efforts in the United States are not only more divisive, they are also less democratic. American projects do not show the same respect for teachers nor a comparable sensitivity to their concerns and desires. Most of the curriculum reforms are intended to structure change *for* teachers. Typically, they place materials in the teachers' hands and then attempt to teach the teachers how to teach with them. No safeguards are enforced by organizations representing classroom teachers, and little choice is left open to the individual instructor. His only real choice is to cooperate or to resist. With the tendency for district-wide adoptions, he is not free to select from among many strategies, nor do adopted strategies commonly offer a number of alternative ways of meeting his goals.

The only people in the United States who talk like members of the Schools Council are those professionals affiliated with the Associations for Supervision and Curriculum Development. During the 1960's members of the A.S.C.D., which largely represents professors of curriculum and school-based curriculum directors, were on the defensive. They had difficulty coping with the demands of specialists in the disciplines for a greater share of the learners' time and of the budget for school resources. In that decade an academic backlash had brought together a number of dormant but long-standing critiques of teacher education. "Educationists" have long been suspect members of the academic community; academicians who have proper traditional disciplines to impart have enjoyed greater university prestige. Many members of education departments attempted to become more respectable by concentrating on the contribution of specialized disciplines to education and were reticent about openly defending the concerns of curriculum leaders working in the public schools. Few prominent people spoke out convincingly for maintaining a balance in the curriculum or were able to dramatize the concern that something more fundamental than tampering with content might be necessary to improve ways in which people relate to one another. The recent groundswell of American interest in informal English primary education is one of the most noteworthy countertrends of the 1970's.

The one area of curriculum development in which America seems superior to England is research. Far more money in the United States is devoted to educational research, much of which is independent of specific curriculum projects. Although England has a National Foundation for Educational Research, its funds are limited and the dissemination of its work appears restricted to a single series of publications (N.F.E.R., 1970).

SOCIAL CONDITIONS FACILITATING OR BLOCKING CHANGE

Educational changes in England do not seem to meet with the same resistance from powerful forces that blocks them in the United States. England is essentially free from school board politics and control by laymen over curriculum decisions. Since the head teacher is virtually autonomous, he is not expected to be subservient to a central administrative machinery. There are no organizations in England comparable to the John Birch Society and other right-wing groups that have applied pressures on American schools. Upper-middle-class parents in the United States serve as local opinion leaders and school officials dare to tread but lightly before them; in England these parents simply do not care what happens in the state primary schools. Many potentially vocal critics from the upper middle class have opted out of state education and have chosen instead the private preparatory and public schools to try to better ensure a privileged future for their children.

Teachers in England do not appear to be afraid of parents, nor do they act as if they are afraid of the children. Therefore they are much more inclined to follow their professional inclinations. Many teachers in the United States are so worried about what the public will think that they do not dare to follow their professional hunches. Parents of the "crank" variety obviously exert too much power in the United States. Ironically, the English are seeking greater contact with parents, in the belief that close home-school relationships are one aspect of the American system that the English would do well to adopt (Plowden, 1967; D.E.S., 1968; Goodacre, 1970).

Deep-seated resistance to change among some teachers in the United States must stem from distrust, fear, and, in some cases, downright hostility toward children. How else can we explain the widespread formalism, mass instructional procedures, obsession with discipline, and heavy reliance on textbooks? Without such props they fear the children will run wild, "climb the walls," disturb other teachers, arouse the disapproval of the principal, or, worst of all, carry complaints back to the parents. Such apprehensions are not all imaginary.

Many American teachers must deal with children who come from more diverse subcultures than those found in England. Children in both countries reflect differences in child-rearing patterns related to social class, but American children reflect pervasive racial, ethnic, regional, and religious differences as well. American children are exposed to a great deal more television with its excesses of violence and clever advertisements. Since elementary schools in America tend to be larger than English schools, it is easier for American children to be neglected. While some neighborhoods in English cities reflect conditions of severe poverty, seldom does the breakdown of conventional social controls parallel those occurring in comparable neighborhoods in American cities. All these conditions combine to make classroom discipline a more harrowing experience for a number of American teachers.

Can there be any actual difference between the behavior of English and American children? One would not get that impression from comparing the amount of noise on the playground during recess. Occasionally, especially when comparing schools in working-class neighborhoods, one has the fleeting impression that American children might not respond as well to freedom, might be used to stronger controls from authority figures.

Are English children, then, generally easier to control, more outwardly conforming, less aggressive? To even attempt to answer such suppositions, one would have to look at the two cultures with the insights of a trained anthropologist, preferably one with psychoanalytical grounding, and compare child-rearing practices and cultural norms for childhood behavior. If there are differences, they can only be differences of degree, with wide areas of behavioral expectations overlapping between the two cultures. English children *are* given a great deal of freedom in many primary schools, and most seem to respond to it positively. American children are given very little real freedom in most elementary schools, so we do not know how they might respond.

Are English parents more placid, more deferential, and less aggressive in relation to the school? There appears to be somewhat stronger support for this hunch, traceable to traditional parent-teacher relationships in England. In the past there was a wide social distance between parents and teachers. The old-style, working-class parent was particularly deferential toward the schoolmaster. Teachers still have had more formal education than most of the parents, and deference, even among middle-class parents, is still strong, despite current efforts to form P.T.A.'s in England and to enlist parents in the support of the school. A most progressive school head, whose school reflects a great many of the current practices and provides widespread freedom for children, recently organized a P.T.A. After the constitution had been adopted, he welcomed all the new members but warned them that if they started to interfere with his school, he would have no hesitation about dissolving the P.T.A. forthwith. The parents accepted this warning as just and proper.

Listening to American teachers, one might come to the conclusion that some American parents have moved completely out of line. Not only do they run the P.T.A. (which is, after all, desirable) but increasingly some think that they can dictate to the profession about professional matters. They complain to the teachers; they complain to the principal; they complain to members of the school board; they write letters to the editors. They even believe that they have the right to suggest to teachers how to teach beginning reading.

American school personnel apprehensively attempt to appease the most vocal critics. Elaborate campaigns to enlist the support of parents in bringing about even a modest change—for instance, the gradual switch from grade-level expectations to a nongraded organization—seem almost ludicrous. Yet the American elementary school principal knows full well that he dare not make a change without first convincing the parents that "no real change" is taking place.

Certain conditions in America are potentially more explosive than in England. Teachers sense the danger, and, fearful of parental reactions, they become cautious about freedom for children. The potential and actual violence, the levels of environmental and vocal noise, the heterogeneous, clashing subcultures, the authoritarian child-rearing practices (or the inconsistent middle-class practices of overcompensation), all produce greater frustration and greater aggression among children. In England fewer people openly act out their anger.

Not so long ago English children were regimented in rows of desks, expected to be silent, grouped by ability, dominated by teachers, and disciplined by the threat of the cane. English primary schools are no longer organized in these ways. Even traditional English schools have undergone reform, and the majority of English primary schools are moving toward considerable freedom for children. If these changes have become widespread in England over the past twenty-five years, similar shifts might well take place in America.

Americans frequently ask if informal methods are used in English primary schools that serve poor children in industrial cities. Since the publication of the Plowden Report in 1967, an increasing number of central-city schools have been moving in this direction, although the percentage of children affected may be lower than in suburban or rural communities. It is not the absence of informal methods or flexible programing that tends to defeat the transformation of schools in working-class neighborhoods; it is rather the cultural disparity between middle-class teachers and the poor. American educators tend to be more optimistic about counteracting the effects of environmental conditioning.

The major difference between schools serving the poor in London and Manchester compared with similar schools in New York and Chicago is that English schools and neighborhoods are not as segregated along racial lines. In most large English cities there are pockets of West Indian, Pakistani, and Hindu settlement, but almost never do those children constitute a majority of the school population. Even though individual English teachers may be racist, English society is not pervasively ingrained with racism. England has its politicians who look for scapegoats and play on racial fears; until very recently, however, the prevailing strategies of most "colored" spokesmen as well as those of English teachers have been assimilationist. The strategies are changing, but England is far from experiencing a black revolution or a white backlash.

England has not experienced widespread racial segregation, has few minority groups, and is without a tradition of either cultural pluralism or ethnic conflict. Teaching difficulties in English inner cities are tied to class-related problems (discussed more fully in Chapter 11). Still, many primary schools in industrial areas are intriguing institutions for Americans to visit. They are struggling to overcome many handicaps, including sometimes appallingly grim buildings, inadequate playgrounds, shortages of teaching materials and visual aids, excessive turnover of staff, and a high percentage of probationary teachers. They are gradually becoming more informal. The Inner London Education Authority and the University of London Institute of Education have both demonstrated marked leadership in promoting educational change among central city primary schools. It is within secondary education in industrial areas that many teachers and pupils lose confidence in educational opportunities.

THE UNITS OF CHANGE IN THE TWO COUNTRIES

The unit of change in England is the individual school, and it may be that the individual school is the only viable unit in either America or in England. It serves as a miniature society in education, where power and authority are made visible. Furthermore, in England the smaller size of the individual school contributes to its effectiveness, allowing the head to establish more intimate working relationships with the staff and the teachers to interact more directly with one another.

Power and authority in England reside with the head teacher, not in a district central office responsible to an elected school board of laymen. Trappings of local community control exist in England, but these do not generally affect the individual school. The Education Committee of the Local Education Authority, which has both lay and teacher representation, exercises power by partial control of financial matters. This power can be substantial. Nevertheless, the laymen seldom exercise control over the curriculum, which is considered to be strictly a matter for the profession. Each school has its own board of managers, but the members have largely become supportive officials. Managers perform a necessary function only in the choice of a new head. After his appointment, they almost always listen to him. Managers who are appointed for their potential contribution to the school do serve as a safeguard against mismanagement and can be used as an avenue of communication to the Education Committee of the local authority.

Curriculum reform in America has had a dismal record precisely because authority and power do not reside in the local school. The larger the school district, the more dismal tends to be its record. When a bureaucratic machine establishes policies on a district-wide basis, the proposals seldom become the personal concern of the teachers and the principals who are supposed to carry them out. Too many elaborate curriculum proposals exist on paper and not within people. The school district, even the small school district with jurisdiction over a few schools, may be the wrong unit for curriculum change.

It would seem that the simplest way to incorporate into the American system what is admirable in English reform is to turn more individual schools loose so that staff members may bring about the kinds of changes that they want. This does not mean that individual schools cannot receive help from outside sources, such as the curriculum staff of the school district or a nearby university. Through the provision of greater autonomy the potential for professional decision-making within a school faculty can be mobilized in a setting in which face-to-face communication is at least possible.

3

Six English Critiques of Current Reforms

The Report of the Central Advisory Council on Education in England, *Children and Their Primary Schools*, familiarly known as the Plowden Report in honor of its chairman, was the most important government-sponsored document about primary education published in thirty years. The Council carefully gathered evidence from a wide spectrum of sources over an extended period of time. In 1970, three years after its publication, most people acknowledged that the Report represented a fair summary of enlightened professional opinion. Few felt that it was very far in advance of common practice; rather it gave semi-official endorsement to changes already underway and made modest recommendations for more widespread implementation during the 1970's. There is some indication that *Children and Their Primary Schools* represents a combination of positions of the enlightened, middle-of-the-road members of the educational establishment.

Perhaps "establishment" is not the right word to describe leaders in primary education. The people usually referred to as the Establishment—England's social, economic, and political elites—care little about primary education; if they care at all, it is that not too much money be allocated for the supporting budget. The educational establishment in the professional sense refers to many of the influential leaders who make important decisions that affect the primary schools. These include Department of Education and Science civil servants, Her Majesty's Inspectors, the Chief Education Officers of the L.E.A.'s and members of their primary school advisory staffs, leaders of the Schools Council, College of Education principals, professors in the university departments and schools of education, and leaders of influential organizations such as the National Association of Head Teachers, the National Union of Teachers, the National Association of Schoolmasters, and the Association of Teachers in Colleges and Departments of Education. The membership of the Central Advisory Council that produced the Plowden Report represents a fair cross section of this establishment.

British educators use the Plowden Report as a frame of reference. Traditionalists deplore its liberalism; progressives decry its conservatism. College of Education students use it as a required reference book. Quotations from it appear frequently in articles, speeches, and statements issued by professional bodies. Following the publication of the Plowden Report some intriguing essays appeared that doubted the soundness of many of its basic assumptions. This chapter brings together critical comments expressed in these articles along with opinions of College of Education tutors and students taken from interviews and informal discussions. The criticisms can be linked to branches of educational disciplines and in some cases to philosophical viewpoints.

Most of the articulate spokesmen critical of the more orthodox positions of the Plowden Report are members of university and college departments of education, but they include some outspoken head teachers and some of the more dissatisfied classroom teachers. In most cases they offer constructive criticism, intended essentially to push the primary school leadership toward greater critical awareness.

THE CHILD–CENTERED CRITIQUE

Early-childhood educators have a long-standing affinity with the child-centered philosophy, dating back to the days of Froebel's English disciples (Lawrence, 1969). Rousseau is still read in English

Learning How to Learn

Colleges of Education (Rousseau, 1911), and a recent book reaffirms the importance of his ideas in the history of educational thought (Dobinson, 1969).

Advocates of the child-centered approach claim that primary schools are still too teacher-dominated and too often ignore children's potential for self-direction. Rather than being too free, the schools are not yet free enough. (This critique may seem far-fetched to visiting Americans impressed with the amount of freedom provided and the number of teachers who identify themselves with a child-centered philosophy. They wish the schools in America were half so free.) The Plowden Report itself seems vulnerable to the opposite attack. A favorite jibe is that teachers can be seen in only two of the forty-six illustrations. The pictures give the impression that children educate themselves. If only children can be seen in the pictures, these critics ask, who is doing the teaching?

How child-centered are the English primary schools? A number of English teachers are able to remain in the background and yet exert control for a good part of the time. Despite an affirmative endorsement of the child-centered position by many English teachers, they seldom place the interests and needs of children at the heart of the learning process. Most English teachers still do a lot of direct teaching. Some manipulate situations so that the children only appear to be making their own choices or following their own inclinations. Teachers still prepare individual assignment cards. Teachers for the most part orchestrate integrated days. Teachers arrange environments. Teachers for the most part evaluate the children rather than help the children to evaluate themselves. It is so difficult for adults to function with children without dominating them that, even within very relaxed atmospheres, teachers are still very much in command.

Child-centered proponents maintain that since the period of childhood is intrinsically valuable, it should not be sacrificed to the pursuit of adult-determined goals. Suspicious of the authority of teachers and of an adult-conceived curriculum, some doubt whether it is really possible for anyone to teach anyone else anything (C. R. Rogers, 1961). A child learns only what he chooses to learn through what he directly experiences. Education should not prepare for the future, except insofar as present concerns prepare children to meet future challenges. The freely chosen activities of children have a right to exist for their own sake; if play is the primary way in which children learn, they should be given full freedom to engage in play.

The child-centered critique basically asks that greater respect be shown for the maturity and good sense of children and that children be allowed to make more of their own learning decisions, with the teacher serving largely as a helpful adult guide and resource (Ashton-Warner, 1963). Many teachers in England have learned to provide options, offer choices, individualize expectations, enrich resources, and stand back, rather than hover too closely over the children at work. Child-centered advocates contend that more teachers could do more of this more of the time.

In what ways is a thoroughgoing child-centered position vulnerable? Schools that do not establish some constraints can hardly discourage egocentric behavior. Is not education, as a formal institution, created by society for the deliberate, systematic dissemination of skills and knowledge and the clarification of values? If so, the teacher has responsibility for structuring experiences, extending interests, helping children to define learning goals, and drawing on basic generalizations from established fields of knowledge (H. Entwistle, 1970a). Important concepts are not learned informally through chance encounters but develop progressively with deeper understanding through deliberate planning (Bruner, 1966a, 1966b). Self-discipline and self-direction are not inborn characteristics but are the products of extensive learning opportunities.

This does not take away from freedom of expression or the educational importance of children's interests. Interests can be the basis for motivation; the curiosity and spontaneous questions of children set the stage for concrete experiences. Children's questions are the products of learning and correspond to concerns long identified with established fields of knowledge. The interests of children and adults are not in opposition; indeed, children want to grow up as fast as possible and from an early age seek to model themselves after adults. Children's interests in this regard become means as well as ends.

Historically, the child-centered movement has helped to counteract formalism, authoritarianism, didactic teaching, and the arbitrary separation of learning into subject matter compartments. It has helped to underline the importance of taking into foremost account the current concerns of children. Since *learning by doing* means that children internalize or personally possess knowledge as

Learning How to Learn

they use it, the movement has helped to encourage problem-solving behavior (Dewey, 1938, 1959, 1961). This is not to say that learning by doing is restricted to the child-centered movement, for even traditionalists can involve learners in activity as an instrumental teaching technique. Most important, the child-centered movement has helped to extend the concept of the rights of man to the child; it respects the child's individual integrity and denies any teacher's right to exploit him, no matter how high-sounding the purpose.

Arguments about the child-centered position range from outright philosophical rejection to sympathetic concern for clarification to zealous advocacy. A penetrating analysis of both the claims of the child-centered movement and the criticisms of it has been brought together by Harold Entwistle (Entwistle, 1970a). Avoiding the either-or dichotomy of proponents and opponents, he settles on the concept of "learner-centered education" to allow for the intervention and authority of the professional teacher. Entwistle makes a convincing case for not being satisfied with child-centered education. He wants the teacher to raise the child's horizons and to enlarge his realms of meaning. The teacher acts as mediator of a richer, wider culture, concentrating on that knowledge that has most transfer value in developing self-instructional habits. He draws on fundamental generalizations from the disciplines, ethical principles, and allegiance to the scientific method, values that are historically rooted and go beyond either the teacher or the child at the center of the learning process. By Entwistle's standards English schools are seldom *either* child-centered *or* learner-centered.

SOCIOLOGICAL CRITIQUES

The educational sociologist tends to accuse primary school leaders of glossing over complexities by ignoring sociological theory and research. Their aspirations are too ambitious; there is a heavy strain of evangelical "do-goodism" and a tendency to brush aside disconcerting realities. The sociological critique is best expressed in an essay by Basil Bernstein and Brian Davies in which they accuse the Plowden Report of giving insufficient recognition to the social dimensions of the problems it discusses (Bernstein and Davies, 1969).

Specifically, the Report is accused of playing down subcultural differences, insufficiently grasping the varieties of family background, neglecting the implications of the social dimensions of age-grouping, and paying too little attention to class differences in language, values, forms of social control, and views of the school. The Report gives little attention to major research interests and insights of educational sociology; it ignores the social organization of the school, role strains of teachers, and forms of social conflict, while glossing over components of social structure and oversimplifying school-community relations. These critics find most pernicious the Report's assumption that parental influence in working-class neighborhoods that have been designated as Educational Priority Areas can be altered and controlled by school authorities.

An amusing yet penetrating critique of educational priorities is the satire *The Rise of the Meritocracy* by the sociologist Michael Young. It takes the form of a scholarly report, written in sociological jargon, of English society in the year 2033, when the English educational system has finally arrived at the ultimate extension of existing trends. Merit is at last fully recognized. Wealth, social position, and egalitarian sentiments can no longer influence the child's life chances. The book traces the history of the rise of a new elite based on brains, the erosion of the independent public schools as bastions of privilege, the discrediting of comprehensive, or all-inclusive, secondary schools, and the decline of the Labor Movement. Workers are forced to become domestic servants again, and the salary differential becomes so great that highly placed bureaucrats receive rewards and privileges equal to their station. Unfortunately, the report ends abruptly, since the "author" of the treatise is killed at an uprising at Peterloo while gathering data about a protest demonstration organized by incoherent dissidents from the lower classes (Young, 1958).

Young's utopian report does not pit itself against the prevailing primary school philosophy; its major targets are secondary and higher education. It lambastes both the special pleading of conservatives and the timid tampering of socialist reformers. The critique goes beyond the Plowden Report to call into question the pervasive acceptance of selectivity and a limited pool of talent, the worship of intelligence and verbal skills, the weight given to examination results, and the schemes of social planners who accept the broad outlines of the existing system and attempt to modify it by substituting academic ability for inherited privilege.

William Taylor has written one of the few sociological books devoted to Colleges of Education, the institutions attended by most English primary teachers (W. Taylor, 1970). He deals with the economic restrictions under which the colleges developed, their social structure and social control, the changing roles of the principal, conflicts among staff members, and the changes taking place among students.

The most penetrating of his critiques is summarized in the concluding chapter, which deals with the values of teacher education. He contrasts the missionary spirit of many educators of primary teachers (Floud, 1962) with the university lecturers' high regard for intellect. He draws on the analysis of Talcott Parsons, who characterizes the ethos of the university in terms of affective neutrality, self-orientation, universalism, achievement, and specificity (Parsons and Shils, 1961). By implication, educational missionaries reject many of these values and demonstrate affective concern rather than neutrality while defining their goals diffusely rather than specifically.

Missionaries try to convert prospective primary teachers to become agents for social cohesion. Beginning teachers are enjoined to show concern for interpersonal relationships, to trust their intuitive feelings, to aspire to intangible goals, and to promote social betterment. Within the ethos of many Colleges of Education, cohesion is preferred to conflict, school loyalty to personal disengagement, and stability to change.

Some college tutors resent the controls that university boards maintain over college syllabuses and examinations. A number of tutors are not products of the universities themselves, but have been recruited to teacher education from the ranks of successful teachers and heads. College of Education lecturers exist outside the university status system with its distinguishing marks of social success and community esteem. They reject an exclusive concern for intellectual modes of arriving at truth; some college tutors have become dedicated through a sense of commitment. They do not merely instruct; they aspire to fulfill a worthy vocation. The needs of the learner rather than the demands of the subject become foremost; the whole student rather than his intellect alone is in need of development.

The missionary spirit is losing adherents as students and staffs exhibit greater diversity than before. Student social life has become more private and more passive. Students gather in the privacy of their rooms and less often as members of college organizations and societies. Many educational sociologists are themselves at war with educational missionaries. They are joined in battle by subject-matter tutors in academic departments whose loyalties are more closely consistent with the university ideal.

Taylor overstates the dichotomy between those who respect the demands of the intellect and the child-centered progressives in the Colleges of Education. It is unfair simply to characterize child-centered educators as being opposed to intellect. They cannot be concerned exclusively with the intellectual development of children, for they have to foster diffuse professional commitments—the primary teacher's roles are unavoidably diffuse. Taylor does, however, identify some of the strains within an institution undergoing rapid change. The small, isolated, single-purpose, single-sex, conservative institutions for preparing primary teachers began to change rapidly during the 1960's with the expansion brought about by the introduction of the three-year course. The colleges will very likely change even more markedly should they evolve from single-purpose to multipurpose institutions more closely associated with the universities.

Taylor's analysis is most telling in the implied criticism of the orthodox position among primary educators (so well summarized in the Plowden Report). Value positions of members of the educational establishment are vaguely stated and remain largely unexamined; they owe more to missionary zeal than to philosophical rigor. Functions that primary schools are expected to assume continue to multiply and become elusive. The Report's proposed solutions for social problems, whether those encountered by children or those besetting society, appear to be utopian in conception and superficially analyzed. It largely ignores the distribution of power and social conflict in the schools. Insofar as the missionary spirit still inspires members of the educational establishment, their uplifting words will fall on the tuned-out ears of an increasingly secularized student body. Neither educational nor religious missionaries are much in fashion among youth in modern Britain.

Recently, the teaching of the sociology of education has been expanding in the Colleges of Education (Musgrave, 1965; Cotgrove, 1968; Shipman, 1969; R. King, 1969; Hoyle, 1970; Ashley, Cohen, and Slatter, 1969). But the perspectives of the discipline have not reached many teachers who have been out of college for ten years or more. Sociologists have scarcely influenced the thinking of a large majority of the educational establishment, many of whom seem to have a pronounced tendency to underestimate the difficulties involved in bringing about social change.

PHILOSOPHIC CRITIQUES

Educational philosophers complain that aims for primary schools are seldom stated explicitly. When stated, they are often confusing and even contradictory. The Plowden Report has come in for its share of attacks. R. S. Peters has cogently dissected its "recognisable philosophy" into four components:
1. the child has a "nature" that will develop in the appropriate environment;
2. self-direction is crucial to this development;
3. knowledge cannot be compartmentalized but should be pulled out of an integrated curriculum;
4. the teacher must serve as a guide rather than an instructor.

He challenges each of these assumptions. He is worried that a semiofficial, widely accepted ideology restricts investigation into a variety of teaching strategies (Peters, 1969). Are all activities that can conceivably take place in schools equally viable? How much is known about the ways in which independence and creativity develop? Is learning by discovery a method applicable to all fields of knowledge at all ages of development? Can the principles of mathematics and science be learned informally through integrated activities? Can one overall teaching strategy be applied to all fields of inquiry? Can teachers function simply as "child-growers," standing back while children proceed from one self-initiated discovery to another?

In the same collection of essays Robert Dearden documents the lack of concern that the Plowden Report shows about the specific statement of aims. The Report disguises aims in recommendations. Value positions go largely unexamined, often presented as if they were tested principles rather than largely untested beliefs (Dearden, 1969). Both Dearden and Peters have developed coherent, more conservative philosophies of education in books that are closely related to the long-standing concerns of philosophical inquiry (Peters, 1964, 1966; Dearden, 1968).

The practicing primary school teacher is not a philosopher, in

England or anywhere else. Few teachers take the time to question in any systematic way what they are doing; they just do it. This criticism is leveled by a number of tutors who teach in the Colleges of Education. Partly as a result of this concern, the prospective teacher in England is increasingly exposed to a good dose of philosophy of education; it is probably the most effectively taught discipline in education departments. It is replacing an earlier emphasis on the history of educational ideas that was descriptive rather than analytical. The philosophy of education is a subject well suited to tutorial teaching, for both students and tutors enjoy arguing about issues and principles. The reflective mode of inquiry is highly regarded, and there is an extensive library of professional literature to draw on (O'Connor, 1957; Reid, 1962; Bantock, 1965a, 1965b; Peters, 1964, 1966, 1967; Archambault, 1965; Nash, 1966; Langford, 1971; Peters and Hirst, 1971).

Even though younger teachers have been exposed to the rigors of philosophical inquiry in preservice education, it is difficult to apply the discipline in school situations. It may be unfair to accuse overworked primary teachers of lacking clarity about educational objectives, but it is not at all unfair to make a convincing case against a document that proposes to deal with the future of primary education at a national level (Dearden, 1969). Dearden points out that a professional body with the reputation of the Central Advisory Council should have been under greater obligation to issue a coherent, noncontradictory, philosophically defensible statement of implicit and explicit aims.

THE LEARNING THEORY CRITIQUE

Some critics complain that not only do primary educators have trouble defending their objectives, they do little about measuring the achievement of the objectives that they do espouse. Many popular teaching practices lack intellectual rigor, are imprecisely defined, inefficiently organized, carelessly evaluated, and based on inadequate psychology.

This critique needs to be distinguished from the traditionalist attack (Bantock, 1965a, 1965b; Cox and Dyson, 1969; Froome, 1970), which expresses disapproval in similar language but stems from a different set of assumptions. Traditionalists tend to admire formal subject-matter and skill-development objectives. They deplore a watered-down curriculum. They favor a teacher-dominated classroom in which learning is disciplined by categories of traditional subjects. They abhor activity for its own sake and the teachers' apparent lack of concern for the strict acquisition of knowledge.

The learning theorist is not so concerned that children are given too much freedom to play as he is that teachers are unaware of well-established principles of learning. Not enough attention is devoted to the social contexts in which learning takes place, including the effects of family and neighborhood environments on language acquisition, the importance of the peer socialization process, social class influences on motivation, and the emotional or nonintellectual concomitants of learning. The contribution of social psychology to the understanding of group behavior is ignored. Furthermore, evaluation processes are so subjective and objectives are so rarely stated in behavioral terms that appraisal of learning defies measurement. Critics claim that too much of what goes on in many primary classrooms is tangential to recognized learning principles; too often it is a waste of time for children and teachers alike. Some learning theorists are comfortable with developments in programed learning and the pursuit of academic goals that are possible to quantify and assess.

Educational psychologists are not at all happy with the apparent psychological basis of the Plowden Report, which leans heavily on developmental theories and the work of Piaget but pays too little attention to other areas of current psychological theory and research (Foss, 1969). Piaget's work has been widely disseminated in England. Many of his experiments have been replicated with English children, and modified norms and implications have been drawn (Lunzer, 1960; Brearly and Hitchfield, 1969; Beard, 1969). But Piaget's theories tend to be used as an excuse to postpone cognitive learning. Jerome Bruner is now widely read by students in English colleges (Bruner, 1966a, 1966b). His criticism of the lack of intellectual rigor in many classrooms is just as valid in England as in America. English children are ready to carry out studies of a more disciplined nature than they are frequently encouraged to do, but someone needs to help the children to establish procedures and to interpret what they are learning.

The learning theory critique is in some ways opposite to the child-centered one, at least in terms of the teacher's function.

While child-centered critics want to give children greater freedom from teachers, learning theorists demand that primary teachers, as mature adults familiar with the rational organization of content and method, guide learning with a surer hand than they frequently do.

RADICAL CRITIQUES

Radicals claim that primary schools are conformist, teachers timid, middle-class traditions overbearing, the curriculum too intellectual, and the mental health of children often ignored.

The radical critique has been most forcefully presented in the writing of A. S. Neill (Neill, 1953, 1960, 1967) and his admirers (Perry, 1968; Snitzer, 1968; Begefjord, 1970). Neill's major battles were with the Scottish schools that he remembered from his early days in teaching (Skidelsky, 1970), which did not show much change until after the Second World War. Even today the schools of Scotland are seldom as enthusiastic as the English about endorsing the Plowden perspective (Scottish Educ. Dept., 1965). But primary schools in England are also still a long way from approaching Summerhill, Neill's progressive independent school. Progressive English state schools are seldom therapeutic institutions, either in intent or in practice. They maintain adult controls and supervision over pupil behavior. They respect tradition and uphold adult standards of work. A number of Americans confuse progressive practices in state-maintained English primary schools with the radically different but isolated example of the fee-paying boarding school at Summerhill. Neill himself, however, is well aware of the great gulf that separates his school from the English mainstream.

Despite Neill's conviction that no one in England listens to him, he has inspired a number of native disciples. Some of them are teaching in state-maintained schools. One of the joys of reflecting on the autonomy of English education is that some heads and some teachers are following Neill, at least in a modified way, within local schools, and they are getting away with it. Such a phenomenon is virtually inconceivable in the United States.

One college tutor has described a Neill-type school in his neighborhood as illustrating the "disintegrated day" (to distinguish it from the integrated day). He tells stories about children running loose in the village with the head teacher's blessing; yet this school is regularly used for practice teaching and the head teacher retains the confidence of the parents, at least of the majority who have kept their children in the local school.

A growing number of college students and a few lecturers criticize the majority of English primary schools from Neill's perspective. They charge the teaching profession with being exceedingly conformist. There may be beards on the chins of English college lecturers and teachers, but they are almost always neat beards. Tutors strongly encourage college students to clean up their appearance and cut their hair before undertaking practice teaching. Like schools the world over, English schools overemphasize intellectual components of learning, sometimes at the expense of the mental health of the children. A number of teachers make casual references to slow children and backward readers in front of the children themselves.

The radical critic seldom provides a fully developed alternative curriculum, but he does offer a needed anecdote against complacency or enthusiasm for minor achievements. Radicals will never permit the English establishment to crow too loudly about happy children in informal primary schools. To the radicals, the children are not all that happy nor the schools all that informal.

THE PESSIMISTIC CRITIQUE

While granting that primary schools are becoming more pleasant places, pessimists wonder what long-range difference current developments will make. If the English educational system is elitist in the state sector from the secondary years onward and in the private sector from the beginning, what good is it to modify the state primary schools? Children attending relaxed primary schools may well suffer the consequences in those secondary schools that are highly academic, dominated by examinations, unconcerned about social issues, and dedicated to selective grouping practices.

The conviction is still widespread in England that the state schools are only for the masses; the private schools cater to the important classes. Upper-class and upper-middle-class Englishmen still seem obsessed with secondary education; the old school tie has yet to become a joke. The battle over selective secondary schools remains a political issue. The Conservative Party victory in the 1970 general election slowed the rapid swing toward comprehensive secondary schools and probably saved state support for the semi-independent, direct-grant grammar schools (Wansell, 1970). Whether English state-maintained secondary education can become fully comprehensive is in question, particularly if direct-grant and selective grammar schools draw off the most able students. Even comprehensive schools have not eliminated selection; they have merely disguised or postponed it.

Can the primary schools of England make a difference in later education? It is still too early to tell. People are fond of describing the progressively upward influence of the increase in freedom. The nursery schools freed the infant schools; the infant schools are freeing the junior schools; the junior schools will free the middle schools or the first few forms of the secondary schools. Finally, comprehensive schools will give more attention to less academic streams, and the elitist academic tradition will eventually become diluted. But will it?

Even though some changes are taking place in the lower forms of the secondary school, eventually the students still have to face the rigors of the examination system, with its selection at G.C.E. O-levels, its equivalent selection by C.S.E. examinations, its selection at G.C.E. A-levels, and the restricted opportunities for higher education. All these hurdles culminate in the career pecking order established according to the subtle, distinguishing reputations of the various categories of university honours degrees.

This helps to explain the anomaly of some College of Education tutors, themselves devoted to preparing teachers for the state educational system and engaged in a struggle to help bring about greater equality of educational opportunity, who still drain their limited incomes by educating their own children in independent or direct-grant grammar schools. As long as knowledgeable people "invest" money in a private education in order to increase their children's life chances, changes in the primary schools may not count for much. Primary education may only be an insignificant preliminary to the real competitive battle of educational selection that lies beyond it.

THE NEED FOR CONTINUING CRITICISM

Too much writing about English primary schools tends to be uncritically enthusiastic. The schools of England are by no means as child-centered as they at first appear to be. Most English teachers could provide far more self-direction for the children. If they were not so overworked and if they had the necessary patience, teachers could well spend more time studying how people learn by listening carefully to children. A thoroughgoing child-centered philosophy may play down societal expectations, teachers' prerogatives, and the values a teacher has gained by virtue of his maturity, yet critics can with some justification accuse a number of teachers and heads of hypocrisy. Many that claim to be child-centered are simply providing some well-regulated options.

The sociological critique exposes the Plowden Report's advocacy of a not too subtle form of social engineering. Unless the warnings of sociologists are heeded, many of the Report's best-laid educational plans will go awry. It is far more difficult to manipulate working-class people in Educational Priority Areas than reformers with the best of intentions seem to realize (Bernstein and Davies, 1969). Lessons from the shortcomings of compensatory education for the disadvantaged in the United States should not be ignored in this regard. Teachers are also subject to a blindness to class-related phenomena, often associated with shockingly stereotyped references to working-class and immigrant families (Goodacre, 1968).

Educational philosophers can justifiably accuse many practitioners of stubborn muddle-headedness. There is a persistent anti-theoretical, anticonceptual tendency at work among many British teachers. Teachers complain that philosophical discussion may be appropriate for ivory-towered lecturers and college students in the shelter of their tutorials, but the classroom teacher has a job to do and he cannot wait to consider ethical or epistemological implications while coping with a continuous crisis. Nevertheless, the recommendations of the semi-official Plowden Report should at least stem from defensible premises and an explicit statement of aims.

The learning theory critique is closely related to the philosophical one. Practitioners rarely question *why* they are doing what they are doing. Even when they do, they seldom systematically measure what they have achieved. Teachers just go along as they have been doing; the children carry on; the whole process is grossly inefficient. Furthermore, the meager amount of funds supplied for technological aids and newer learning materials hampers the more widespread use of methods that could improve learning efficiency.

The radical critique should help to keep the schools honest.

The primary schools of England are far too conformist, too verbal, too timorous. The radical perspective can push the schools in the direction of long espoused but seldom realized goals—to show greater concern for the mental health and all-round development of children.

The pessimistic critique expresses doubts about long-range results. Even if the emphasis on examinations and the thinly disguised selective grouping practices of secondary schools give way in the future to broader forms of assessment and wider opportunities for higher education, the middle-class bias of the schools will continue to overwhelm the majority. Primary schools can become more humane places for more children, but experiences in secondary schools will still lead most students to view themselves as educational failures or, at the very least, as learners without much promise.

No doubt American schools can be subjected to the same criticisms; in some respects the complaints are even more relevant. There are almost no child-centered teachers left in America. The child-centered philosophy was abandoned long ago. The radical critique against American schools is far more virulent; it has recently claimed many more American adherents because the schools are so regimented. Some of the best writing about education in the United States during the 1960's stemmed from the radical critique (Friedenberg, 1963; Goodman, 1964; Hentoff, 1966; Kozol, 1967; Kohl, 1967; Holt, 1964, 1967, 1969; Gross and Gross, 1969; Postman and Weingartner, 1969; Dennison, 1969). Radicals have far more reason to complain in America than they do in England; as a result many young American radicals have decided to opt out of public school teaching.

The critiques of English education should not lead Americans to underestimate the appropriateness of current, widely dispersed English reforms, modest though they be. English primary schools do provide much greater freedom for children. They are certainly less repressive than American schools; they have killed off fewer children at an early age (Kozol, 1967). While England is officially ridding itself of corporal punishment in the primary schools (Plowden, 1967; Sproule, 1970b) the practice continues unabated in the United States.

The moderate English changes, the low-keyed, gradual process of reform, the more functional preservice teacher education, the greater professional autonomy, are all potentially transferable to America. If these modifications would occur on a reasonably broad scale, the pessimistic critique would be less pertinent in America than it is in England. Some of the very factors that pain the English pessimists are of lesser importance in the United States. American secondary education has long been comprehensive. Open-door enrollment policies adopted by many American universities are diluting the remaining vestiges of elitist selection within higher education. Extensive funds are available to support educational research, curriculum innovation, technological improvements, and varied learning resources. On the other hand, the English might point to the lack of "value for money" in America, for extensive expenditures in support of innovation seldom reach many practicing elementary school teachers (Bassett, 1970). This should be cause for a different kind of pessimism. A great deal of money and energy in America are spent to promote change, but the divisions in American society, the controversies sparked by racial segregation, the property taxpayers' revolt, all increase resistance to change. Why spend all that money if teachers receive little help in their daily work with children?

4

The English Head Teacher and the American Principal

The autonomy of the English primary school rests on the authority vested in the head teacher. He makes curricular decisions. He may be advised by others, but he is almost never ordered. The freedom to make decisions, recognized through long-standing customs, is accompanied by genuine authority, power, and status. The head's educational ideas and personality often make an indelible impression on the school. What the head personifies—his spoken wishes, his written communications, his interests, and his aversions —is inclined to become part of the character of the local school.

The head's influence often extends beyond the school into the local community. This can be particularly important in rural areas where there are few competing institutions and where there may be a paucity of social service agencies. In the small village school the head teacher exercises a considerable degree of community leadership, and the school is afforded a highly regarded place in the minds of the local citizens. Rural schools have pioneered in the development of a number of currently popular practices, such as environmental studies and the renewal of interest in folk art and industry.

Most heads are recruited from within the ranks. This means that primary heads are almost invariably products of the Colleges of Education, not the universities, and they do not hold degrees. A head teacher's first appointment is usually to a small school. Since the scale determining the head teacher's salary is based on the enrollment of the school, there is a great deal of competition for appointments to the larger schools. Vacant positions are publicly advertised in the professional journals, such as the *Times Educational Supplement*. The Board of Managers of each school, acting with the advice of the Chief Education Officer of the Local Education Authority or his representative, interviews and selects the best qualified applicant from a "short list" of previously screened candidates. A head generally has ten or more years of teaching experience before he receives his first appointment. Typically, he changes schools a few times and then settles down at one school in the middle of his career.

Formal education for leadership positions seldom includes the specialized study of administration. The head has probably taken a number of brief in-service courses. If he is fortunate, he is offered "secondment" for a year's leave with pay to take a course that will qualify him for an advanced diploma under the jurisdiction of a School or Institute of Education within a university. The diploma is not considered the equivalent of a university degree, nor does the content of the course deal much with school administration. The course usually combines the academic study of disciplines that contribute to educational theory with a thesis and opportunities to visit schools and curriculum centers.

A position that is held by thousands of practitioners inevitably reflects the full range of educational philosophies, from staunch traditionalism to doctrinaire progressivism. The majority of heads probably could be classified as moderates; it is they who have led the primary schools in England to make the moderate changes described in this book. As key change agents they are not necessarily the people who originate new ideas, but they are most instrumental in carrying them out.

When comparing the American elementary school principal with the English head teacher, the American seems to have much more in his favor. He is a graduate of a university, and he probably holds an advanced degree as well. In most cases he has taken many educational administration courses. His salary is far higher, and he is provided with a much larger budget for supplies, books, and furniture. Yet the elementary school principal in the United States exerts far less leadership than the English head. The American's contribution is particularly deficient at the heart of the educational process—the leadership of the instructional program.

To American youngsters the principal has become a symbol of school discipline. He rarely teaches children directly. He may know the names of most of them, but he is seldom well acquainted with their learning difficulties or special aptitudes. In curriculum matters he may not be of much help to teachers, particularly if his experience has been in secondary schools and he has chosen elementary school administration as an opportunity for quicker promotion.

Many American elementary school teachers complain about principals. Some even blame them for *holding back* educational change. Although teachers are fairly loyal to their own principals, they tend to distrust and dislike administrators as a breed. But the image of the roadblocking school principal may only serve as a convenient scapegoat, an excuse to rationalize the teacher's own wish to perpetuate old patterns.

In matters of authority the American principal is the middleman, caught between the demands of increasingly militant teachers and the regulations of the central office, charged with carrying out the policies of an elected local school board. The symbolic authority of the principal is further compromised when he is asked to serve as the front-line educational salesman, the official responsible for keeping the parents content. To gain the allegiance of his staff, he must prevent parents from climbing onto the teachers' backs. To keep the parents happy, he must make himself accessible to listen to their concerns. To his staff he must appear to support the professionals at all times, whether he feels that they are right or wrong. The English head must also deal with these expectations, but to a far lesser extent. He retains more leeway than the American to fulfill his primary responsibility, that of providing educational leadership.

Few principals are well known as educational leaders outside of their own communities. It is the school superintendents who get the publicity, both good and bad, in the United States. In England people are continually advising visitors to go to see a specific head teacher's school. In the United States people rarely identify a school with its principal. Rather, the school is supposed to "belong" to the neighborhood.

Most disturbing of all, very few principals in the United States act as if they have the freedom to bring about any far-reaching changes. So often they defer to school board policy. In both England and the United States the expectation of leadership resides in the position. Both English head and American principal act as father figures to the children and, in some cases, to the teachers and parents as well. Yet the English head is not hampered in carrying out his professional sense of obligation, while the American principal frequently feels restricted.

It is as dangerous to generalize about American elementary principals as it is to treat English head teachers as if they were all more or less alike. While this chapter will make bold contrasts between principals and heads, it is recognized throughout that a great variety of individual responses accompany the fulfillment of any administrative office. One reason for using contrasting models is to highlight to Americans the *potential* for change that resides in this pivotal leadership position, a potential more often tapped in England than in America. This chapter compares the English head teacher and the American elementary school principal in three respects: the leadership of instruction, the maintenance of authority, and the establishment of relationships with school clients.

THE LEADER OF INSTRUCTION

The English Head Teacher

In England a school has only one recognized teacher in charge —the head teacher. All the other teachers are officially classified as assistant teachers. The meaning of this distinction is clear: all other qualified teachers assist the head in the process of teaching. The older terminology, headmaster and assistant masters, which is still used in private schools and most secondary schools, underlines the distinction even more forcefully. The English head is the person responsible for the curriculum. Leadership for the instructional program is considered to be his *primary* function.

Furthermore, the head teaches. He is required by law to do so. Many heads, particularly in the smaller schools, take a class of their own for most or part of the day. They preside over the daily assembly each morning in the hall. They coach teams and they supervise after-school activities, such as country dancing. Visitors to schools often find the heads working with special groups of children. Heads may provide remedial work for children with learning difficulties or teach the more talented children creative writing, drama, science, or fine arts. Heads nearly always accompany the children and teachers on week-long trips to the Continent or to other parts of England. It used to be a common practice for heads to drill the more able older juniors each day to get them ready to "pass" the eleven-plus examination for entrance to secondary school.

Since teaching materials and supplies are selected by the individual school rather than the district, the head is responsible for ordering new equipment, furniture, books, supplies, and teaching aids. The alert head must be aware of new developments; his intimate knowledge of the latest curriculum materials helps him to provide instructional leadership. Local control of how money is spent preserves the individuality of each school.

In many authorities an English school can no longer hire a supply (substitute) teacher until a regular member of the staff has been absent due to illness for at least a week; it is the head teacher who typically takes over the absentee's class or sees that it is covered. He also fills in if a teacher is released for an afternoon to attend a course. In sections of the Inner London Education Authority, where there is a relatively high rate of absenteeism, some heads are seldom free of teaching commitments and their effectiveness in carrying out other responsibilities is hampered. The regulations restricting the employment of supply teachers, which are no doubt designed to save money, would be much more damaging to effective school leadership were it not for team teaching and the willingness of teachers to fill in for one another. Head teachers have not complained bitterly about the restriction, because they accept the expectation that they are responsible for the entire instructional program at all times, whether they are working directly or indirectly with children.

Head teachers participate directly in teacher education. At Berkshire College of Education twenty-four local heads devote one day each week to serve as cotutors for the first-year primary education course. The National Association of Head Teachers has called for an even more active role in teacher education. At present they work closely with practice teachers, they supervise first-year proba-

Learning How to Learn

tionary teachers and new teachers, and they work with all the staff concerned during the introduction of new programs.

The head frequently sponsors innovation, and this is the most important difference between the leadership roles in England and America. The head's part in spreading curriculum changes across the country has become crucial. Some heads encourage new ideas in every area of the school. They promote organizational modifications such as team teaching, suggest new instructional strategies based on integration of content, demonstrate new teaching aids, purchase new scientific equipment, develop methods for more descriptive evaluation of children, and publicize opportunities for in-service courses. When innovations gain acceptance by other teachers, it is frequently the result of the head's initiative.

The head can do all this because he believes that he has the freedom to do so. The assistant teachers, the parents, the school managers, the Chief Education Officers, and the representatives on the Education Committees of the Local Authorities support the head in this assumption. This does not mean that the head has unlimited power in the instructional area nor that he does not frequently consult with other teachers. Even a traditional head relies heavily on the deputy head and the experienced teachers in the school. Less traditional heads are becoming more aware of the desirability of pooling staff ideas and sharing authority.

It should be stressed that English primary school heads can set themselves for or against change. There are very traditional schools in England with very authoritarian heads. A determined traditionalist can be almost impervious to suggestion. Even head teachers with pronounced symptoms of mental illness would be difficult to remove. In some large secondary schools the head enjoys such an exalted position that it is apparently possible for him to isolate himself from the students and staff, working from his study and making an appearance only on ceremonial occasions, such as school assemblies.

The unevenness of curriculum change across England is partly due to the fact that it takes such a long time for an old-fashioned head to pass on or retire. Generally his replacement helps the school catch up with the times. Whatever the reasons, schools in England do change when a new head takes over. In fact, rather profound changes take place within a year or two. Some L.E.A.'s have tried to induce these changes by encouraging movement among heads, but hardening of the arteries is a disease not confined to the aged and the infirm.

English observers are not as impressed as Americans by the influence of head teachers as a group. They would qualify most of the above assertions. They maintain that only some heads, rather than most heads, are influential. The prime movers tend to be the younger, newly appointed heads, those interested in making a reputation, and those who have returned to schools from a year's leave at an advanced diploma course. But the potential does reside in the office of the headship. English observers would soon find that the autonomy of head teachers, taken for granted in England, hardly exists in the United States.

The American Principal

One of the first axioms in educational administration courses used to be that all other responsibilities should be considered secondary to the leadership of instruction. Since the curriculum lies at the heart of the school, one might be justified in concluding that the main job of the school principal is to provide curriculum leadership. This may no longer be sociologically possible.

Visitors to the United States easily come to the conclusion that the instructional program proceeds relatively untouched by the elementary principal. After the books have been distributed, the schedule of classes for music and physical education posted, and the district-wide forms properly explained, the principal goes about his other duties. In the United States the curriculum is not under his jurisdiction; legally its determination resides with the local board of education. Moreover, the textbooks are so lavish, the curriculum guides so thick, the teachers so independent, that there seems to be little left for a leader of instruction to do.

The principal who has little impact on the curriculum has little effect on the character or atmosphere of the school. To confirm this, visitors need only make a tour of neighboring schools within an American school district. They will find the instructional program to be very similar from school to school. Visitors in England, on the other hand, will find neighboring schools within the same Local Education Authority to be quite different. American education has become much more centrally determined, yet Americans are the ones who speak more earnestly about local control.

In order to promote curriculum changes, Americans create elaborate machinery consisting of various combinations of assistant superintendents for instruction, curriculum coordinators, subject matter consultants, curriculum committees, curriculum councils, curriculum documents, curriculum resource guides, and curriculum task forces, buttressed by impressive theories of curriculum change, and well oiled with federal or state financial grants. Seldom is the elementary school principal central to this machinery. Instead, curriculum planners are careful to "involve" him, to "go around" him, or simply to secure his permission. His official status is still that of leader, but he is not considered crucial to program innovation.

Elementary school principals commonly protest that they would like to work more with the children and be of greater service to teachers. They would like to devote more time to the curriculum, but there are just too many administrative details for them to handle. Often they cannot convince the teachers that they are the leaders of instruction, for they are not really head *teachers* in the English sense. American teachers do not believe that principals can teach beginning reading or modern math or creative drama more effectively than anyone else in the school. Some American principals avoid teaching because they feel more comfortable serving as functionaries in a bureaucratic system.

AUTHORITY, POWER, AND STATUS

The English Head Teacher

In the decentralized English system, the individual head has authority (the right to make decisions) and power (the ability to carry out decisions). He has a recognized status, which, while not as exalted as that of headmaster of the independent preparatory school or public school, is indisputable. His status does not need to be earned, except in a modified way; it is largely ascribed to the office. The respect of the children, the parents, the Board of Managers, and the central administration comes with his appointment. If he is successful, he can enhance his prestige. He can build a favorable reputation that will make his job easier and more effective.

The status springs from a hierarchical tradition that tends to recognize authority where it is supposed to reside. Most people accept the head's prerogatives. Even though the social distance between primary school and local community is decreasing (D.E.S., 1968; C.A.S.E., 1970), the distance remains. The mums wait patiently for their children after school outside the school grounds; few bother the head unless they have very good reason to.

If some older, more traditional heads resent current reforms, it is because they recognize in them threats to traditional authority. Some are not at all happy about forming P.T.A.'s and try to discourage parental involvement in school affairs. They foresee a number of growing threats to their autonomy—from Local Education Authority advisers to Department of Education and Science officials to leaders of curriculum development groups such as the Schools Council—yet all these people function in a *very* advisory capacity.

In public, primary school heads tend to endorse the idea of forming an official link between parents and the school; privately they tend to be skeptical about possible interference. When one mentions that American P.T.A.'s are the least of the principal's worries and that local P.T.A. chapters often serve as staunch supporters in bond issues, tax-assessment votes, or as a line of defense against community attacks by hostile groups, the English respond with amazement. They associate the reputation cantankerous parents have established on the other side of the Atlantic with the P.T.A. They need to be reassured that it is other pressures—from certain aggressive parents, from right-wing attacks on public schools, and from outspoken critics with direct access to school board meetings—that constitute the more dangerous threats of interference. In a country in which school policies and revenues are at the mercy of school board elections and taxpayer revolts, it is not the P.T.A. so much as antischool forces which constitute the gravest danger.

The American Principal

The American elementary school principal has much less independent authority. He is restricted by the forces that act on him. Although he has considerable status within his school and the surrounding neighborhood, within the school district bureaucracy he is considered merely an administrative functionary. The most important distinction is that the American principal seldom acts as if he has power to make far-reaching decisions. He restricts the use of his authority to solving immediate problems and to making decisions that will keep the machinery going. He serves more as a trouble-shooter than an innovator.

What are some of the negative conditions that prevent elementary school principals from exerting greater influence? It is difficult to develop close personal relationships in a large school with more than five hundred children and a staff of more than twenty-five teachers. Large schools make demands for a multitude of administrative decisions that are carried out impersonally, often according to written rules and regulations. The principal may serve as the front man to the parents, but he is the middleman between the teachers and the central administration. He serves a centralized bureaucratic system and is charged with carrying out district-wide policies.

The ethos of the American elementary school does not encourage a comfortable, self-confident style of leadership. The principal of a central-city school knows that he is sitting on a powder keg, as parents get ready for battle, pressure groups exert demands, and the children act out emotional problems and perform inadequately on city-wide achievement tests. As the status leader, he is badgered from all sides. He is more than satisfied to perform a holding action against a world that seems increasingly alien to traditional objectives. In the suburbs the position is not quite so precarious, but a common defensive response to pressures is a desire not to rock the boat. A good day passes when the expected storm is weathered.

RELATIONSHIP TO THE SCHOOL'S CLIENTS

The English Head Teacher

The English head would not use the term "client." The word implies a professional relationship to a nonprofessional public, similar to that which a lawyer offers a client who pays for his services. The English head teacher does not exist to serve the public. He deals with the same people as those with whom an American principal deals, but he relates to them in rather different ways. No one disputes his authority or challenges his status. Heads do not act out of fear of their clients' power, nor are they inhibited about exercising the power of their office.

To the children the head is not merely a symbol of authority; he is their teacher. And he knows them as a teacher knows his students; he is acquainted with their interests and hobbies, their academic progress, their creative achievements, and their learning problems. Many heads ask class teachers to keep fairly detailed anecdotal records about children, and they regularly discuss the children's progress with the teachers.

To the parents and community members, the head may at times act in a high-handed manner, but they seldom try to tell him what to do. One of the differences between England and America is that in England the office of the head has not become a focal point for conflicting community power forces. The head, therefore, does not need to worry about pleasing (or appeasing) the school's clients. Since taxes for education are raised more indirectly than in America, there is not the necessity in England to keep the voters contented in order to ensure the approval of a tax assessment.

The American Principal

The principal's symbolic role of leadership is not as secure as is the head's in England; the American has to maintain his status by not antagonizing the clients—the parents, the teachers, the community, the school board, and the children. When his position is threatened by potentially hostile forces, the principal needs to win them over. He therefore learns to rely on public relations techniques. He tries simultaneously to serve the teachers, to pacify the parents, and to follow faithfully the policies of the central administration.

To innovate and make changes, to exert strong curriculum leadership, to express educational opinions forcefully, can only agitate already troubled waters, which is precisely what the principal does not want to do. He wants to calm the waters, not upset the people whom he feels he must please. Job security among American principals is not as threatened as many fear; few are fired for incompetence in public relations. Yet the principal who wants peace of mind learns very soon that controversial issues are best avoided. Enough troubles arise in the normal course of events without stirring up additional ones through advocating change that might make others feel insecure.

Teachers give the principal the message, "Leave us alone and let us teach." And, on the whole, he does leave most of them alone.

His support of the staff consists of providing supplies and services, giving recognition to the more effective teachers, and bailing out the inadequate ones. Teachers in an English school would rarely send such a message to the head, especially not in open-plan infant schools, where too many moving children are seeking attention from too few adults. English teachers tend to welcome all the help that they can get, particularly from the widely experienced head teacher.

THE HIERARCHICAL TRADITION

The acceptance of ascribed status permeates English middle-class society. Few Englishmen see any inconsistency between democracy and a highly structured hierarchical system (Raynor, 1970). The English concept of democracy is largely based on middle-class respect for property rights and parliamentary forms and, more recently, the expectation of services from the welfare state. Many Englishmen, even intellectual socialists, are suspicious of equalitarian principles. There is a widespread feeling that mass education, mass spending power, and mass means of communication are threats not only to privilege but also to the quality of life. Many fear that to cater to mass desires will inevitably result in depressed standards.

The educational system is part of the hierarchical tradition. In such a tradition the impetus for change frequently originates at the top and moves downward. The tradition of opinion-making from above is certainly on the decline, but it is still very strong. Because resistance to authority in England is as yet diffuse and poorly mobilized, suggestions that originate from higher echelons still carry a great deal of weight.

The hierarchical tradition serves as a bulwark for the educational advisory services. In England no one in education orders anyone about. There is no need to issue directives or enforce administrative decisions or distribute policy statements through the chain of command. Advisers spread new ideas informally through conferences and publications; heads take them up if they choose; teachers carry them out if they think them feasible. This attitude is what leads tourists to remark that England seems to be such a very civilized country. Authorities seldom resort to coercion; it is usually sufficient to carefully make their wishes known. People are attuned to suggestion. In this subtle system of muted communication the head receives messages and transmits them down the line.

CHANGES AFFECTING HEAD TEACHERS

Contrasts between English head teachers and American elementary school principals have been somewhat overstated in the above discussion. Actually, there are several ways in which English heads are prevented from exercising arbitrary authority, and American principals are not quite so helpless in carrying out their designated functions.

Current developments in England are likely to transform administrative practices so that they are closer to the American pattern. In an increasingly urban society the exercise of power arouses countervailing power forces (Cotgrove, 1968). The parents, the teachers, and community groups will not remain acquiescent for long.

Even when his authority is respected, the head still spends too much of his time performing routine administrative duties. Many primary school heads learn to become amateur carpenters. If they want to modify the structure of the building, add shelf space, install new teaching areas, or construct hutches for outdoor pets, they generally supervise the construction themselves. They become adept fund-raisers. They are required to keep records of all kinds of petty financial accounts. They spend too much time responding to memoranda from Local Education Authorities and other advisory bodies. Even with an efficient secretary, the head cannot escape from the routine demands that plague state-maintained institutions.

The head's potential for misusing power is gradually being reduced. Authoritarian head teachers are on the wane; upon retirement they are increasingly being replaced by men and women with more benevolent dispositions. No longer do heads cane children, keep the parents at arm's length, or arbitrarily inspect the work of teachers. Progressive heads predict further shifts of this sort. Heads are becoming more inclined to work cooperatively with teachers and to serve as group leaders at meetings that pool suggestions from various staff members.

Heads are increasingly dependent on parents to help raise auxiliary funds. Budgets provided by the authority for supplies, materials, furniture, and resources are spent at the head's discretion, but they can purchase only a fraction of what the staff requests. Expensive audio-visual equipment and technological resources must be financed through voluntary contributions. Hardly a week goes by without some school sponsoring a jumble (rummage) sale or fair in the community. A number of primary schools have launched major fund-raising schemes to construct school swimming pools. Increasing parental support is matched by the increasing presence of parents in schools. Not only are parents welcome on Open Days; some schools actually encourage parents to drop into the classrooms for informal visits. This was almost unknown a generation ago. Parents serve as voluntary helpers and part-time teachers. A number of heads are beginning to take seriously the Plowden recommendations about involving the community in the school (Plowden, 1967).

LEFT–WING TEACHER CRITICISM OF THE HEADSHIP

According to members of Rank and File, an organization of left-wing teachers within the National Union of Teachers, the changes that have so far taken place are far from enough. They warn that it would be irresponsible to rely on the head's benevolence. They claim that enlightened heads represent little more than kindly paternalism, and traditional heads may represent authoritarian despotism.

Can an assistant teacher directly challenge the authority and power of the head? The assistant has little recourse for his grievances; he cannot even go to his own union. The N.U.T. executive committee is largely composed of head teachers who will not intervene in a dispute among members unless there is an obvious breach of professional conduct. The authoritarian head, on the other hand, can often count on the support of the Local Education Authority as well as fall back on law, local custom, and school traditions.

Although it has not received much publicity, a Teachers' Charter promoted by Rank and File proposes to protect the class teacher's right to oppose administrative authority (Rank and File, 1970). It is designed to give the assistant teacher a greater say in decisions that directly affect his work, such as those relating to discipline, the curriculum, and his teaching assignment. The Charter calls for the election of an executive officer, or officers, by the teaching staff to replace the appointment of a head. The executive is elected to remain in office for a prescribed period and is subject to recall by the electorate. Only a nominal pay differential between the executive and other teachers is provided. Teachers, parents, secondary students, and members of the community are to become the Governing Body that establishes school policies. The executive officer is charged with carrying out the Governing Body's decisions.

This Charter is in bold contrast to prevailing practices. At present the head is responsible for the curriculum, school discipline, and the establishment of school policy. He has the right to make the rules and enforce them. He is legislature, executive, and judiciary rolled into one. The Charter would make the former head's functions executive in nature while stripping him of legislative powers. He would be transformed from the master to the servant of the teachers' association.

Such a stance is attractive to young, militant teachers, particularly those working with nonacademic groups in secondary schools in industrial areas. But a reassessment such as the Teachers' Charter would almost certainly be unacceptable to the Chief Education Officers of the Local Education Authorities, to the Education Committees and Borough Councils, to the National Association of Head Teachers, and to community power forces. It is also totally contrary to tradition. If the solution proposed in the Charter seems contrary to the ways in which executive power is exercised in most formal groups (Mills, 1956; Cotgrove, 1968), it is particularly at odds with the English hierarchical tradition.

The American principal works within a basic paradox. His authority is severely limited by regulations and unwritten expectations, yet he holds a position in which he is expected to assert leadership. Furthermore, there is no other defined leadership position at the local school level, despite the existence in larger districts of an elaborate administrative machinery working under the superintendent of the central office. If instructional leadership is declined by the American principal, who is left to exert it?

In England the head is accorded so much authority and can exert so much power that abuses are permitted. Power can be used to promote or to retard change, to punish as well as to reward. In

England dissident teachers have too little protection from opinionated heads; in the United States principals who want to provide instructional leadership need to deal with too many conflicting demands.

5

The Class Teacher

The class teacher is obviously the crucial figure in any educational system. In England the position of the teacher is even more crucial than in most countries, since he is responsible for determining the curriculum. Americans and some Englishmen tend to be overly impressed by the curricular influence of the head. For all practical purposes, a head teacher does assume responsibility for the school's program, and he has much more influence than the American elementary school principal. But in the final analysis it is the class teacher who carries out the program, exercising considerable independence along the way.

Too many descriptions of English primary education imply that a dedicated band of superior teachers with unlimited reservoirs of love, wisdom, and ingenuity provide a smoothly flowing program for responsible children who have largely learned to manage themselves. This picture seems all the more dubious when hard-bitten critics of American education imply that if the English system were transplanted, American schools that had been bureaucratic, rigid, deadly dull, and authoritarian would suddenly be free, open, relevant, and child-centered.

English teachers are pleased to hear positive impressions about their schools, but they are even more pleased when others recognize the frustrations and problems with which they have to cope. Their job is not particularly socially rewarding. They are certainly underpaid. Primary teachers are afforded low status in the English school system. Employment conditions give rise to multiple dissatisfactions, particularly among men (Rudd and Wiseman, 1962). In spite of all this, more and more teachers are gradually adopting new methods, and many are endorsing current reforms with strong conviction.

That the class teacher is at the heart of reform has been best expressed by John Blackie. He describes the crucial point of contact in English education as the personal relationship between teacher and children: "It is to make this contact as fruitful as possible that everything else—authority, administration, inspection, curriculum exist. . . . Innovation, under such a system, may come more slowly than when it is imposed from above, but it comes more surely because it is initiated by the teacher and based on, and tested by, his own experience" (Blackie, 1969, pp. 4–5).

In the United States lip service is paid to the teacher's professional autonomy, but others define the curriculum for him. G. W. Bassett, an Australian who compared American and British primary education, makes a point similar to Blackie's. Professional associations, university professors, research teams, curriculum specialists, bureaucrats, and publishers in the United States promote reforms (Bassett, 1970). These influences try to get the teacher to change. In England the focus of attention is on the school itself, and the innovators are the teachers themselves. They tend to resist the proposals of outside bodies, since interference conflicts with their idealized image of professional responsibility.

The interchange of ideas among class teachers has become one of the most potent ways to diffuse new practices. Teachers are more likely to accept suggestions from other teachers than from college tutors, advisers, or publications. Heads are considered teachers rather than administrators, and they help to publicize new ideas while encouraging teachers to visit other schools and attend short courses at the Teachers' Centres. Staff room conversations, interroom visits, team teaching arrangements, after-school meetings, corridor and classroom displays, all help to circulate practical suggestions. Advisers tend to organize short courses as workshops where they emphasize the production and display of new teaching materials.

One criticism leveled at classroom teachers by heads and college lecturers is that they are unaware of research reports and do not do a great deal of professional reading in the more theoretical journals or books. Popular writing for primary teachers tends to be anecdotal, descriptive, and methodological rather than theoretical or empirical. Since teachers are not obligated to take advanced courses in education, and since there are few opportunities to do so, it is unlikely that conditions will change. The gap between research and practice will probably grow even wider. The gradual diffusion of modern practices has been dependent on the convictions of nontheoretical practitioners, much to the chagrin of college and university lecturers devoted to the educational disciplines.

FREEDOM FOR THE CLASS TEACHER

The degree of freedom accorded teachers in England does not exist in any other advanced industrial society (Blackie, 1969). In consultation with the head, class teachers carry out whatever curriculum interpretations appeal to them. They have genuine autonomy.

American teachers claim that when they close the classroom door, no matter what is stated on paper, regardless of who is stalking the hallways, they determine their own program, for the curriculum is nothing more than that which takes place in the classroom with a group of children. In this sense any teacher has autonomy, but what counts is the atmosphere under which he exercises it. In America, freedom for teachers generally involves a subversive act behind closed doors; in England it is *expected* that the primary class teacher will assume responsibility for formulating his own curriculum objectives.

These objectives can be broadly or narrowly defined. The teacher may choose to adopt informal methods; he may choose to retain formal ones. He has freedom not to change as well as freedom to change. No one will attempt to coerce him; the only influences brought to bear will be personal and advisory in nature.

Chief Education Officers like to joke about American exchange teachers who seem at a loss when first plunged into an English primary school. Americans ask: "Where is the course to study?"

"What kind of lesson plans are required?" "Which forms need to be processed?" It takes a while before some of them find out that restraints are of a very different order. No one will tell them what to do or how to do it. In some cases they are left so much on their own that they feel neglected. The exchange teacher program suffers in a number of ways through inadequate communication, especially with regard to changed expectations. Many Americans feel completely ignored at first, whereas it is likely that their English colleagues believe that they are respecting their privacy by leaving Americans alone.

English teachers cherish independence. They resist imposition. They are opposed to attempts to exert overt direction and are suspicious of commercial teaching packages, guides, or manuals. No one in England has yet tried to promote a "teacherproof" curriculum reform. No one dares to imply distrust of the class teacher's judgment to such an extent!

One of the most important implications of a locally determined curriculum is that there are no common minimum expectations throughout the country, county, or borough. Each teacher has leeway to adapt his program to his particular children in a particular school located in a particular neighborhood. Such flexibility offers the teacher freedom to gear the curriculum to the children and to the local community setting. On the other hand, a teacher who is unaware of particular community needs may provide an inappropriate curriculum. In this respect teacher autonomy provides for a relevant or irrelevant curriculum. There are no district-wide safeguards or restrictions.

CONSTRAINTS ON THE CLASS TEACHER

English teachers are not quite so free as it seems at first. They work within a hierarchical social structure that reinforces the power and authority of the head, whose leadership is recognized by the Local Education Authority, the parents, the children, and ultimately the teachers themselves. The limited rights of class teachers offer little protection should they disagree with the head. Because the head usually wins in a showdown, confrontations are avoided.

Teachers' organizations have so far asserted little power. They seldom serve as collective agents for class teachers in disputes with the school administration or the governing education committee.

Their power is further limited by having to negotiate nationally over matters of salary with representatives of the education authorities.

Differences within staffs divide teachers and reduce their potential combined strength. There are the usual sociological distinctions based on age, sex, and marital status (Blyth, 1965). Social distance between older and younger teachers, differing interests among men and women teachers, economic and social discrepancies between married and single teachers, all prevent teachers from discovering common ground for collective action. Many other differences arise over educational views and degrees of support for or antipathy toward the head.

The greatest constraint on collective political or economic action, particularly that advocated by young teachers fresh from college, is traditional attitudes. English schools, like almost all schools, are conservative institutions clinging at least to the forms, if not to the feelings, of the past. English primary teachers may be more politically conservative than secondary teachers (Vaizey, 1962); certainly they overwhelmingly adhere to middle-class values. Most primary teachers are women; they tend to look with suspicion on militancy and tend to be unsympathetic to radical postures in dress, manners, or political tactics. As College of Education students have become more politicized, their image has suffered, even among the teachers whose economic cause they seek to support.

A constraint on rural teachers is isolation. There are still hundreds of one- and two-teacher schools in England in which there is little contact with other professionals (D.E.S., 1970) and few opportunities to attend meetings or courses during the school term. A few local authorities like the West Riding of Yorkshire have attempted to bring rural teachers together, but the majority of primarily rural counties depend for outside contacts on the very occasional stimulation of visiting H.M.I.'s and county advisers.

THE STATUS AND CAREER PROSPECTS OF THE CLASS TEACHER

The teacher in the United States certainly has greater career prospects than the teacher in England. His most important advantage is the option to switch careers if he so chooses. He has a university degree and his qualifications enable him to seek employment elsewhere if teaching does not prove satisfying. The American teacher is relatively well paid, at least during the early years of his career, in comparison with manual, sales, and clerical workers. If he becomes dissatisfied with salary or working conditions, he may turn to unions or professional organizations which are successfully pressing demands for a fairer share of economic benefits. The teacher in England has only one prospect, and that is to become a head teacher. His qualification, the teaching certificate, has no transfer value to other professions. He is locked into teaching.

Salaries of primary teachers are generally low and have been deteriorating in relation to salaries of secondary teachers since 1945, when primary teachers were finally placed on a common professional salary scale (Blyth, 1965). University graduates, almost entirely confined to secondary schools, receive a sizable bonus for possessing a degree (although this advantage may be reduced in future national negotiations over salary). There are many more graded and special responsibility posts available in the secondary schools. In fact, the whole concept of graded posts, supplying additional remuneration for additional responsibility, is foreign to the organization of primary education.

The primary teacher's role is anomalous; he assumes responsibility for a great many different functions and the whole range of the curriculum in an age of increasing specialization (B. Wilson, 1962). Higher status in English education resides within secondary teaching, where an emphasis on specialized subjects and adoption of more limited cognitive objectives decrease diffusion. The highest status and the highest pay scales belong to public (independent) school and grammar school teachers, who are mostly men and mostly university graduates. The teacher in the primary school cannot escape comparing his more diffused and lower-prestige position with that of others in teaching.

Curiously, some former avenues for increased status have been taken away. In the days of streaming, or grouping by ability, the community attached higher status to those who taught the high streams of the older juniors. The reputation of the junior school depended in part on the examination results of these older, more able children. But streaming is now on the decline while family grouping is decreasing the importance of age differences. There are few remaining distinctive marks of esteem for the career teacher.

The ambitious teacher devotes a good deal of energy to trying

Learning How to Learn

to qualify for promotion to head teacher. He can add to his paper qualifications by taking additional short courses. If he is fortunate, he may be "seconded" for full-time study at a college or university. He tries to move from school to school in order to add to his experience. With no college employment service to aid him, he must fill out numerous applications for advertised posts, sometimes trying to hide his search from those who might interpret it as dissatisfaction or disloyalty. If he is young, he knows that he must wait several years for promotion. Few headships are open to persons under thirty. A deputy headship, which remains a full-time teaching post, is often as far as an individual can advance on the salary scale in his first ten years of teaching.

Many of the more militant men teachers have joined the all-male National Association of Schoolmasters, which attempts to speak for male career teachers in matters of salary and working conditions (N.A.S., 1970). This further fractures the solidarity of teachers' organizations, which are split into many unions that cater to men or women, degree holders or non–degree holders, heads or assistants, private or maintained sectors, college or university lecturers, and so forth. The N.A.S. struggles for a salary structure that will reward career teachers, while the larger National Union of Teachers fights for smaller across-the-board increases in the basic salary to attract beginning teachers and reward the large percentage of women within the membership. The N.A.S. is more militant, but its bargaining tactics are such that they seek special concessions, which members of the N.U.T. consider to be special pleading at the expense of the total profession.

It is not that men teachers suffer discrimination; it is more likely that women do. Women career teachers are offered even fewer financial inducements (U.W.T., 1970). Their prospects for advancement are considerably less. Their chief outlet for recognition is classroom performance. They attempt to gain respect from their peers or come to the attention of the authorities by adopting currently popular patterns. Blocked opportunities, then, may have fostered the spread of modern ideas. Men turn to them to enhance career opportunities, and women have few other satisfying outlets to achieve distinction.

THE HEAVY DEMANDS OF THE NEW METHODS

It is up to the class teacher to make the new methods work. How can he manage the highly differentiated and dispersed activities of individualized teaching along with small, shifting groups?

The teacher used to have a set curriculum and common assignments through which he controlled the goals, pace, and instructional procedures. Now the teacher must bring a vast repertoire of abilities to implement the new methods. Former props to the teacher's authority have been removed, increasing his fallibility. Restrictions on children's movement have been lifted. The teacher needs to be well aware of the learning performance and interests of a large collection of individual children. He needs background knowledge in a great many disciplines. He must feel comfortable with problem-solving procedures and indirect teaching methods.

The teacher who is able to function under these demanding expectations turns himself into a human resource. He feeds in new data and guides to additional references, responds to a variety of questions, and stimulates further probing. He tries to help the children learn to make intelligent choices, assume increasing self-control, and follow through on awakened interests. If he wants to foster the scientific method, he has to keep the search for knowledge open-ended. He has to help children form hypotheses, organize investigations, collect data, and devise tests for verification. Children are continually asking questions for which the teacher has no answers. Even if he has the answers, he recognizes that it is not his job to do the children's thinking for them. It is no easy matter to locate adequate, up-to-date resources for solving the many problems under investigation.

Problems of management are exceedingly complex, especially in outmoded buildings. The learning environment has to be so arranged that the children as well as the teacher have ready access to sources and materials. The sheer quantity of work that children produce is extensive, and they expect a response. If the teacher is going to do more than acknowledge and praise, he must respond in ways that will encourage the children to carry on further investigation.

All this requires a flexibility of personality and a patience in interpersonal relationships that too few members of the general population possess. Some accounts imply that informal teaching is so much more rewarding than formal teaching that teachers naturally gravitate to it. Teachers who have switched to an informal program almost invariably admit in interviews that it is much more difficult than formal teaching, but they are quick to acknowledge the increased satisfactions.

RELATIONSHIPS WITH CHILDREN

A number of teachers who have adopted new procedures believe that their major function is to establish congenial working relationships with children. Interpersonal contacts become crucial. If the teacher no longer merely stands up and teaches, if instead he tries to help children learn how to learn, he must reach them on a somewhat different plane.

There is certainly a different quality of interaction in many English classrooms as compared with American ones. There seems to be less fearfulness. The children are not afraid of the teacher, and the teacher is not afraid that the children will take advantage of him. There seems to be greater mutual respect. The teacher is less hesitant about turning responsibility over to the children. Unlike so many American teachers, he does not feel that turning children loose will cause chaos. The title of a most sensitive book, *Alongside the Child in the Primary School* (Marsh, 1970a), idealizes the changed relationship. The teacher works by the side of the children—with them, not above them. He relates to them without placing undue emphasis on his adult status.

The teacher spends a lot of time talking informally with children, and he often goes over their work with them. He seldom talks *at* children; he talks things over *with* them. A nonimposing, accepting quality of spoken and unspoken communication is a distinguishing mark of the ability to relate comfortably to children. The teacher encourages the children to carry out their own tentative plans. Children check with the teacher from time to time, but he will seldom deter them, except to point out where they may be taking on too large a commitment. Respect for a child's ideas implies a basic respect for his integrity as a person.

The changing relationship has released the teacher from some former expectations. He cannot escape his authority as the teacher, but he can relinquish authority as the final arbiter of right and wrong, of true and false, of appropriate and inappropriate. He is free to make mistakes. He is free to admit uncertainty or lack of understanding. He retains the right to be fallible. Even so, the teacher remains an important adult model. He shows interest, offers encouragement, provides support. His implied approval becomes a powerful motivating force, particularly with children who have experienced feelings of failure or rejection or suffered from unfavorable comparisons.

Cognitive objectives do not assume as high a place in English schools as they do in the United States. English primary teachers claim that they are more interested in fostering *attitudes* toward learning (although there is little sophistication about how attitudes might be measured). How a child feels about himself and how he feels about fields of inquiry are more important than how much knowledge he acquires. To foster a self-generating attitude toward learning, relationships that encourage children to think for themselves are preferred to those that maintain children's dependence on adult direction.

More and more primary teachers are talking along these lines, but few English secondary teachers talk this way, nor do they behave in accordance with these more supportive terms. For the most part, secondary teachers rely on their authority with the pupils they govern and with the subjects they teach.

The less formal, more equalitarian relationships between primary teachers and children may increase feelings of satisfaction, but they also add to role conflict. What are teachers supposed to do with children who are more familiar with authoritarian adults or who cannot comfortably assimilate increased freedom?

Unfortunately, a great deal of rubbish, to use an English phrase, has been written about the modified relationship between children and teachers in modern primary schools, as if there were no pertinent differences between adults and children and as if everyone were gathered together in one great big, happy learning laboratory. Even if some adults are unwilling to admit it, children at least are aware of the social distance. They do not call teachers by their first names, nor even by their surnames. English children still address teachers as "Sir" or "Miss."

ROLE CONFLICT

A few sociological constructs should put into perspective some of the never-never-land descriptions of the English primary teacher that occasionally appear in print. Sociological definitions for the

Learning How to Learn

term "role" are more specific than that given by popular usage (Cotgrove, 1968). The teacher performs many roles, both ascribed and achieved, and some of these roles come into conflict, particularly in modern primary schools. The following discussion is adapted from W. A. C. Blyth's *English Primary Education* (Blyth, 1965) and from his primary sources when appropriate.

Blyth draws on Talcott Parsons' analysis of *ascribed* roles, those roles that are given by definition, which the teacher does not have to earn but does have to carry out (Parsons, 1961). First, the teacher is an *instructor.* Since the primary teacher works with younger children, the role of instructor is less prominent than it is in secondary schools. Nevertheless, the teacher still has to teach the children something, even when he concentrates on teaching children how to teach themselves.

Second, he is a *parent substitute.* He must supplement the home as a source of affection and nurturing. Women teachers in nursery, infant, and junior schools function as mother substitutes, while male teachers and heads in the junior school become father substitutes.

Third, the teacher is an *organizer.* He sets patterns to simplify classroom management in order to avoid confusion. In this context he needs to establish procedures for effective classroom control and discipline.

A fourth role is that of *value-bearer.* Since the school for the most part fosters middle-class values, the teacher, in effect, supports some homes and contradicts others. He helps to transmit aesthetic values along with the English national religious heritage, although this last is primarily the function of the head teacher.

Finally, the teacher is a *classifier.* This role may have become less important than it was at one time, but primary teachers still talk about good and bad pupils, those who do well and those who have difficulty. They continue to make many comparisons, both invidious and appropriate. Evaluation procedures are for the most part subjective, largely taking the form of written and verbal anecdotes. Classification systems tend to be influenced by social class membership, for it is generally the middle-class children who are classified as more academically promising.

In addition to ascribed roles, the teacher takes on *achieved* roles. These he earns for himself, and they usually take time to acquire. Teachers gradually earn individual reputations within the staff room and in the surrounding community. One teacher becomes the football coach; another the most skillful craftsman. One takes on the role of remedial expert, another that of the school's leading artist. One teacher is the organizer of social events, another is the staff room wit. Achieved roles depend on skills, interests, and personality characteristics.

While roles need not be in opposition by definition, they often involve the teacher in role conflict. It is difficult, for instance, for a teacher to be both a supportive parent substitute, who must care for all his children equally, and a classifier, who distinguishes the more successful from the less successful. Some teachers try to get out of such a bind by emphasizing one role at the expense of another. Infant teachers tend to be more dedicated to affective, supportive relationships, while teachers of older juniors tend to concentrate on more impersonal cognitive and skill development goals. Teachers want to treat children as equally worthy members of the family group, but they have difficulty disguising their preference for conforming, achieving behavior. It is hardly possible in the primary school to abandon either the parent substitute or the classifier role, although some secondary teachers try to escape the first by withdrawing from emotional involvement with pupils. They thereby function as very aloof parents.

Another source of conflict arises between the roles of instructor and value-bearer of the school-approved subculture. Middleclass values and motivational patterns, such as reliance on verbal and written explanations, place working-class children at a disadvantage in acquiring instructional independence.

How does a teacher in a primarily working-class area manage learning through informal relationships with children who encounter strict adult regulation in the home? This situation involves a four-way role conflict between organizer, value-bearer, parent substitute, and instructor. It is little wonder that middle-class teachers in urban areas with large proportions of immigrant children are ambivalent about their objectives. Role conflict, value differences between home and school, changed relationships to authority, expectations of parents, and philosophical commitment all become entangled in a web of misunderstanding.

Occasionally, a strong head teacher's expectations conflict with an assistant teacher's definition of what is desirable. The traditional teacher senses disapproval in an atmosphere that fosters

Learning How to Learn

open teaching, while an informal teacher is often frustrated within a traditional setting.

A further source of conflict arises between the teacher's emotional identification with children who badly need support and the impersonal objectivity of the professional stance. The teacher has his own personal life, his own family, his own obligations; yet he recognizes emotionally deprived children greatly in need of affection. Much of the discussion in English books about teacher-child relationships is amazingly nonsociological. It almost assumes that teachers can become emotionally involved in nurturing relationships with roomful after roomful of children without suffering stress and conflict. Can a teacher really substitute for a neglecting parent?

Finally, there is conflict created by *role-set* in teaching. Role-set is a term developed by Robert Merton to identify the series of people involved in carrying out a role (Merton, 1957b). The fact that so many people are affected by the teaching act, that so many people think they know what a teacher ought to be doing, only multiplies the conflicts for the primary teacher. The parents have aspirations for their children. The head has his particular point of view. The way that a teacher functions affects his colleagues. The children themselves have many different expectations. The teacher cannot please everyone.

SOME DIFFERENCES BETWEEN ENGLISH AND AMERICAN TEACHERS

Some qualities common to many English teachers seem rare in American teachers. There is naturally a good deal of overlapping behavior between the two countries, yet certain traits impress American visitors, particularly educators who have become hardened to the negative perspective so often expressed in America.

One major difference is that English teachers do not seem obsessed with problems of discipline. Management of learning and the control of classroom behavior are considered integral to the teaching process. While all teachers need to establish boundaries or limits of acceptable behavior, and while classroom management problems are always a cause for some concern, experienced teachers in England soon learn to take such matters within their stride. True, some English teachers scream at children in class. There are some softhearted teachers whom children quickly learn to "play up." Proper handling of discipline problems becomes a part of the teacher's repertoire of response. English beginning teachers have trouble; experienced teachers have learned to cope. American beginning teachers have even more trouble, yet experienced American teachers continue to fret or resort to crude and sometimes brutal forms of coercion. Americans are amazed at how smoothly many informal classes are run and are impressed by the apparent lack of tension.

Another contrast, perhaps related to differences over classroom procedures for establishing effective discipline, can be found in staff room talk. American teachers complain and sometimes relieve their frustrations by berating administrators or children; English teachers do much less grumbling. At least they do not complain too much while having coffee or tea during the morning break. When staff room talk gets around to children, which it frequently does, positive comments are heard more often than negative ones. The teachers work very hard without much verbal catharsis. One even becomes a little suspicious of so little complaining, for the frustrations of the job are many and the relaxing moments are few. Many English teachers let out aggression through witticism or conceal it under the social amenities.

Why have so many more creative teachers developed in England than in America? Many have been struck by this difference (Kallett, 1966; Featherstone, 1967; Ulin, 1969; Rogers, 1970). English teachers respond creatively to challenges that would discourage many Americans. They use their ingenuity to overcome a shortage of supplies or inadequate facilities. Most important, many are able to bring out the children's talents (Marshall, 1963). They are able to recognize and respond to creative potential. Many primary teachers contribute their own artistic gifts to the school program. Most primary schools have teachers who are gifted in creative movement, folk singing, pottery-making, and dramatic improvisation.

There is much creative teaching in American elementary schools, and American teachers do not by any means constitute a monolithic body of conformists. Many American teachers are dedicated and inventive people. The trouble is that a great many more *potentially* creative teachers are sidetracked, discouraged, blocked, or even intimidated by sources of authority that reside outside their jurisdiction. By acquiring the autonomy that English teachers possess, thousands of creative American teachers could express inventiveness with little fear of outside interference.

Americans marvel at the adaptability of many English teachers. Why does team teaching work so well in English schools when it so often becomes routine, departmentalized, and bureaucratic in the United States? One answer is that English teachers are used to improvising on the spot. They shift organizational patterns from term to term. If a new idea seems to work in a neighboring school, they will adapt, modify, and revise it until finally it may emerge in a quite different form. Each teaching team adapts the pattern to the particular staff, the building, and the traditions of the school.

Considering all the praise heaped on English teachers from abroad, it is gratifying that so few become complacent. English teachers tend to be a self-questioning, self-critical lot, and teachers who are self-critical are less inclined to be self-satisfied. This may be one reason why English schools have been improving over the years.

English teachers are a long-suffering breed. They are patient with children, patient with stupidity or arrogance on the part of out-of-date heads, reticent about making complaints. Why don't English teachers get ruffled more easily? Are they really as placid or as good-humored as many appear to be? One visit to an infant school turned up four teachers who had lost their voices, not from hollering at the children; perhaps it was from the flu bug, but possibly it was an internal defense against aggression.

Finally, Americans marvel at how English primary teachers have put up so long with exploitation by the rest of society. One frequently hears teachers proudly maintain that helping children is its own reward. Teachers give of themselves, but English society does not give much in return. Many young teachers and some older ones pedal to work on a bicycle; some cannot afford to own an automobile on a teacher's salary. There is little doubt that primary school teachers are an exploited group in England; they are at the bottom of the pecking order in a profession that is notoriously underpaid and undervalued in relation to entrance requirements. This may be one of the greatest professional weaknesses. English teachers have been very slow about demanding their rights, reluctant to enter the power struggle. To remain powerless will further depress a sector within an educational system that has too long placed financial improvements for primary schools near the bottom of its national educational priorities.

6

Nursery Schools

Tax-supported nursery schools constitute only a small part of the English state system of primary education. But since the state schools serve as models for private nurseries and play groups, their importance stretches beyond the children they serve directly. Nursery schools were the first to practice on a fairly extensive scale the philosophy and methods currently associated with English infant schools. Early recognizing the fundamental importance of play, they developed programs catering to children's interests, providing opportunity for free choice and free movement while supplying unobtrusive assistance from supportive teachers. Such practices stemmed from the writing and teaching of pioneer early-childhood educators, including Rachel and Margaret McMillan and especially Susan Isaacs, whose contributions will be examined later in this chapter.

NURSERY EUDCATION IN ENGLAND

Although nursery schools in England earned an international reputation, all proposals for growth in the state sector were blocked by financial restrictions for twenty years after the end of the Second World War (N.U.T., 1964). In response to the Plowden Report's recommendation that more state nurseries be supplied for Educational Priority Areas (Plowden, 1967), a modest start in new construction has been made. A research team under the direction of the distinguished sociologist A. H. Halsey is studying the effect of nurseries in energizing community members to improve local living conditions (Halsey, 1970). But nowhere near the recommended number have been provided nor are they likely to be in the foreseeable future. Moreover, most of the existing buildings are old; many are makeshift wartime facilities. In spite of these handicaps, state nursery schools maintain a continuity with original purposes, and the goal of extensive expansion is continually reiterated (Plowden, 1967).

Through the years the nurseries have offered a program based on a relatively unstructured day, providing considerable freedom for the children to explore a varied and stimulating environment. Head teachers have spent allowances wisely over the years on well-constructed equipment, and they have used ingenuity in reclaiming from the scrap heap the relics of technological progress. Outdoor apparatus includes, in addition to the usual playground facilities, climbing frames, sandboxes, wheel toys, old boats, old cars, truck tires, and cement pipes. Indoor toys, books, puzzles, counters, kitchens, housekeeping corners, imaginative play props, musical instruments, and artistic supplies are in abundance.

Head teachers of nursery schools developed close relationships with mothers long before many of the state infant schools opened their doors to parents. Contacts are reinforced daily when mothers deliver and call for children. Parents often serve as helpers, and parent associations support the school as fund raisers and as sources of pressure when local authorities periodically threaten to close the buildings to reduce expenditures. There is always plenty of work for volunteers to do, and there are plenty of matters for parents and teachers to discuss. Because many mothers are struggling to cope with difficult social and economic conditions, it has been natural for them to seek help from the school, and for teachers in turn to show an interest in the children's family life. If the barriers between parents and teachers in later sectors of the primary school are reduced, it will be in part because state nursery school teachers have long recognized the benefits of close home-school cooperation.

Nursery schools have also pioneered in parent education. Many teachers share materials about child development with parents. Written reports to parents often discuss stages of development and provide anecdotal comments dealing with the individual child's pattern of growth. The Plowden Report recommends that nursery schools become centers for adult education, where concerns about health, nutrition, and childhood behavior may be shared in a setting that focuses on the nursery child but has implications for the entire family (Plowden, 1967).

Since state nursery schools and classes come under the jurisdiction of the Local Education Authorities, a number of L.E.A.'s employ nursery school advisers. Most have been nursery head teachers and have had considerable experience in helping schools achieve appropriate standards. Nursery advisers have also given an extensive amount of help to the volunteers who staff the play group movement. There is no counterpart in the United States to these experienced leaders.

The Froebel Foundation is another force that has strengthened English nursery education through publications, courses, meetings, and particularly teacher training. In earlier days only selected colleges were recognized as qualified to grant the Froebel Certificate. Among these the Froebel Foundation maintained national standards of examination and course development. England was one of the few countries in the world that provided more education for teachers of young children than for teachers of older pupils (Lilley, 1967; Lawrence, 1969). For many years the training college course for primary and secondary teachers was two years long while the course for the Froebel Certificate lasted three years. All certificate courses are now three years in length, and the Froebel colleges have been incorporated into the state system.

Should the government decide to do so, England would be well prepared to expand its state system of nursery education. Colleges of Education in England have long offered well-established programs to prepare nursery teachers. Private colleges and state colleges of further education, which cater to sixteen-year-olds who have left school, provide two-year programs to prepare nursery nurses, one kind of nursery assistant. Existing nursery schools serve as model training centers for practice teachers and nursery nurses in training. Holders of the Froebel Certificate have responsible positions within all segments of the state system. Head teachers and nursery advisers are endowed with a wealth of first-hand experience. With such a core of experienced personnel, England is in much better shape than the United States, where there is a shortage of teacher educators to staff newly created university positions in early-childhood education.

The Neglect of Nursery Education

Why has nursery education in England been so neglected since the Second World War? There has never been enough money to go around, and neither the economics of education nor the current sense of national priorities makes early-childhood educators optimistic about the future. Expansion of state nursery schools would involve heavy expenses. New schools or additional nursery classes in existing schools and new teachers take money away from other stages.

The competition for educational funds is already heavy. Successive governments have in turn financed the replacement of war-damaged facilities, the expansion of higher education, secondary school reorganization, and primary school rebuilding, areas in which built-up demands had become overwhelming. Furthermore, the change in the school-leaving age from fifteen to sixteen, the continuing demand for increased opportunities in higher education, the more aggressive demands from the teaching profession for increased salaries, the equally persistent efforts to reduce class size, will in all likelihood claim priority over educational provisions for the early years.

The number of working mothers with preschool children is increasing and is likely to continue to increase. The number of young children who require special assistance is far in excess of nursery places available. This need for greatly expanded nursery education in England has long been documented (Van der Eyken, 1969). But the critical importance of preschool learning is not even officially recognized by the Department of Education and Science, for to do so would fortify past promises with actual commitment. Even voluntary efforts by local groups to aid willing L.E.A.'s have until very recently been blocked by D.E.S. decisions. By contrast, the federal government in the United States is shifting more and more of its

attention through sponsored research and professional development contracts to preschool children, especially the children of the
poor.

The Importance of Nursery Education

Critical development during early formative years shapes basic
personality structure. The potential for fruitful language acquisition, healthy psychosexual development, and the development of
active curiosity are largely determined before the child reaches
school age (Bloom, 1964). If he has suffered social deprivation, linguistic poverty, mistreatment, economic neglect, or restricted learning opportunities, his future learning potential may be severely
stunted (Megson and Clegg, 1970). Concern about early deprivation has led to the greatly increased attention given preschool
learning in the United States.

But it is not just the socially and economically disadvantaged
who may be handicapped; children who come from a "favorable"
home environment may also lack sufficient stimulation and professional guidance. Parents may not be sensitive enough to recognize cues of disturbance, and even if they do recognize them, they
may not have the time or ability to provide the necessary communication, stimulation, and challenging activities. When a baby makes
demands, a mother may find it hard to attend to an older pre-
schooler. Homes with one or two children cannot offer sufficient
social interaction, and parents must make special efforts to find
playmates for their youngsters. Parents of only children are among
the strongest advocates of nursery education, for they know the
hunger with which most three- and four-year-olds reach out for the
company of other children. If the early years are as crucial as we
have come to believe, how much greater potential might be developed in a highly favorable setting drawing on the combined insights and practices of psychoanalysts, learning theorists, sociologists, and gifted nursery school practitioners?

The waiting lists in England for any kind of nursery—state,
private, or play group—are long. Mothers register children a year
and sometimes two years in advance. State nurseries, where
stringent regulations require that only those with the greatest need
be served, must turn down approximately two qualified children for
every one accepted (Van der Eyken, 1969). Even neighborhood
play groups, in an attempt to stretch facilities as far as possible, ra-

tion places carefully, allowing the youngest children to attend only one morning per week and gradually allowing older children to attend no more than three mornings per week.

Although England has established family need as a determining criterion in allocating places in state nursery schools, one government regulation seems to involve a contradictory criterion; it serves as a kind of fringe benefit to members of the teaching profession. In order to encourage qualified teachers to return to work, the state offers nursery school places to the children of teachers (Van der Eyken, 1969). Where a serious shortage of places exists in some counties, the state schools may have a large proportion of teachers' children. Thus, those children from verbal, middle-class, professional homes can conceivably take places from working-class children who are suffering from multiple environmental handicaps. On the other hand, the view that state nursery schools are a form of special education for the needy is a limiting concept that in England has historical roots. In a number of other countries there is a growing conviction that the right to attend nursery classes is a matter of parental choice for all children.

Affluent families are able to send children to private nursery schools, but even these have waiting lists, despite the substantial fees. Private schools range from acceptable ones, which carry state recognition as being efficient, to questionable ones, which largely resort to seat work, with children confined in cramped, nonfunctional quarters.

The lower-middle-class response to the lack of provision of nursery education has been to organize voluntary play groups (Keeley, 1968). The best of these take their lead from the state and the private nurseries. They offer a program patterned after the informal activities associated with nursery education. "Play group" is a well-chosen name; the term itself helps the organizers to adopt a philosophy and program consistent with recommended patterns. Equipment is often limited, facilities makeshift, and the training of teachers leaves something to be desired, but the play groups have succeeded in stimulating parent involvement to a very large degree. Play groups are comparable to Cooperative Nurseries in the United States. They tend to appeal to the same social levels and depend on parental help on a rotating basis. The play groups charge a small daily fee to cover expenses; but even this modest cost prevents them from serving the majority of working-class children.

The Plowden Report recommended that at least 15 percent of the three- and four-year-old population be offered places in state-maintained schools (Plowden, 1967). This modest figure was based on a combination of deprivation and need factors. The recommendation is not likely to be implemented very quickly. Today the percentage amounts to 5.7 percent, according to Van der Eyken, whose estimate is somewhat lower than official statistics, since Department of Education and Science figures include "the rising fives," who account for almost half the official total (Van der Eyken, 1969). English infant school head teachers have the power to admit children before they reach five years of age, and many heads use their discretion to admit children a term or two early if the school is not overcrowded.

The Future of Nursery Schools

Recently, Local Education Authorities have begun to build new nursery schools in Educational Priority Areas, particularly where non-English-speaking immigrant populations and long waiting lists underscore the need.

Some difference of opinion exists about whether it is better to have separate nursery schools, with their own head teachers on their own grounds located a distance away from other schools, or whether nursery classes should be attached to existing infant schools. England provides for both arrangements within the state system. An experimental school that has received considerable publicity is the Eveline Lowe School in London, which caters to children from the ages of three-and-a-half to nine (D.E.S., 1967). Children may attend for a half day until they reach the age of five, after which they begin a full-day program.

At present the play groups receive a considerable amount of volunteer advice from nursery school heads, Local Education Authority advisers, and College of Education lecturers. They may get a much-needed boost in the form of state aid or a modest subsidy. Financial support for play groups would be the cheapest, if not the best, way to increase facilities. It would be just too expensive to provide in the near future enough nursery school places for even the realistic and limited recommendations of the Plowden Report.

Two organizations that have developed increasingly powerful lobbies are the National Campaign for Nursery Education and the Pre-School Play Group Association. These groups publish journals and newsletters, carry out petition campaigns, demonstrate before and submit evidence to government advisory groups, and bring pressures to bear on parliamentary and borough council representatives. It is middle-class parents who tend to be most vocal about blocked nursery provisions, even though working-class parents have fewer opportunities for voluntary forms of preschool education and must rely largely on demonstration of need to qualify for the state-maintained system. That there still remains a bias in the state sector in favor of working-class parents is a tribute to the original welfare concerns of early nursery school advocates, including Maria Montessori and the Macmillan sisters.

THE INFLUENCE OF SUSAN ISAACS

It is not the nursery school movement in England itself that commands attention. It is rather the influence that the nursery schools have had on infant schools. To place this influence in historical perspective, the contributions of Susan Isaacs will be discussed in considerable detail.

First, however, acknowledgment should be given to two other pioneers who have had a profound influence on the education of young children in England: Rachel and Margaret McMillan. They were social reformers who campaigned against child labor and for school health and welfare services (McMillan, 1927). They are often credited as the most influential founders of the nursery school movement, but their influence has been important at all stages of primary education. They established a nursery school that encouraged imaginative play, adventure, movement, artistic expression, good food, and adequate rest. The introduction of the subsidized school meals service resulted in part from their campaigns to overcome some of the detrimental effects of poverty. They also helped to promote the provision of school nurses and a school medical service. They made teaching the children of the poor a respectable vocation for the daughters of the middle classes. In this they were helped by the early leaders of the national Froebel movement in England.

A convincing case can be made that Susan Isaacs has been the most important native English figure associated with the changing face of primary education. Dent lists her among the fifty most important educational figures of the past hundred years, and his list includes a number of foreign educators as well as Englishmen concerned chiefly with secondary and higher education (Dent, 1970). English primary school educators mention her name consistently in interviews. But she is not well known in the United States outside of the relatively specialized area of child psychology.

Her major field work took place during the 1920's; her most important reports were published during the early 1930's; her work as a teacher educator took place prior to the Second World War. From the beginning, her writing was highly regarded by nursery teachers in England and abroad. She tutored a number of primary education lecturers who held positions in the Teacher Training Colleges; they in turn imparted her ideas to English teachers, future heads, and future primary school advisers. Her students and the students of her students have helped to spread her views. A sensitive biography was written by one of her best-known students, Dorothy Gardner (1969), her successor at the Department of Child Development at the University of London Institute of Education. The book describes Susan Isaacs' struggle to obtain an education and traces her pervasive influence on teaching and research dealing with the early years of childhood.

The Malting House School

The source of data for Susan Isaacs' two most important works, *Intellectual Growth in Young Children* (S. Isaacs, 1930) and *Social Development in Young Children* (S. Isaacs, 1964), was a privately financed nursery in Cambridge known as the Malting House School. She became the school's first director in 1924 and remained in charge of it for three years. The school served as a living laboratory of source material in child development (Gardner, 1969).

Malting House started with ten boys ranging in age from two years, eight months to four years, ten months. It was expanded to include twenty children ranging from two years, seven months to eight years, six months. A few girls joined the group, but there were never less than four boys to every girl. The children came from professional families in the Cambridge area, and their IQ's ranged from 114 to 166, with a mean score of 131.

The school site consisted of a large hall, four smaller rooms, and a surrounding garden with plenty of indoor and outdoor space for playing, running, and climbing. Plots of land were set aside for communal and individual gardens. The small rooms were used for construction and academic work; one room served as a scientific laboratory.

The school was organized along relatively free lines. Children were not admonished for the open expression of feelings toward one another. They were encouraged to express their fantasies in dramatic play and construction. These teaching methods are now common in nursery schools but during the 1920's were not yet widely applied. Educational toys suitable to the age group and materials for arts and crafts were abundant. Children were urged to carry their work outdoors whenever possible. The curriculum was unstructured, based on play; the children were expected to find their own answers and follow their own interests. The younger children spent a great deal of time running about, conversing, and working with materials. The older children used special rooms for reading and for number work; they made use of scientific apparatus for experiments and tools for construction. Some of the older children wrote their own textbooks.

Teachers at the Malting House School kept detailed daily records of the children's behavior, carefully separating anecdotes from subjective interpretations. They jotted down notes as the incidents occurred and later the same day dictated a fuller account. During the last years of the school stenographers took verbatim notes, but this did not make the original recording methods less useful. The publication of *Intellectual Growth in Young Children* in 1930, based on these data, made an immediate impression on educators and psychologists.

Intellectual Growth in Young Children

One of the distinctive features of the school was its emphasis on scientific thinking. Both Susan Isaacs and her husband, Nathan, were convinced that preschools neglected cognitive growth and scientific interests by their admirable but too pervasive emphasis on artistic activities and self-expression (N. Isaacs, 1961). A major aim of the school, as stipulated by its financial backer, Geoffrey Pike, was to discover the beginnings of the scientific spirit and the scientific method (Lampe, 1959).

The children's active curiosity was encouraged through sensitivity to the joy of spontaneous discovery. Play was conceived as the children's natural form of work, providing opportunities for both cognitive learning and the release of emotions. Equipment included balances, pulleys, ropes, lenses, maps, pendulums, levers, machines, Bunsen burners, tripods, flasks, glass rods, dissecting instruments, jars for specimens, and a human skeleton. Live animals included mice, rabbits, guinea pigs, cats, a dog, snakes, salamanders, frogs, a fresh-water aquarium, and a wormery.

The children were given many opportunities to observe, question, and seek answers. They showed persistent curiosity about living things and physical objects in the surrounding world. Malting House children experimented with water, weights, gas, and fire and studied plants and animals. They took part in the dissection of animals; the scientific laboratory was dubbed the "cutting-up" room. The boys showed an intense interest in automobiles, engines, airplanes, and radios. They appeared to have more familiarity with the technological world of the twentieth century than adults were willing to give them credit for.

Above all, the children's values were not to be imposed by adults but were to be developed through their own experience. There was no punishment and little admonition to obey adult-imposed codes. The role of the teachers was to respect the children's discoveries, not to substitute their own purposes. The teachers were also to provide support by minimizing physical danger and emotional anxiety.

The only restrictions on the children's freedom were those considered essential, and they were administered in a flexible manner. Since children played freely with mud and clay, they were asked to wash their hands before dinner. Although the teachers did not wish to seem more concerned about the children's safety than they needed to be, certain safety precautions were taken. Children were not allowed to play with fire or to turn on a Bunsen burner unless an adult was present. Only one child at a time could climb a ladder or a tree or get on the roof of the summer house. Tools used as weapons were taken away. Relative equals were allowed to settle their own quarrels, but bullying of weaker or younger children was discouraged, as was cruelty to animals. Teachers used positive suggestions rather than prohibitions to bring about alternative behavior.

Incidents of cognitive behavior were classified according to a system designed to chart the beginnings of the processes of discovery, reasoning, and thought. These classifications included (1) the application of prior knowledge to new situations, (2) the increase of knowledge through problems, experience, observations, and discussions, and (3) the social interaction of knowledge, including children's "why" questions.

Social Development of Young Children

Even more fascinating than *Intellectual Growth in Young Children* was the sequel, *Social Development in Young Children*, first published in 1933. A member of the British Psycho-Analytical Society, Susan Isaacs was well aware of the sexuality and hostile impulses of young children. She did not claim to run a psychoanalytic nursery; indeed her writings carefully distinguished between the role of the therapist and the role of the teacher. But as a scientist she was interested in *all* the behavior of children and unwilling to select out only one part.

Malting House children were encouraged to discuss and act out their fantasies. Their aggressive and sexual interests were never suppressed. Nor were they prevented from freely expressing joy and delight. Feelings were allowed to appear out in the open; teachers were asked not to intervene unless children needed protection from the consequences of too much anxiety over hostile acts and impulses.

Another classification system was used to order and analyze the extensive anecdotes about the child's emotional life. His behavior was categorized among the following topics: primary egocentric attitudes; hostility and aggression, including forms of individual hostility such as possessiveness, power, rivalry, and inferiority, and group hostility toward strangers, neighbors, adults, younger children, and temporary scapegoats; friendliness and cooperation; the deeper sources of love and hate. The last category included incidents of sexuality such as oral eroticism and sadism; anal and urethral interest and aggression; exhibitionism; sexual curiosity; sexual play and aggression; masturbation; castration fears, threats, and symbolism; family play, including ideas about babies and marriage; and "cosy places." A final category dealt with guilt and shame (S. Isaacs, 1964).

The objective record of incidents was separated from the theoretical interpretation, and it is this two-hundred-page theoretical

Learning How to Learn

section that is probably the most stimulating part in the book. There is now a widespread awareness of psychosexual incidents such as those reported, but at the time of publication such knowledge was hardly part of the popular culture.

The material in this book was more controversial than the earlier book on cognitive development. Its basis was just as well established through child studies, but acceptance by even the professional public was much slower. An abridged edition of *Social Development of Young Children* appeared in 1951 for use by students in English teacher-training colleges. Most of the material on hostility and aggression was included, but much of the material on children's sexuality was omitted, ostensibly on the grounds that young girls in training colleges needed more background in psychoanalytical theory to interpret the material adequately.

Susan Isaacs' Contribution

Susan Isaacs communicated on different levels to different audiences. Her more technical contributions appeared in psychological and psychoanalytic journals, government reports, and professional reviews (S. Isaacs, 1932a, 1939, 1943). Her two books on child development, written with careful scientific precautions, were widely read by students and lecturers in colleges and universities. She was able to reach an even wider audience through popular books and articles for practicing teachers, nurses, and parents (S. Isaacs, 1932b, 1950).

A new department was created for her in 1933 at the University of London Institute of Education, where she was highly regarded as a stimulating lecturer, tutor, and research director. Through this post and through her writing, her philosophy came to influence many leaders concerned with the education of young children.

Her educational perspective was far in advance of her time. Along with her husband, she early recognized the crucial importance of stimulating language in fostering cognitive growth. The Malting House School encouraged extensive communication through discovery approaches to learning. The school combined sensitive teacher support with freedom of choice and movement. Critical of the methodology in Piaget's early experiments (Gardner, 1969), she still respected his contributions to the understanding of the stages of children's thinking.

The most far-reaching result of her work was to establish play in its foremost position in nursery education. She helped teachers realize that children need to express hostility and give vent to aggressive impulses, and she demonstrated how teachers can help channel aggression through role-playing, craft work, and fantasy. She transformed the educational methods of Dewey from adult-conceived activity projects to child-conceived investigations based on the children's own interests.

Schools are a long way from allowing children to express emotions openly and reveal their sexual impulses, despite an abundance of psychological evidence of children's sexuality. Few teachers have been able to create an atmosphere that encourages the spontaneous revelation of a child's feelings. Typical stages in freedom for young children were charted at Malting House. Children were found to pass quickly from a disbelieving, submissive stage to a wildly active stage before settling down to a third, more purposeful, answer-seeking stage. Usually the second stage blocks teachers from experimenting with the limits of freedom. Other educational methods used in the Malting House School have been widely accepted within English nursery and infant schools. Many teachers now avoid the excessive use of prohibitions; instead they offer guidance through constructive suggestions.

How Applicable Are Susan Isaacs' Ideas?

Susan Isaacs was guided by two powerful theories, those of John Dewey and Sigmund Freud. She was able to temper both of them through conclusions drawn from first-hand experience in a nursery-infant school setting. But can the principles that worked so well at Malting House with a small number of economically favored, able children in the 1920's be applied to children representing a complete range of social, intellectual, and economic attributes within the schools of the 1970's? Are educational traditions based on the theoretical writings of Dewey and Freud, as modified and popularized by Susan Isaacs, viable in the education of older children? A crucial question that warrants further investigation is, How effective are free methods with the children of the poor?

The Malting House School was based on learning through discovery, currently a popular term. The environment was rich with stimulating apparatus. Many opportunities were provided for the natural expression of language. The supportive atmosphere denied the necessity for any form of punishment. The possible extreme interpretation of a permissive, child-centered philosophy was tempered by the pragmatic approach, scientific spirit, and psychoanalytic insights of Susan Isaacs. The freedom given children was to be accompanied by adequate protection against anxiety. In this she was influenced by Melanie Klein, who maintained that children need support for their constructive and loving impulses and protection from too severe anxiety caused by their hostile impulses (Klein, 1952).

The Malting House research, a study of the growth and development of bright children, has been confirmed by other studies of gifted children that demonstrate their impressive capabilities in early cognitive learning, while showing that they go through the same sequence of learning as other children. If bright children are like other children except in the earlier appearance of some manifestations of cognitive growth, would a program similar to Malting House be effective with children of average ability? Would an environment rich in scientific apparatus, technological toys, and living things be as challenging to their curiosity and scientific interests?

Progressive education in England has never been considered a dirty word, nor is John Dewey viewed as a corrupting influence. How did they become considered as such in many quarters in the United States? Progressive American educators divided between the child-centered, permissive wing, which seemed to lack an adequate theoretical basis, and the social reconstructionist wing, which asked schools to perform too radical a function. Both wings came up against the traditional organization of the disciplines and the reluctance of educational conservatives to endorse freer methods. The schools in America were transformed through Dewey's influence, but his methods and objectives have largely been lost in the process. To the contrary, his educational philosophy as well as adaptations of his methodology have found a fertile ground in English primary schools.

NURSERY EDUCATION IN THE UNITED STATES

The child-centered, nonpressuring philosophy of education has long been challenged in the United States. Although support for that philosophy is found in both private nurseries and public preschool and kindergarten programs, the advocates are frequently put on the defensive. They must contend with the intrusions of academicians who advocate early reading and other formal disciplines in both nursery and kindergarten programs (Pines, 1967).

In the United States nursery schools have developed outside of the state system. They take the form of expensive private schools or cooperative, middle-class nurseries similar to English play groups. Kindergartens attached to public elementary schools introduce five-year-olds to a half-day program, but they often are conceived as a preparatory stage for entry into a graded school system. American kindergarten teachers have little power or status to influence the rest of the primary school curriculum. In many schools they are not even taken seriously by the principal and the other teachers. In England nursery head teachers and advisers work with considerable independence. English infant schools have gradually evolved a program that is not too far removed from nursery school methods and objectives.

Too many Americans assume that deprived children are essentially incoherent, communicating in grunts and blocked in the ability to learn. Although language facility is clearly essential for verbal learning, learning in the nonverbal area may be related to the psychosexual development of economically disadvantaged children. It may well be that aggressive and sexual interests, particularly among boys, provide a basis for stimulating their active curiosity, even if language development has been severely restricted. If, in addition, they are intrigued by machines and technical equipment, if they are fascinated by their own bodies and other living things, could not such avenues be more adequately explored? Some investigators have been so concerned with language deprivation that they have concentrated preschool attention on the verbal domain, hoping to prepare children for competition in the language-dominated grade school. Language development can never be neglected, but there are many other ways in which children learn. The first-hand experience and powerful drives that urban children bring with them to a preschool setting may be far more extensive than is commonly recognized. The conditions that produced *Social Development in Young Children* might well be replicated in settings involving the urban poor.

Part of the failure of preschool intervention programs to counteract the culture of the poor may be due to inherent shortcomings in the methodologies, which fail to capitalize on the cognitive skills of the children involved (Baratz and Baratz, 1970). There has been misleading publicity about some programs supported by federal tax money. The publicity makes headlines for the compensatory preschool programs, but it often leads to both overstatement and understatement of their results (Sugarman, 1970).

Day care, until recently a "poor relation" of preschool education (Caldwell, 1971), is now gaining cautious acceptance from both the social service and education professions. New legislation that would provide day care for preschool children promises to overshadow the interest of the late 1960's for a push in "early-childhood education." The likelihood of funds as well as public endorsement is opening possibilities for a previously neglected field.

The issues surrounding preschool education in the United States are far from settled. They center around the questions of content, methodology, and the stage at which the child is to begin school. Unanswered is the question of who will be in charge of implementation and assessment (Evans, 1971). There appears to be a growing awareness that the *general* preschool experiences and personal characteristics that develop during the early years of life are more accountable for differences in early academic achievement among children than are experiences in institutions such as schools (Kohlberg, 1968).

7
Infant Schools

The discussion in this chapter and the next represents a division related to English primary school organization—that of the infant stage (five- to seven-year-olds) and the junior stage (seven- to eleven-year-olds). This chapter discusses how infant schools have gradually been shaped by the informal classroom practices that first became widespread in nursery schools. The discussion of junior schools in the next chapter continues the theme that freedom is extending upward through the age range. Two new terms, the "first school" and the "middle school," have been suggested by the Plowden Report to replace the infant and junior schools and to extend the age brackets by a year or two. A few Local Education Authorities have changed to the new names and age spans, but essentially the provision of separate facilities for younger and older children in the primary school has been retained.

The extension of freedom and the informality of nursery school teaching to older children is by no means common in the United States; in some respects, in fact, the reverse process is true. The push of academic pressures is downward, affecting the kindergarten program and at times resulting in an academic emphasis even at the preschool level. Why do the two countries seem to be moving in opposite directions? Some of the difference may be the result of historically determined, fortuitous circumstances. Other changes have come about through the influence of advisers, and these changes have been cumulatively reinforced over the years.

Despite American admiration, English educational leaders are far from self-satisfied. They know that infant schools are not as free as they appear to be to casual observers. Most infant class teachers and heads identify their positions as middle-of-the-road. They are neither traditional formalists nor devotees of learning by discovery. Few are as relaxed about learning skills as nursery school teachers tend to be. Seldom is reading or mathematics deemphasized in favor of self-expression, creative exploration, or social interaction. Even so, the middle of the road in England provides much more leeway than does the middle of the road in the United States.

The first infant schools were established by volunteer church groups to care for the children of the poor. State support for education began with modest aid to these charity schools (Blackie, 1969). Government support for elementary schools reflected the Victorian concern for "gentling the masses" by inculcating respect for authority along with basic elements of the four R's (the fourth being religion). People who were able to educate their children in private schools were expected to do so, an expectation that still survives in some social quarters. Elementary education was considered terminal schooling for the working classes, whose members were supposed to remain in their place.

Schools initially offered a baby-minding service for working mothers; children commonly were allowed to attend from the age of three. But gradually the younger infants were dropped from the school rolls, and the early formal methods began to be less rigid. The Hadow Report in 1931 encouraged the less formal education that was being developed by pioneering teachers. By the time of the Plowden Report thirty-six years later, these informal infant teaching methods were establishing pace-setting standards. Since the publication and semi-official endorsement of the Plowden Report, informal methods have spread even more widely. Backlash from traditionalists occurs only at the outer periphery of the state system and has done little to stem the expansion of new methods. Only independent schools have profited from consumer dissatisfaction (Cox and Dyson, 1969a; Glennerster and Wilson, 1970). Private schools compensate upper-middle-class parents for the fees by offering small classes, traditional methods, and socially selected peer associations.

CHARACTERISTICS OF
ENGLISH INFANT SCHOOLS

The first eight of the characteristics of English infant schools listed below are products of historical traditions that have few counterparts in continental Europe or in the United States. This does not mean, however, that some of the features cannot be transferred in a modified form to another country.

1. A Full Day at School from the Age of Five

While infant schools once catered to three-year-olds, it became established that a full day of school would be available during the term after the child reached his fifth birthday. Since there are presently three terms of entry in each school year, and since head teachers can admit children before they reach their fifth birthday, English children start a full day of school much earlier than do children in the United States or most European countries. When English schools were more formal, the immaturity of young children might have caused problems. Perhaps the difficulty of imposing a long formal day on five-year-olds helped to encourage the shift toward informal methods and more relaxed expectations.

During the days when streaming by ability was common in junior schools, Jackson showed that in addition to social class and other factors, the accident of date of birth helped to determine which children were eventually placed in the top streams (Jackson, 1964). Since the transfer to junior schools occurs only in the autumn, children born prior to the autumn term may spend three years in infant schools, whereas children born right before the summer term are limited to two-and-a-third years. Extra time in the infant school gives some children a kind of "head start," which results in significantly different placements in the higher streams. Streaming in junior schools is rapidly decreasing, largely because of the decline in importance of the eleven-plus selective examination for secondary school placement. Accident of date of birth may no longer be as important as it once was. At any rate, before too long English be as important as it once was. At any rate, before too long English infant schools may adopt the American practice of a single date of entry per year (Plowden, 1967).

Are children ready for a full day of school at the age of five? Few English children return home during the noon hour; the great majority stay for the subsidized hot school meal. No doubt during the first few weeks of school many children are tired in the late afternoon. On the other hand, children who are even younger attend a full day of nursery school, although the present recommended practice in nursery schools is for those whose mothers are not working to attend for only half a day.

2. The Absence of Grade-Level Standards

Since 1926 England has had neither a national curriculum nor established grade-level standards or expectations (Razzell, 1968). The old standards had been thoroughly discredited through the system of "payment by results"; under this system children were regularly examined by His Majesty's Inspectors, and the results determined the remuneration paid to their teachers.

The organization of classes on the basis of chronological age is decreasing with the spread of cross-age vertical, or family, grouping. In schools that group by chronological age new entrants each term tend to be placed in a reception class, but there is little expectation that children will begin reading shortly after they enter school or that they will achieve a set standard in reading by the end of the first year or, for that matter, by the end of the second or third years. Standardized group tests of achievement are rarely used; children are not expected to arrive at arbitrary grade-level norms.

The distinction between the reception class and other classes is muted because many activities overlap. Seldom does one find the dichotomy between the "play" or "readiness" emphasis of the American kindergarten and the formal reading expectation of the first grade.

3. A Separate Infant School

The infant school is housed in its own building with its own head. It functions as an autonomous unit, free to devote itself to the education of young children. The junior school may be located just across the playground, but it too functions as a separate, autonomous unit. Not all schools are separated in this way. Many primary schools, particularly those affiliated with religious bodies, take the complete age range from five to eleven, but if they are large enough, they tend to have infant departments with one teacher having special responsibility for the infant age group.

A change in organization suggested by the Plowden Committee is to add an extra year or two to the infant school, renaming it the first school, and add an extra year or two to the junior school, renaming it the middle school (Plowden, 1967). The advantages and disadvantages of these modifications are discussed in the next chapter, but the changes do not alter the school's essential autonomy nor its particular focus of attention on a limited age range.

4. Women Head Teachers

Women heads seem less concerned than men heads with matters of status or with maintaining a social distance from the parents. They are often less ambitious and are inclined to be somewhat more child-centered. This is not only a reflection of the age groups for which they tend to be responsible; women heads, women inspectors, and women primary school advisers have in general been more instrumental than men in spreading the progressive educational philosophy (Blackie, 1969).

The infant head teachers have had a great deal of teaching experience with young children. Drawing on their own extensive past and present teaching experience, they are able to help new teachers with the specifics of infant teaching. As head teachers, they do not shy away from teaching but frequently work with groups of children and with individuals in need of special attention. They set the curriculum and establish the patterns of organization. Because the schools are small, seldom exceeding 250 children, the children are well known and the program becomes adaptable.

5. The Autonomy of the Class Teacher

Although subject to the sometimes very persuasive influence of a strong-minded head, the infant school teacher is much more free than the American teacher from external demands or expectations. The class teacher usually welcomes help from the head but is aware that the final determination of the educational program remains largely up to him.

There is nothing comparable to American school district policies, a predetermined course of study, a district-wide testing program, or parental interference, either threatened or actual, which so often detract from the American teacher's sense of autonomy. Few controls restrict the teacher's professional initiative; few restraints block him from making desired innovations. Some might argue that freedom from interference allows the class teacher to remain in a well-worn rut, but British autonomy seems to offer greater encouragement for spreading innovation than do American or European attempts to impose change through directives from above.

6. Each School Determines Its Own Curriculum

Like all schools throughout the English system, infant schools are free to switch to more flexible and informal curriculum practices. If the head teacher and the staff wish to introduce family grouping, or the initial teaching alphabet as a reading medium, or structural mathematics, or if they wish to purchase a new set of reference books or more versatile furniture, they need not seek permission from anyone. If staff members are convinced that a change is desirable, they are free to put it into effect, subject only to the financial limitations imposed by Local Education Authorities.

Curriculum ideas spread from school to school through the voluntary initiative of teachers and through courses and conferences organized by the advisory services. This gradual diffusion, which has neither external sanctions nor rewards, results in curriculum change that eventually seems to take hold at a more fundamental level of teacher commitment than do more widely publicized curriculum projects in the United States.

7. The Influence of the Nursery School Philosophy

Infant schools must cope with large numbers of young children for a full day. Nursery schools and day care centers have set an example by dealing with even younger children through organizing many centers of interest and a wide range of learning activities. The infant school has become more like the nursery school as it has adopted its methods, classroom organization, and close teacher-child relationships, first with the five-year-olds and later with the older children.

Infant schools have borrowed from nursery schools their familiar home-centered equipment, including play houses, blocks, wheel toys, dress-up clothes and props, construction equipment, puzzles, and games. Parents in the United States view the first grade as the time for children to settle down to formal schoolwork. In England teachers introduce children to the tools of learning gradually, according to their readiness rather than their chronological age or grade placement. Some five-year-olds may begin reading, but few six- or seven-year-olds are denied opportunities for activities generally associated with play.

The child-centered philosophy, which was first widely accepted by nursery school teachers, has spread rapidly into the infant school (Simpson and Alderson, 1960; Stone, 1963; Gardner and Cass, 1965). Just why this philosophy has become so widespread is not clear. Perhaps teachers who themselves are free from external pressures are inclined to accept a philosophy that invites children to follow their natural inclinations. Most children enjoy school and all children learn through play. Informal activities and relaxed expectations seem to work for many infant teachers. The return to teaching of married women who can draw on their own experiences in child-rearing has probably reinforced this trend and has added greater stability and maturity to the teaching force. (Prior to the Second World War, many Local Education Authorities had discouraged married women from teaching.)

8. Teachers Are Products of the Colleges of Education

Almost all infant teachers have been prepared at small, single-purpose institutions that seldom enroll more than a thousand students; formerly designated as Teacher Training Colleges, they are now called Colleges of Education. Whatever criticisms can be leveled against the Colleges of Education, they have not been remiss in emphasizing vocational preparation.

Many college lecturers, particularly those in the Education Departments, have been recruited from headships in the primary schools. They have the background to acquaint young teachers with changes in content and the wide variety of teaching materials currently available. College tutors help prospective teachers in tutorials and during practice teaching to establish teaching patterns that will enable them to fit into changing infant schools. Schools in the United States are not changing nearly as rapidly, but even if they were, the preservice preparation of teachers would be ill suited to provide much in the way of a practical induction into school-based work. (Contrasts in teacher education are developed in greater detail in Chapter 9.)

9. Family Grouping

Although family grouping has been practiced in English infant schools for the past twenty-five years, it is currently one of the country's most influential developments. Chiefly a change in class organization, it also influences the curriculum and teacher-pupil relations (Ridgway and Lawton, 1969). Family grouping (also known as vertical grouping) cuts across the age range to bring children together into classes; it thus breaks with the tradition of organizing classes on the basis of chronological age. As in the family, older children interact with younger ones. Now widespread among infant schools, the pattern is moving into many junior schools, at least on a modified basis. It has, of course, always existed in one- and two-teacher village schools.

Family grouping eases the recurring problem in English infant schools of assimilating the reception class for five-year-olds each term. Instead of having to form a new reception class as many as three times a year, the schools spread new entrants among existing family groups; generally no more than five or six newcomers are added to each class. In this way new children become better known sooner to each of the teachers, and older children help introduce new members to classroom routines. The older children develop a sense of responsibility by helping socialize younger ones, following the family pattern in which older siblings serve as models for younger brothers and sisters. When an older child reads to a younger one, he has a live, appreciative audience, while the younger child receives attention and learns through imitation.

Vertical grouping can hardly be recommended to formal teachers using traditional methods. The wider age span increases heterogeneity and compounds instructional complexity. Family grouping is particularly effective in a learning environment based on work in small groups and a relatively unstructured day. Since the children in a family class often stay with the same teacher for two or three years, established work patterns provide considerable self-direction for children, freeing the teacher to work with individuals and small groups.

These provisions seem to help teachers to relax and to devote more attention to children's interests (Ridgway and Lawton, 1969). Family grouping has a self-generating liberalizing effect. The greater the heterogeneity, the greater the need to attend to individual differences, the greater the reliance on self-instructional methods, the greater the inclination to provide a variety of choices for the children. The more years a teacher spends with a child, the better he understands the child and the better he understands infant children as a group.

Head teachers claim that a shift to vertical grouping provides an opportunity for them to offer more help to beginning teachers and to improve staff communications (Ridgway and Lawton, 1969). Part of the improvement can be traced to the enthusiasm of new converts, but family grouping does give a teaching staff a chance to reexamine and discard outmoded age-level curriculum expectations.

In some ways family grouping holds the same potential for multiplying changes as the practice of nongrading, which is spreading in American primary classes. Nongrading, as described by Goodlad and Anderson and as exemplified in the Laboratory School at the University of California at Los Angeles, is similar in conception to family grouping in England (Goodlad and Anderson, 1959). As it is practiced in most American schools that claim to be nongraded, however, differences quickly become evident. In America nongrading often means little more than reducing the pressures on initial reading in the first grade. Nongraded classes in the United States are seldom vertically grouped. Instead, levels of achievement in reading are substituted for grade-level expectations, with children moving through the levels at differing rates according to their aptitudes. Children are grouped by achievement in reading, and the classes may become disguised forms of ability groups. The emphasis is almost entirely on developmental reading, which is often tied to a relatively formal, graded basal series. The potential for flexible, multi-age, multi-ability groups in a wide range of curriculum areas is practically untapped in American nongraded classes.

By contrast, family grouping in England has allowed children to work together within various age ranges in different small groups throughout the day on a variety of activities with no more emphasis on reading than any other skill. The various small groups are temporary and often are heterogeneous by age and ability.

10. The Non-timetabled Day

The "integrated day" is a popular term in England for the pattern that results when the timetable for separate subjects is obscured. The term "integrated day" means so many different things to different people that the term "non-timetabled day," while less glamorous, is probably more descriptive (Marsh, 1970a). At one time the English primary curriculum was timetabled, as the secondary school curriculum still is. Each subject was allotted a certain time period, and the school assembly hall was tightly scheduled for activities such as physical education and religious instruction. With the removal of the time schedule, the blurring of subject matter distinctions, and the more varied use of the assembly hall, the curriculum has become much more fluid. Fixed points are now at a minimum. Children interrupt their work only for a morning break, and they are free to continue working if they wish. Some schools have even done away with this break. Instead of clearing up, changing books, and settling down to a new period five or six times a day, with all the management and control problems that entails, children put away their work only at the end of the day.

The whole class seldom works on one curriculum area at a time. Infant teachers rarely resort to mass methods of instruction. Children tend to work as individuals or in small groups of from two to six members. The teacher arranges a number of centers of interest in the room; the children may move from activity to activity, sometimes on direction of the teacher but often on their own initiative. Opportunities are provided for cooking, sewing, painting, modeling, construction, dramatic play, and block building, as well as the more traditional school subjects—reading, writing, mathematics, and science. Children know that sometime during the week they will get a turn to cook or to work at the easels.

Well-organized teachers maintain a record-keeping system to check whether each child is participating in a fairly balanced program during the week (Webb, 1969). Such an organizational plan rests on the assumption that children will grow in self-direction when they have the chance to establish their own work rhythms.

The concept of the integrated day is discussed at greater length in the next chapter, on junior schools. It is based on an expectation that class members will coordinate much of their work around an integrating theme. Such an expectation is less common in the infant school, where children tend to make fewer distinctions among subjects. Younger children approach learning without separating out subject matter differences; they do their own integrating by seldom chopping learning into artificial segments.

11. The Decline of the Textbook

At one time very prominent in English primary schools, textbooks have now come into actual disfavor in many classrooms. The wide variety of approaches to initial reading instruction, the greater reliance on individualization, and the increasing importance placed on manipulating concrete mathematical materials have made the standardized textbooks less appealing to teachers.

The expensive, disposable workbooks that commonly accompany basal reading series in the United States are rare. Instead, children write in a number of small, blank notebooks provided by the Local Education Authorities. The children often have half a dozen different booklets, one for mathematics, another for creative writing, another for project work, another for vocabulary-building, and so on. When the children have completed their assignments, they place these notebooks in various baskets for the teacher to check. Well-organized teachers find time to check the work individually with the child as the day passes.

The decline of textbooks has allowed English schools to use their instructional budgets to purchase a wide variety of information booklets, storybooks, and standard children's reference works. English classrooms and school libraries are well stocked, even though the budget for materials and instructional resources is limited. Money saved by not buying large collections of common textbooks and workbooks can be used to purchase a great many more titles for a much wider range of reading interests and abilities. The quality and variety of children's books are most impressive. English textbooks do not compare favorably with American textbooks according to publishing criteria, but trade books are at least as attractive, and information books tend to be more authentic.

12. Daily and Weekly Assignments

When children are allowed to pace themselves by choosing their own order of work, teachers need only provide general expectations and offer the children plenty of time to carry them out. This is one reason that so many different activities can take place simultaneously. Children know that they are expected to complete a series of assignments within the week. They pace themselves accordingly, determining their own daily balance based on some patterns established by the teacher or the older children in a family group.

Each day older children do some writing; each day they engage in some mathematics work. Those who can read independently select their own books; others join small groups to receive instruction from the teacher. Arts and crafts, construction, imaginative play, movement, and physical exercise balance more sedentary activities. Older children often carry out independent projects based on topics of interest.

The teacher of young children may start out by assigning work schedules that last for half a day; he may then gradually increase the time to cover the whole day and eventually establish weekly expectations. Under this system the teachers are more likely to do homework than the children.

13. Individualization

Each child works at his own pace according to his own pattern. He tends to choose his own materials, select his own books, determine his own projects, and establish his own priorities. The initial impulse for the children's work comes from the learning goals the teacher helps them to set and from instructional procedures he has provided on workcards.

Many teachers make up their own individual workcards; others rely on commercially prepared materials. The individual workcard dates back many years to a time before current methods became popular. At one time they must have been used as a cheap substitute for workbooks and as a convenient way to keep children busy. They still serve these purposes, but many workcards are attractively constructed, differentiated according to difficulty, and challenging in intent. Experienced teachers have hundreds of workcards available, which they frequently cover with plastic film.

A child selects his own card from among a series arranged according to difficulty and designed to appeal to a variety of interests. The instructions may be designed to spark interest in creative writing or to promote further scientific investigation. Individualized mathematics workcards take the place of exercise books or common class assignments.

A number of newer instructional devices encourage either individualization or working in pairs. Tape recorders, filmstrip projectors, puzzles, matching games, programed books, and teaching machines add to the variety of resources that can be used by children without much direct teacher supervision. Even young children have little difficulty manipulating the knobs and push-buttons of audio-visual aids.

14. Small-Group Work

Individualized learning is augmented by small-group work. Children either seat themselves or are arranged by the teacher at tables or other work stations for four to six children. At times groups work cooperatively; at other times the children merely work on similar materials at a common table.

The teacher moves from group to group, where he does much of his direct teaching. He gathers together one small group to better explain a mathematics relationship, another to extend their sight-reading vocabulary. He asks a different small group to communicate the results of a scientific investigation to the rest of the class; then he helps another group of children compose a new song.

Some teachers organize their classes according to ability and differentiate activities for fast, middle, and slow groups, but the more highly recommended practice is to allow children to group themselves heterogeneously. The working group usually has four to six members, about half as many as a typical American reading group. American teachers spend a great deal of time sitting in a reading circle listening to children take turns struggling through a basal reader while the rest of the class is kept occupied with workbook exercises or busy work. Many American primary teachers devote so much time to developmental reading instruction, trying to push three reading groups through their daily paces, that the rest of the curriculum suffers through neglect. Reading in English schools is seldom neglected, but it tends to be much more flexibly organized so that it does not dominate the daily schedule.

15. Flexible Work Space

Arrangements for centers of interest can be traced to nursery school practices. The classroom is divided into numerous teaching areas where many small groups can carry on a variety of learning functions simultaneously. Classrooms tend to have so little floor space that teachers often construct temporary dividers to form work bays that separate one activity from another. Many heads have created extra work areas in older buildings by erecting temporary walls or by converting cloakrooms and passageways.

Some of the newer schools have been planned specifically to accommodate more openness. These schools attempt to use almost all covered area as teaching space. Semiprivate bays and working spaces are skillfully arranged so that the teacher can maintain eye contact with various corners of the extended classroom (D.E.S., 1961). Instead of teaching from the front of the class, the teacher moves about from bay to work area to library corner, stimulating investigation, answering questions, and offering encouragement.

Open- or semi-open-planned schools are designed to promote team teaching with a variety of learning activities planned for purpose-built corners and sections. There are quiet areas for reference work or contemplation, noisy areas for construction and dramatic play, messy areas for pottery-making and painting, well-organized areas for scientific investigations. Children can carry their work outside of the classroom into cupboards, corners, hallways, and outdoors. The library corner is often carpeted, tucked out of the way of traffic, and furnished with comfortable chairs or benches. One village school has been furnished in a manner similar to a home; it has a bedroom, study, kitchen, and sitting room with electric fireplace, which should help to ease the transition from the warmth and familiarity of the family setting (D.E.S., 1961).

16. Versatile Furniture

One solution to an overcrowded class with too many desks blocking easy movement is to remove some of the traditional furniture. Some teachers no longer consider it necessary for each child to have his own desk. Children sit at work tables, stand at tabletops or easels, or lean over workbenches. Instead of forty cluttered desk drawers hiding the children's paraphernalia from view, there are trays stacked in accessible storage racks, which save space and allow children to move from one work area to another. Corners, tabletops, booths, countertops, sinks, and shelves are devoted to pottery, scientific collections, libraries, structural apparatus, handicrafts, and props for dramatic play.

Neat rows of desks no longer separate children from one another in order to prevent talking. Children spend as much time on their feet as they do sitting down, and the furniture is arranged to promote conversation rather than restrict it. Children seem to survive well enough without desks of their own; the added space allows for a much wider use of the learning environment. More traditional teachers balk at the thought of not having a desk for every child. They claim that each child wants to possess his own little space. More likely, it is the teacher who wants to restrict the child's movement. Children seem happy with the opportunity to move about, and their sense of private ownership is seldom offended by the request to share furniture.

17. The Display of Work

English primary schools commonly use the walls, corridors, added bays, and room dividers either to display the completed work of children or to provide stimulation through charts and pictures constructed by the teacher. College tutors say that they can get a feeling for the curriculum and philosophy of a school by studying the displays near the end of each term, when every available inch of wall seems to be covered.

Displays serve a number of related purposes. They allow groups to share the results of their investigations with other members of the class. Teacher-constructed wall charts, word lists, and mathematical representations become handy instructional references. Displays motivate children by offering recognition for their more conscientious efforts. They contribute to the attractiveness of the surroundings and the brightness of the room. They serve as focal points to arouse interest in new topics and help to stimulate further study.

The teacher sets an example for the children by the ways in which he displays work. When the teacher sets high standards, displays are attractively laid out, the general effect is pleasing, and the children take pride in their best achievements. Poems and stories are carefully revised and neatly rewritten; tie-dye or block prints are carefully hung; paintings and three-dimensional craftwork are tastefully arranged. Some teachers, on the other hand, deliberately display work in various stages of completion to show that perfection is not the goal. In any case, an infant teacher needs discretion and an artistic sense of proportion to avoid a cluttered look.

110   *Learning How to Learn*

There is a marked contrast between the amount of work displayed in English and American classrooms. English teachers would be amused to hear American teachers grumble about a requirement that they change the tiny classroom display cabinet in the corridor once a month or to notice that displays are confined to the classroom bulletin boards. The whole room, often with the temporary walls provided by bays and dividers, serves as the English bulletin board. Whether children are aware of this bombardment of visual stimuli or whether they become immune to it after a while is debatable. There can be no doubt, however, that a visitor is keenly aware of the great variety of learning activities as soon as he enters an English classroom. There are both two-dimensional and three-dimensional displays. Collages, pottery, woodwork, models, and papier-mâché puppets and animals are more common in English classrooms than in American classrooms, where construction activities are often associated with excessive noise and time-wasting.

18. Freedom to Talk and Move About

One of the most difficult features of the British school system for inexperienced exchange students from America to appreciate is the freedom given young children to follow their natural inclinations. The room seems noisy and chaotic to students who are used to more formal methods of classroom control. Children are not expected to remain in their seats or ordered to remain quiet or admonished to get down to work. They know what they are expected to do, and they are free to go about it on their own terms. They move about naturally from supply cabinets to work spaces to teacher to storage trays. They get their own milk, put away their own workcards and games, take responsibility for housekeeping duties. They work alone, in pairs, or in small groups; they learn from each other, read to each other, compare notes, and communicate freely.

Not all teachers are able to establish conditions in which purposeful talk and movement remain at a reasonable level of noise. Not all young children are capable of self-direction. Many traditional teachers in England and America struggle mightily to settle children down and prevent communication in order that children do not "disturb their neighbors." In family-grouped classes there is greater likelihood that patterns of communication can be transmitted from older children to younger ones without as many teacher reminders. Relaxed English infant teachers spend less time reminding and admonishing children to hold the level of noise within reason than formal teachers spend in trying to block talk insofar as possible.

It is not true that children want to talk all the time. They need to communicate on a great many occasions, but they will frequently seek quiet corners where they can engage in solitary reading or play. They become so engrossed in an activity that they will ask other children to go away and leave them alone. In this regard they are establishing their own rights to privacy and freedom from interruption, rather than being subject to teacher-imposed regulations that separate children from one another.

19. Relaxed Discipline

Discipline problems do not disappear in an atmosphere of greater freedom. But rather than growing out of the curriculum and the arrangements for learning, the problems tend to be associated with children who have unfulfilled emotional needs or who are too immature to exercise much self-control.

Secondary teachers complain more about discipline than do infant teachers. This can partly be attributed to the increasing defiance of adolescents against adult-imposed social controls, but part of it must spring from the differences in curriculum, classroom organization, and teacher-learner relationships. When the curriculum capitalizes on children's interests, when the classroom organization provides informal access to other children and materials, when the teacher's manner invites approach through acceptance, the number of discipline problems decreases. Perhaps, also, the infant teacher needs to exert less control because of the increase in the number of "teachers" in the guise of older children in classes devoted to family grouping.

Inexperienced American exchange students who visit English classrooms sometimes express concern about their inability to maintain discipline in the freer, more relaxed, more informal atmosphere of an English infant school. American undergraduates have seldom observed children moving about freely, nor have they assimilated the noise level occasioned by the continuous hum of conversation; they are unfamiliar with centers of interest replacing rows of desks and are taken aback by the greater reliance of the teacher on pupil initiative in choice of activities. Such conditions may actually promote greater self-discipline, so much more marked among English than American children, particularly after they enter the junior school.

20. The Teacher as Arranger of the Environment

The English teacher spends little time standing in front of the room or sitting in a reading circle, talking at children and telling them what to do. He spends much more time creating the conditions that will enable the children to get on with their own work. How he arranges the learning environment, supplies materials, sets out clay, paints, apparatus, games, and puzzles, arranges displays, responds to written work, settles disputes, keeps evaluative records, and establishes patterns for replacing equipment is a tribute to his organizational skills. Experienced infant teachers manage to find opportunities to respond to most of the children individually each day. With young children the teacher can hardly confine himself to encouragement or nondirective reflection. But his teaching is for the most part indirect.

Many teachers spend many after-school hours preparing workcards, matching games, vocabulary aids, and challenging charts. They seldom sit down during the day except for morning coffee; they seldom have time to go over all of the work that children hand in until after the school day ends, although they try whenever possible to go over it with the child as soon as it is finished.

21. Selective Intervention

Some would accuse the informal infant teacher of responding passively through a kind of laissez-faire indifference. But this is just not true. Few young children teach themselves, and very few infant teachers can follow Susan Isaacs' Malting House program of not intervening until the children seek out help in the process of discovery. Only with fewer children could some teachers offer this kind of nondirective support. Informal infant teachers are moderate progressives; they do both direct and indirect teaching, but a good deal of this occurs with individuals and small groups. This is not to say that infant teachers avoid taking the whole class for some activities; movement, singing, story time, preparation for field trips, and follow-up discussions are convenient total class activities. Otherwise, the teachers intervene on a selective basis.

In selectively intervening a teacher often initiates the communication by sitting down with a group or with an individual child to help take the learning one step further, to help recall specific details, to point out useful resources, or to overcome a hurdle that seems to be blocking progress. With young children at a mathematics table, it means helping to establish meanings within number relationships. With children building independent reading skills, it involves solidifying patterns. With children creating a mural, it means suggesting a changed perspective. With children making a block print, it involves a direct demonstration. The teacher who selectively intervenes draws on his maturity to extend meanings, establish new relationships, sustain creative effort, or challenge further investigation. With young children this intervention may simply take the form of frequent supportive communication when children seek the teacher's approval.

22. The Influence of Piaget

Jean Piaget has been highly influential in providing theoretical and empirical support for changing goals in English primary education, and at no stage has his work been more influential than in the infant school. Infant school children are for the most part passing from Piaget's stage of intuitive thought to his stage of concrete operations (Piaget, 1962).

In the infant school there has been a definite move away from learning mathematical facts and combinations to developing mathematical understandings based on the manipulation of concrete objects in meaningful situations (Dienes, 1960; N. Isaacs, 1960; Churchill, 1961; Lovell, 1961). Learning materials for counting, classifying, comparing, and grouping come in a great variety of forms, including three-dimensional apparatus such as Stern blocks, Colour Factor rods, Cuisenaire rods, abacuses, counting frames, and Dienes Logic blocks. Children tend to work at tables arranged according to stages of mathematical maturity. (Mathematics seems to be far more functionally presented in English primary schools than it is in the United States. Chapter 8 contrasts modern mathematics in England and the United States at the junior school level.)

Piaget's influence can also be seen in learning strategies that stress first-hand experience and vivid sense impressions. Teachers enjoy stimulating children through poetry, pictures, recordings, television programs, and field trips, providing sense impressions before children begin painting, writing, or describing what they have experienced. English interpreters of Piaget have also helped teachers to avoid moving prematurely toward abstractions and generalizations (Brearley and Hitchfield, 1966; Beard, 1969).

23. Language Development

Since language ability is based on usage, children who freely communicate acquire confidence in verbal expression while extending their knowledge of words and concepts. Children from homes in which language development is restricted are especially in need of opportunities to speak (Schools Council, 1970d). Dramatic play with dolls, blocks, wheel toys, or household objects offers natural occasions. Each day teachers read or tell stories that stretch the imagination, provide a pleasurable shared experience, and demonstrate the magical power of independent reading.

There are almost as many different reading schemes in England as there are in the United States. The older look-and-say methods based on carefully controlled vocabularies are giving way to more imaginative approaches (Gattegno, 1969; Roberts, 1970; Roberts and Southgate, 1970). Some recent programs build on structural analysis of language patterns as discovered through the science of linguistics (Schools Council, 1969; *Breakthrough to Literacy*, 1970).

Especially popular in some flexible infant schools is the initial teaching alphabet (i.t.a.), which has the added advantage of stimulating more extensive writing at an earlier age. While claims for i.t.a. are a matter of continuing controversy (Hess, 1968; Warburton and Southgate, 1969), it was never promoted in England in the same way as it was introduced in the United States. In America reading materials written in i.t.a. came up against dozens of other schemes distributed by the highly competitive publishing industry, which forced promoters of i.t.a. to adopt American "hard-sell" tactics. In England the founders of i.t.a. first approached a university Institute of Education, which conducted a nationally controlled experimental sample to establish a research basis before claims were widely broadcast. The i.t.a. system has been one of the few introductory reading schemes introduced under controlled conditions (Downing, 1966).

Schools in England use all kinds of reading programs; the schools often encourage a combination of many approaches. There is much less reliance on the basal reading series. Instead, children are encouraged to read widely and independently as soon as they are able. Teachers develop vocabulary through the extensive use of labels, charts, games, and teaching aids.

The practice of asking for some independent writing from each child each day has a long tradition. Only a part of this written communication should be termed creative writing (Marsh, 1970a). For many infants it serves as one way to relive experiences. If there were more adult listeners in the form of auxiliaries and parental helpers, perhaps there would be less need to fill up notebooks for the teachers.

24. *Creative Expression*

A number of writers have traced the beginning of the movement toward greater freedom in England to developments in the creative arts (Richardson, 1948; Marshall, 1969; Marsh, 1970a; Blackie, 1971). English writers give high priority to creative expression in primary schools. Some descriptions by teachers with highly original perceptions demonstrate great sensitivity (Marshall, 1963). The arts in England are prized.

Many more English children are engaged in art and craft work throughout the day than children are in America. Art in English schools has not become a special reward for good behavior or a distracting change for restless children, taking place at the end of the week in a special period set aside for it. Nor is it used as a time-filler under the guise of seat work to try to keep young children quiet pushing crayons over Manila paper. Artistic work tends to go on all of the time. Some children, particularly in junior schools, spend a good part of the day engaged in projects that result in two- and three-dimensional forms of expression.

In cases of team teaching, one teacher may take major responsibility for arts and crafts, but most infant teachers provide their own artistic activities. Creativity, however, cannot be confined to the creative arts; it finds expression in dramatic play, movement, language development, and in some measure within mathematical and scientific projects.

INFANT SCHOOL PROBLEMS

A number of the problems discussed below also apply to other stages of English education. They will be discussed initially here and amplified in the next chapter if need be. If they are not discussed again, the problems identified in this section can be assumed to apply to schools for older children as well.

1. Inadequate Financial Support

Many of the limitations hampering English primary schools are aggravated by financial restrictions. These restrictions are the foremost and most vehement complaint of class teachers, heads, and advisers who are interviewed. Primary schools have always suffered discrimination in the allocation of funds. While pupil-teacher ratios are often low in secondary schools, the ratios in primary schools remain very high. Until very recently it continued to be a national goal to try to reduce class size to forty children or less per teacher. This has finally been achieved, but few infant teachers are celebrating when classes remain crowded with forty children. In 1971 the teachers' unions threatened strike action unless class size could be further reduced to thirty-five children, hardly an unreasonable demand (F. Hill, 1970).

In many cities primary schools are housed in outdated, substandard buildings dating back to Victorian days. Ugly, three-story institutions are crammed with children and divided into small, boxlike rooms. Many late Victorian schools were "open-planned" so that most of the floor space was under the scrutiny of the watchful schoolmaster, assisted by his proctors and pupil teachers. In this manner one teacher could oversee the work of a hundred children seated in tiers, two or three to a desk. When the schools were graded these massive rooms were chopped into small classrooms, often without access doors from hallways. In some schools children have to pass through three or four other classrooms to get into or out of the building. It might be some improvement to knock down the wall dividers and restore the open spaces for team teaching. The asphalt playgrounds are tiny, noisy, and sometimes practically bare of equipment.

The English seem to have great difficulty scrapping an outmoded building. Of the many schools desperately in need of renovation, some are hardly worth salvaging. They are especially deficient in usable learning space indoors. Village schools, while less crowded, are often older and even more substandard in equipment and facilities. The new postwar buildings constructed in the expanding suburbs and new industrial towns have taken funds away from schools in older, urban centers and the rural sections of the North and West (Burgess, 1970).

The planning of new buildings, while nationally controlled, often breaks down at the local level. Time after time the authorities wait until people have settled an area before they complete construction of new school buildings. The time lag ranges from a few months to a few years. Consequently, existing schools in expanding areas are constantly overcrowded with shifting school populations. The English "solution" to overcrowding is to erect cheap "Terrapin" huts, a trade name for a type of prefabricated building that can be moved from site to site within twenty-four hours. They do provide a minimum of teaching space, but they hinder such activities as team teaching, and the physical separation of the huts isolates the teachers and children from the rest of the school's resources. Added to the strain on the overcrowded schools is the corresponding insecurity of children waiting to be shifted to a new location.

Regulations governing school construction sometimes require smaller schools to be built in stages, a process that is inefficient and greatly increases the overall cost. In the space of a few years one school had three additions budgeted as minor works projects, and workmen disrupted the site on three separate occasions. Population projections are available to chief education officers but the competition between schools and other institutions for the services of the building industry leaves them with little power to effect long-range site planning.

Allowances for books, teaching aids, supplies, and equipment are pitifully small by American standards. Head teachers attempting to stretch meager budgets are frustrated by the excellent but increasingly expensive educational equipment continually appearing on the market. They consequently devote too much energy to finding ways to raise additional funds through voluntary contributions. Parental efforts at times become diverted by a misreading of educational priorities. Some schools invest thousands of pounds and hundreds of voluntary man-hours to construct outdoor swimming pools that can be used for only a few months of the school year, while the curricular program is desperately in need of additional books and audio-visual equipment.

Salaries in England for beginning teachers are so low that the 1970 campaign for increases widely publicizing the poor pay scale might well have discouraged a number of potential male recruits to the profession. Salaries are determined according to a national scale that counteracts regional inequalities but drastically decreases the bargaining power of teachers. The teachers cannot play one district off against another through selective strike threats. The scale also divides career teachers from beginning teachers, splits teachers' organizations into rival groups that maintain an uneasy truce during national negotiations, and induces the unions to make excessive demands on the national budget, to which the government can hardly accede without spiraling the inflationary cycle (Hughes, 1971).

The second source of funds other than the contribution from the national budget is from local rates, or taxes. Some professionals feel that educational budgets for operating costs are too closely tied to the rates. In negotiations with the local Borough Council Finance Committee, the Education Committee must compete with all other social services and costs of local government for a fair share. Councillors tend to expect "value for money"; that is, they try to buy education at the cheapest possible cost. Because members of the Education Committees are more inclined to support the claims of expanding secondary schools, primary education suffers once again in the allocations.

2. Inadequate Provisions for Special Education

In contrast to the United States, special education in England has been slow to develop as a professional field. Training programs for teachers of handicapped children are not sufficiently available to provide for the number of children who need help. While institutional facilities serve educationally subnormal children, children in the regular school program who are only moderately mentally handicapped are inadequately identified and provided for.

Compared with the United States, fewer psychological services cater to children with social and emotional problems. School psychologists largely confine their attention to severe cases. There are few visiting teachers or school social workers and not enough child guidance clinics. Few programs prepare class teachers to work with emotionally disturbed children.

Children with learning difficulties are not given enough expert professional attention. Most English primary schools only go as far as to organize remedial classes under remedial teachers. In earlier years, when streaming by ability was common, schools had slow classes for dull children, indiscriminately perpetuating the stigma of backwardness by segregating slower children from others and placing them under teachers with little special preparation.

The prevention of learning disabilities in reading and other areas and the diagnostic approach to learning problems are poorly developed. Often by the time that children have been identified as needing special help, their self-concepts have been too severely damaged. The infant school is the most fruitful stage for diagnosis and prevention, but identification of disability is still largely left to chance.

Although nursery schools should not be conceived as a form of special education, many English people view them in this light, and head teachers heartily endorse nurseries as a means of preventing future disabilities while providing socializing experiences for children with special needs. Many heads strongly favor half-day nursery school attendance in classes attached to the infant schools, but this request has rarely been heeded.

3. Deficiencies of In-Service Education

The isolation of teachers from one another and from current educational developments is one of the most glaring weaknesses in the English system. Class teachers may talk to the head and to other class teachers within their own building, but not enough have contacts with teachers in other schools or with college and university staffs. Many heads try to encourage teachers to take time off to visit other schools or to attend short courses, but there are few inducements in the form of financial support or higher positions on the salary scale for advanced study.

A teacher has many diverse opportunities for in-service education, but there is great need for some form of national planning along with a better system of incentives. A common complaint is that once a teacher receives his initial certificate, he may cease his professional training. Short courses and conferences seem to be attended largely by the same people, a minority group of ambitious, potential heads and dedicated enthusiasts. Workshops lasting a week or two during school holidays are organized by the Department of Education and Science under the leadership of Her Majesty's Inspectors. Primary school advisers in the Local Education Authorities sponsor in-service conferences and meetings. Colleges of

Education and the Schools of Education attached to the universities are expanding the range of short- and long-term courses. Many of the curriculum improvement projects sponsored by the Nuffield Foundation and the Schools Council require Local Education Authorities to provide Teachers' Centres when testing new materials in pilot trials.

The Teachers' Centres have been viewed as one way to stimulate curriculum development in the local authority. It is apparently a rather novel idea for teachers and consultants to work together on curriculum improvement projects outside their own building. This is the other side of local school autonomy, for interschool cooperation is very limited.

There is very little professional course work in the field of administration for head teachers. Few heads have studied leadership in any theoretical way; they simply build on traditions or follow hunches. There are no such things as administrative credentials or certificates; practicing heads have few opportunities to study about leadership skills. In fact, it is not always acknowledged that such skills exist or, if they do exist, that they are teachable.

4. Theoretical Weaknesses

Infant school leaders seem reluctant or unable to amplify a theory of education that defends current practices. Infant teachers are seldom able to identify what they are trying to achieve except in the haziest of terms. Many claim to follow a child-centered philosophy, but most are probably not as child-centered as they think. At any rate, few defend the position with other than vague generalizations or weak clichés. One shudders to imagine a parents' meeting at which a well-meaning infant head teacher must answer an articulate critic bent on attacking the theoretical supports for a progressive infant school. Perhaps no one would ask a woman head teacher to defend herself at a public meeting. At any rate, the head considers his primary responsibility to be teaching children, not convincing the public. Even hostile critics in England refrain from publicly embarrassing authorities. They would more likely write a caustic letter to the editor of the local newspaper.

Many heads follow current developments because they seem to be reasonable or because others are doing it. The bandwagon effect is as common in England as elsewhere. A school staff adopts vertical grouping because a neighboring school staff has been doing it or because the primary school adviser shows a film that stresses its advantages. People attempt what they think will work; this pragmatic approach to problem-solving is admirable, but it should not permit the innovators to consider a reasoned theoretical defense superfluous.

Infant class teachers have developed methods and created a learning atmosphere on the basis of extensive practical experience, yet few give much systematic thought to subject matter goals. More content might be drawn from current developments in social science, and teachers still often base work in the natural and physical sciences on traditional nature study. Perhaps this weakness is not as important in infant schools as it is in the junior schools.

Modern practices work well with children who learn effectively in an atmosphere of freedom. Most infants respond favorably to such an atmosphere, but there are always some who do not. Here is where the shortage of psychological services and the paucity of inservice education make English schools vulnerable to criticism. How should a teacher deal with children who seem blocked in acquiring systematic reading skills? What does a teacher do with hyperactive children? How many teachers recognize symptoms of dyslexia? Why do so many teachers have trouble with immigrant children? It can be argued that traditional teachers are not any more capable of recognizing symptoms of learning disability and that traditional methods may in fact aggravate the problems. This is still no excuse for practices that fail to deal adequately with specific learning disabilities.

5. The Paucity of Auxiliary Aides

Large classes in infant schools prompted the Plowden Committee to suggest the employment of teacher aides to help with nonprofessional tasks (Plowden, 1967). This became one of the most controversial recommendations in the Report. The National Union of Teachers is firmly opposed to the employment of auxiliaries in the classroom. The suspicions of the N.U.T. executive board about the intent of the recommendation are fully understandable. Much of England's past history in education has been a record of attempts to purchase cheap education for young children; the employment of underpaid auxiliaries to assist the teacher might well be used as a means of undercutting criticism of the high teacher-pupil ratio. The same criticism was pertinent when early programs to introduce teacher aides in the United States were initiated in the 1950's. In any case, auxiliaries without professional qualifications should not be allowed to assume teaching functions, and it can rightfully be claimed that very little of the child-adult interaction in an infant school can be defined as nonteaching. In the United States paraprofessionals are now provided some training, and they work under the direction of certified teachers. American officials do not attempt to justify large classes when additional helpers are provided.

Many head teachers disagree with union officials about the use of classroom auxiliaries. Some infant schools employ assisting nursery nurses, whose two years of professional training entitle them to work with children from two to seven years of age. Many schools make use of the voluntary help of parents, but this is not nearly as widespread as it might be. The preschool play group movement has shown how eager English parents are to assist in the education of young children. Some parents are employed on a part-time basis, assisting with music, cooking, sewing, handicraft, and other activities. Many heads allow parents to listen to young children read, although this is in direct opposition to the N.U.T. position. The danger of permitting parents to participate in reading instruction is compounded when parents underestimate the range of teaching skills required to offer suitable guidance to children with learning problems.

Despite the increasing use of auxiliaries, there are still far too few adults in schools. Even when children can talk freely with one another, they still need to seek out adult approval, support, and guidance. To observe young children crowding around their teacher for attention is ample testimony to this need. Much of the notebook writing that children do may well be compensation for the absence of listening adults. But not all children are able to write down their thoughts, nor do they all need to start writing so early. Children from homes with restricted language need to talk a great deal with sympathetic adults who can help them to acquire the verbal confidence that is necessary for meaningful communication through reading or writing.

English children work a great deal on their own or in pairs. With a limited amount of adult response and without much instruction in the processes of committee work or intergroup relations, they do not acquire the kinds of social skills that many American children exhibit. Some of the differences may be culturally determined. Gregariousness and outgoing behavior tend to be respected by Americans but are considered suspect among the English, at least within the middle classes. English children spend more time responding to inanimate objects, learning resources, materials, and references. They work alongside one another and cooperate to complete a job, but they may have insufficient opportunities to communicate with teachers and other adults or to explore interpersonal feelings, conflicts, and peer allegiances.

6. Problems in Educational Priority Areas

Long overdue efforts to compensate for social deprivation are at last becoming a matter of government policy, thanks to the recommendations of the Plowden Report (Plowden, 1967). A little more money is being supplied. A few old buildings are being replaced. A few more nursery classes have been authorized. But if compensatory education is to make the slightest difference, it needs to be massive in scope. Financial allocations should probably be multiplied at least ten times. More than just money is needed. More pertinent is to channel funds effectively into social services and community projects that might break the cycle of poverty.

Even the modest beginnings that have been made in compensatory education are threatened. The idea of compensating for poverty by spending more money on the education of poor children has not had a very receptive audience in England. If anything, English educational history has consistently illustrated the opposite tendency, to spend *less* money on the education of the poor. In the United States compensatory education grew out of financial, scholarly, and racial demands. One of the aims of the federal government's War on Poverty was to try to correct the imbalance among states and local districts with large proportions of poor children and a low school tax base. Early intervention in the poverty cycle through programs for preschoolers, lower pupil-teacher ratios, and extra pupil personnel services was fortified by studies of the detrimental effects of growing up in multiproblem neighborhoods.

But even with all this attention to compensatory education, there has not yet been any truly significant improvement in the achievement of poor children in America. English critics of compensation and of the designation of Educational Priority Areas have not been unaware of American efforts, claims, and counter-

Learning How to Learn

claims; but any program that calls for extra expenditures on the part of the national government is suspect, and there are few counterpressures from the unorganized poor in England to press forward their demands.

The worst feature of schools in multiproblem areas is the same in England as in the United States: the inability of teachers to relate to the children, the parents, or the community. English teachers are not as affected by the racism that blocks communication in American ghettos, although racial prejudices expressed by English whites toward "colored" people is sometimes even more blatant; there just happen to be fewer "colored" people. What does block communication in England is the lack of sociological awareness of class differences among teachers in deprived areas. England's major educational problem, the class bias of its school system, is discussed at greater length in Chapter 11.

8
Junior Schools

Exciting developments in English primary education are now taking place in junior schools. Educators abroad have heard a great deal about English nursery and infant schools, but as the climate of freedom has been moving upward into the older age range and previous restraints have been lifted, even more intriguing possibilities are opening up. It is not unusual to find a junior school that combines all the currently popular innovations in one free-flowing arrangement—vertical grouping, open-planned building, team teaching, the integrated day, and incorporation of a variety of Nuffield Foundation and Schools Council projects.

This is not to say that the number of informal junior schools operating approaches the number of pace-setting infant schools. A majority of junior schools are more traditional, tending to organize the curriculum by separate activities. Many still stream children by ability, teach by total class assignments, and evaluate children's progress through competitive grading. The junior stage is still the stepchild in terms of facilities and classroom space. But the pace of change has been accelerating since the late 1960's.

Many practices discussed in regard to the infant school—family grouping, individualization, flexible room arrangements, freedom of movement, and creative expression—can also be found in informal junior schools. But because the greater maturity of the children extends the possibilities of these innovations, a number will be discussed further in this chapter. Other continuing developments will not be discussed, since their existence is implied by the description in the preceding chapter. Before discussing the characteristics of the junior schools, a brief historical overview describes the lifting of previous restraints.

HISTORY OF JUNIOR SCHOOLS

Separate schools for juniors developed by accident. Early English elementary schools took children from the ages of five to fourteen. When the Hadow Report on the adolescent (Hadow, 1926) recommended that new senior schools be formed for the older age range, classes for eleven- to fourteen-year-olds were chopped off the old elementary schools; the age range that was left beyond the infant departments made up the school for juniors.

Selective, fee-paying grammar schools had long enrolled children from the age of eleven. Gradually more scholarships were made available to poor children. Competition to win these scholarships pushed junior schools to concentrate on their abler scholarship candidates and to stream classes by ability. When the 1944 Education Act abolished fees for state-maintained secondary schools, pressures on the junior schools retarded experimentation, and they were forced to compete with one another for the limited number of grammar school places. Pressures from middle-class parents willing to risk their children's chances in the state-maintained system were coupled with concerns of aspiring working-class parents who increasingly identified the selective secondary grammar school as a means of improving their children's social and economic life chances.

The Eleven-plus Examination

Although the 1944 Act was supposed to establish a tripartite system of secondary education with schools of equal esteem, almost everyone knew better. The teachers, the parents, and the children spoke of "passing" or "failing" the eleven-plus examination. The majority of children could not hope to achieve a place in a grammar school, since the number of places varied from 10 percent to 40 percent of the school-age population, depending on the local authority, with a national average of about 25 percent. Proportionally, more working-class than middle-class children "failed" the eleven-plus (Swift, 1964). Examinations that put a premium on verbal facility and rapid mathematical reasoning tend to favor the middle classes. Because only a minority of children passed into the grammar schools, the majority considered themselves failures by the end of the junior school.

Selective secondary education became a political issue. Those L.E.A.'s dominated by the Labour Party gradually moved toward comprehensive secondary schools, while authorities dominated by the Conservative Party clung to the principle of selection. At the same time a number of junior school heads were deemphasizing the importance of an externally administered examination and were attempting to free their schools from the associated constraints on curricular experimentation.

Under the national Labour government between 1963 and 1970, pressure was exerted on all authorities to submit plans for comprehensive school reorganization, particularly after the publication of D.E.S. Circular 10/65 in 1965. Since national recommendations are advisory rather than mandatory, authorities varied in their compliance with the circular. Reorganization of secondary schools became the dominant educational issue of the late 1960's. With the Conservative Party victory in the 1970 General Election, Circular 10/65 was immediately withdrawn (Burgess, 1970; *Times Ed. Supp.*, July 3, 1970). Secondary school selection, then, is not yet a dead issue, but during the years of Labour Party dominance the eleven-plus examination disappeared or was deemphasized in many local education authorities. The effect was to unfreeze the junior school curriculum.

Streaming by Ability

Almost all English junior schools were streamed until a few years ago, and the practice was seldom challenged (Daniels, 1961a, 1961b; Jackson, 1961). When Brian Jackson published his research on streaming based on data gathered in the early 1960's, it was almost universal in schools with a two-form entry—that is, with sixty or more children in each age level (Jackson, 1964). Today, one of the most remarkable changes in junior schools is the rapid abandonment of the practice of streaming by ability in larger junior schools. The decline of the eleven-plus examination took one of the props away from streaming, and the departure from total class teaching made it even less defensible.

"Homogeneous" ability grouping in the United States, a practice identical to streaming, has been officially out of fashion for forty years or more, yet it persists. Hundreds of American research studies show that ability grouping makes little difference in the improvement of performance of either able or slow children and that the self-fulfilling prophecy makes the stigma of "slow" stick to those children so labeled (Rosenthal and Jacobson, 1968). Even though university professors of education in the United States have been presenting evidence against ability grouping for years, the practice continues, often in disguised forms, with teachers and elementary principals sheepishly confessing to undercover manipulation of groups on the basis of readiness, "maturity," reading ability, language facility, or other subjective criteria. Even nongrading has become a means to rationalize groups organized by reading achievement.

English schools, then, moved from almost universal endorsement to rapid discreditation of ability grouping (Clegg, 1970) in less than ten years, while American schools have clung to ability grouping in spite of its poor reputation for decades. This says something about the current extent and rate of change in English schools.

It is probable that a modified form of streaming exists in many junior schools, but the justification for it has been irreparably damaged. The Department of Education and Science commissioned the National Foundation of Educational Research to conduct a broad study on streaming, which was finally published in 1970 (Barker Lunn, 1970). In her admirably documented, carefully controlled study of streaming, Joan Barker Lunn followed five thousand children in seventy-two schools throughout the four years of junior school attendance. By the time the study appeared, however, the issue no longer seemed as relevant as it had earlier. This is a common complaint about the rare examples of carefully conceived and painstakingly executed educational research commissioned to help resolve an educational controversy: by the time the study is published, it does little more than confirm the obvious, leaving the controversy as unsettled as before (N. J. Entwistle, 1970). Partisans can pull out of the findings whatever they choose in order to support their own preconceptions.

The Barker Lunn report actually gives little comfort to either side of the controversy (Trauttmansdorf, 1970a). Many of the findings were expected and had been hinted at by previous research in England and in the United States (Daniels, 1961b). Able children do well in streamed or unstreamed schools. Selection for the high streams favored girls, autumn-born children, and children of middle-class backgrounds. A minority of children were wrongly placed at the age of seven. If errors were discovered and children were moved to different streams, those who moved up improved, and those who were dropped down conformed to lower expectations.

The *Times Educational Supplement* stressed the importance of teachers' attitudes and warned against organizational reforms which do not involve corresponding teacher commitment (*Times Ed. Supp.* editorial, January 30, 1970). Only if teachers were in favor of nonstreaming did it bring about the promised benefits for those previously assigned to lower streams. Although teachers who favored streaming were more united about objectives, teachers who favored nonstreaming were better able to improve the attitudes toward school and the social participation of average and below-average children. Teachers in nonstreamed schools who still favored ability grouping and class competition were able to retain these practices within their own classrooms by using such devices as seating arrangements and special assignments for able or slow-learning children (Barker Lunn, 1970).

Able children do well no matter what kind of organization or what kinds of teacher attitudes they encounter. This destroys one of the major defenses for streaming, the contention that able children need the stimulation of other bright children, imaginative teachers, and an accelerated curriculum to prove their mettle. This argument was at one time so powerful that damages done to less able children through labeling, lowered expectations, and errors of placement were ignored (Clegg, 1970).

That there are no really significant differences in academic performance between streamed and unstreamed children may be more than merely a predictable conclusion; it may accelerate the rate at which schools are unstreamed, as fears about lowered standards for able learners are shown to be unfounded. It may, however, take longer to change the *attitudes* of a generation of heads and class teachers oriented to streaming than to change the grouping practices of junior schools.

CHARACTERISTICS OF ENGLISH JUNIOR SCHOOLS

Junior schools moving toward freer methods and a more relaxed atmosphere may not yet represent the majority of English schools, but they are setting the trend. The methods described below are already practiced in a large number of classrooms, and more and more schools are adopting them. Like characteristics discussed earlier, many can be adapted in modified form to the corresponding age range of American elementary schools.

1. Freedom to Choose

Fundamental to informal junior schools is the degree of responsibility given children to exercise a wide range of choices—whether to keep busy or flit about, whether to work alone or with others, what kinds of projects to choose, what means to use to achieve goals. Choice is not always easy. Some children find it painful to be asked to show initiative or to have to make their own decisions about how best to use their time. But for the most part junior children, because they are more mature than infant children, are more capable of exercising judicious choices over longer periods of time.

As in the infant school, flexible room arrangements, accessible materials, available resources, and experience-based teaching strategies maximize opportunities for self-direction. Some children choose to waste time, fool about, or avoid difficult jobs requiring concentration. Critics of free choice worry about these "scyvers," the ones inclined to take the easy path. Defenders say that such children learn as little in highly directed classes, but their resistance tends to be more passive—they give up by shrinking from competition or by playing dumb. In freer classes, because they may pursue either teacher-approved or disapproved activities, tactics may become more obvious.

If given the opportunity, most preadolescents demonstrate an impressive capacity for sustained work. Since rejection of adult models is not yet a decisive factor in the peer group value structure, most are inclined to follow the expectations of a conscientious, admired teacher. Most juniors enjoy school and thrive on responsibility. Those who interpret freedom as license to do as little as they please still enjoy school, although they may show less academic growth.

2. The Workshop Environment

As in the infant school, many classrooms are arranged with the help of bays and dividers to offer various corners where children can work individually or in small groups. The classroom becomes a workshop with different centers arranged for different forms of learning. There are studios for creative expression, study cubicles for writing and reference work, laboratories for scientific experimentation and research. The teacher moves about providing guidance and stimulation.

English teachers emphasize that their most important concern is to help children learn *how* to learn, not to tell them *what* to learn. In the face of an uncertain future, flexibility, self-direction, and inner resources will be needed as the known world rapidly changes. The workshop environment helps meet these needs by providing a learning laboratory in which habits and attitudes become ingrained that most likely will continue after schools and teachers have been left behind.

3. The Slower Pace

As children establish their own work schedules, there is a marked relaxation in pressure. With older children work deadlines can be more distant; some children continue projects through much of a term. They learn to take their time as they discover and explore the deeper meanings and implications of their initial interests.

On occasion a teacher will deliberately slow the pace in order to help children observe more carefully, to develop their powers of concentration, and to foster habits of diligent workmanship. There is an unhurried quality connected with careful investigation. For preadolescents, greater absorption and involvement enhance creativity and result in increased self-control (Tanner, 1966). Whereas a young child may paint a picture that is satisfying to him within a very brief period, an older child's sense of critical awareness will demand fidelity to detail and the unhurried care associated with authentic craftsmanship (Lowenfeld, 1957; Tanner, 1966).

4. Self-instructional Devices

The use of self-instructional materials such as tape recordings made from B.B.C. radio broadcasts, coordinated slide–audio tape programs, coordinated filmstrips and recordings, reading laboratories, teaching machines, and programed materials is becoming more widespread.

Older children are more capable of working for longer periods of time on activities which require little direct teacher supervision. Children evaluate their own achievements and keep many of their own records. The teacher serves largely as a catalyst. He selectively intervenes to carry investigations further than in the infant school. The junior teacher becomes a questioner, a challenger, a doubter, a suggester. He needs to devote less attention to approval, support, encouragement, and positive reinforcement than the infant teacher, although he continues to supply these. He can also temporarily withhold rewarding responses, demanding by implication greater effort and more penetrating analysis.

5. Decrease in Teacher Talk

As total class teaching decreases (except for a few special activities), the teacher spends much more time communicating with individuals. He may even do some work of his own alongside the children. One of the most impressive experiences for a visitor is to observe a teacher working on block prints, mosaics, or sculpture while the children carry on with their efforts. The teacher can continue as artist or learner alongside the children. This form of teaching is analogous to the apprenticeship system. The children model their efforts after the master craftsman. Typically, such a teacher communicates with children through dialogue rather than through talking at them or leading a group discussion.

An interesting experiment would match a selected group of informal junior teachers in England with a selected group of informal later elementary teachers in the United States. These teachers would be chosen to exemplify highly recommended teaching practices in both countries. The experimental design would simply involve coding teacher-pupil communication according to the system of Interaction Analysis outlined by Ned Flanders (Flanders, 1965). The prediction is that while American teachers might be skillful in leading discovery approaches to learning according to innovative curriculum programs in the United States, there would be far less teacher talk in informal English junior classes. Indeed, interaction analysis coders would have a difficult time recording in some of the categories, since the workshop environment encourages simultaneous conversations in various corners of the room.

6. Respect for Privacy

A unique aspect of informal classes in English schools is the respect shown for children who do not choose to engage in social interaction. It is recognized that preadolescents need time to look within themselves and sort out their thoughts and feelings. Children are seldom accused of daydreaming, nor are they jollied into social activity. Schools designate quiet corners for calm reflection, and privacy is respected. Children who want to be alone are allowed to go outside or to seek their own haven.

The negative side of this is that some children need greater socialization, and the retreat from peers may be a form of escape rather than a desire for reflection. Quiet, withdrawn children are not typed as maladjusted, even though some may very well be. On the crowded British Isles there does seem to be less gregariousness in peer behavior and more concern with protecting inner-directedness than in the United States.

7. Creative Movement

Bodily movement is a form of creative expression in English schools that is seldom found in America, particularly not where older boys and girls are involved. In England, creative movement is an art form which starts in the nursery and infant schools and is carried to much deeper interpretive levels with older children (Jordan, 1960). Long associated with physical education in the school hall, it is meant not only for the talented or dedicated few; every child is encouraged to give reign to imaginative interpretation. Creative movement becomes a form of emotional release with dramatic overtones. Junior children have been doing it in schools for so long that they seldom feel self-conscious when visitors are present.

Many English teachers have become highly skillful in directing movement, which in its more highly developed phases becomes a form of spontaneous choreography (Jordan, 1963; Hodgson and Richards, 1966). Music, expressive stories, dramatic themes connected with school projects, or religious celebrations often provide the stimuli. Children become deeply engrossed as they express physically what they imagine. The school hall offers plenty of room, and physical education apparatus, platforms, chairs, and tables are imaginatively transformed into props.

8. Concern with the Process Rather Than the Product

For many years children in English junior schools have been turning out great quantities of work. Older forms of topic teaching resulted in masses of carefully finished writing and painting which looked very impressive on classroom walls.

Today the junior teacher is concerned more with quality and process than with quantity and finished products. Whether a scientific investigation proves or does not prove a hypothesis, the concern is with the process of making a hypothesis. It is not the finished ship model, it is rather the exploration of materials which is the chief concern. The final display or exhibition serves only as a kind of motivating deadline, not as the goal itself; rather it is the work habits, the process of making decisions, the culminating investigations, that are important. It is not so much the finished stories or poems, even though these are sometimes written with exceptional sensitivity (Langdon, 1961; Clegg, 1966; Lane and Kemp, 1967), it is more the confidence to make an attempt which the teacher hopes to encourage.

9. Modern Mathematics and Science

There are definite contrasts in methods and goals in modern mathematics between England and the United States. English mathematics fits well with individualized learning and discovery teaching. Teachers interested in newer developments generally are the ones who also feel an affinity with the goals of the new programs. Just as with infants, mathematics for juniors has been strongly influenced by the work of Piaget (Piaget, 1960, 1964). The conceptualization of relationships is extended and mathematical principles for juniors are more highly developed, but mathematics seldom moves far from practical testing or a concrete, experiential basis.

In England reforms are taking place through the teachers, while in the United States reforms have been dependent on the introduction of new packaged programs and textbooks. If reforms in

England had taken place in the American way, they would have met with considerable resistance. As it is, many English teachers are opposed to too heavy an emphasis on symbolic abstraction and to the tendency to divorce mathematics for older juniors from other learning activities.

It may be illuminating to contrast the Nuffield Foundation approach to primary mathematics with American modern math projects. Nuffield booklets for teachers are narrative in form (Nuffield Junior Mathematics Project, 1967). They illustrate how modern mathematics fits the informal, multi-activity school program. Mathematics is shown to be a language for more precise scientific thinking. Children are encouraged to seek applications of mathematical principles in local studies and project work. Ways to make and use various homemade devices, aids, and measuring apparatus are shown, with more concern devoted to developing appropriate mathematical attitudes among children and teachers than to the reform of content.

In the United States, Sputnik sparked national concern over the quality of science education in America, which led to demands to "beef up" mathematics and science teaching in the secondary school. School mathematics at last became a respectable interest for professional mathematicians. Mathematics was viewed as a separate discipline, important to study for its own sake. The need to turn out more and better mathematicians and mathematics teachers led to a reform movement that brought together mathematicians and teachers interested in designing a new content, which eventually found its way into new textbooks. Developments which first took place in secondary schools were soon transferred to elementary schools. Even programs for young children quickly moved them toward mouthing mathematical abstractions.

There was little or no resistance on the part of American elementary school teachers to the new textbooks and workbooks, except in the form of teachers' complaints that the new math was new to them as well. The answer was to provide in-service courses for elementary teachers. In-service courses tended to emphasize mathematical content rather than new teaching strategies. Teachers have therefore become even more dependent on the commercially distributed, but now mathematically respectable, teaching materials.

In England concern is more with ways of learning than with

what is learned. There has been a deliberate attempt to wed the informality of free inquiry to the demands of the discipline (Marsh, 1970b). It is an uneasy marriage, but it has been kept together by the intervention of a number of forces between primary teachers and the mathematicians (Association of Teachers of Mathematics, 1967). These include the Nuffield Foundation Junior Mathematics Team, D.E.S. advisers, local authority advisers, and College of Education lecturers who have provided term-long, full-time courses for experienced teachers.

Nuffield Foundation schemes in junior science (Nuffield Junior Science Project, 1967) follow the same pattern as the Nuffield Junior Mathematics Project. They build on informal learning methods while preserving sound scientific content. There is the same adherence to practical activities, outdoor investigation, indoor experimentation, and testing through first-hand experience (Whitely, 1970). A group performs an experiment in one part of the room and records its findings in another part, freeing the science corner for use by another group. The extent of change in junior science has not been as pronounced as that in mathematics, perhaps because there was less development in the infant stage to build on and because there are still too few primary teachers with sufficient competence in the sciences or the scientific method (Blackwell, 1968).

10. Discovery Teaching

"Discovery" is a popular word in both countries, but programs to promote discovery are less sophisticated in England than in the United States, and discovery teaching has yet to become an English cause. People talk a lot about discovery, but there is no format or fully developed teaching strategy worked out to achieve it.

There is certainly less danger of teacher domination of the process of discovery in England than in America. This is both a strength and a weakness. Without teacher direction, some of the discovery process is poorly assimilated; with too much teacher direction, it is the teacher, rather than the children, who internalizes the desired habits of thought.

11. Environmental Studies

English children are encouraged to go outside of the classroom and carry their work out into the local environment (D.E.S. Education Pamphlet No. 35, 1969). Sometimes this is called environmental study; in other contexts it is referred to as local field study or rural study.

Children take their work to corners of the school site or investigate phenomena in the surrounding fields. Some urban schools use the streets as a source of data. Field trips are easier to organize than in bureaucratic American school districts. American exchange teachers who are used to limitations on the use of buses are surprised at the ease with which buses are chartered and trips arranged in England. (English children, however, usually have to pay their own transportation costs.) Historical sites, churches and castles, local industries, geological formations, ponds, forests, and farms extend the school program beyond the classroom walls.

American observers have been much impressed by the extensive use of local surroundings. Community surveys, exploration of physical contours, plant and animal life, utilization of local resources, and integrated themes growing from environmental studies all take children beyond the school grounds. Martha Irwin and Wilma Russell were particularly impressed by the school services provided by local museums (Irwin and Russell, 1971). Museum officials encourage visits by children, assist teachers with materials, provide access to primary sources of data, assist children in carrying out field studies, distribute models, kits, and displays, arrange county-wide exhibits, and offer a wide range of other services. Unlike the United States, where such facilities and personnel would be restricted to large cities, many smaller towns and counties provide museum services.

Irwin and Russell develop the characteristics of a community-centered curriculum. Impressed by the involvement of English children in integrated studies, they discuss how American teachers can promote topic-centered instruction, encourage inquiry-based investigations, involve learners in planning and setting goals, and develop resource units while using the community as a learning laboratory.

12. Newer School Construction

School architects are trying to cater to the principle of free choice in school surroundings as well as within the building. Grounds are planned to offer many different centers with natural streams, playing fields, gardens, paved areas, "adventure" playgrounds, places to run, humps to climb, and quiet corners to retreat to.

Newer open-planned or semi-open-planned schools have fewer enclosed boxes and can better accommodate team teaching. A variety of textures are built into floors and walls. Floors are covered with carpets, rugs, tile, or linoleum. Seating and work space is diversified through the use of tables, benches, boxes, platforms, comfortable armchairs, stools, rockers, cushions, benches, and window ledges. Learning space is maximized by utilizing hallways, cloakrooms, and passageways as teaching areas.

13. Camps and Touring

Many junior schools offer opportunities for older children to take week-long excursions. These become the highlight of the term's work, with the preparation and follow-up activities capitalizing on the involvement which such an adventure induces. Unfortunately, children's parents have to supply at least some of the funds, which means that only part of the class gets to go, and those who are left behind often can be relegated to a kind of second-class citizenship.

School-sponsored trips to the Continent during spring holidays are becoming more and more common for older children. Others go camping in England or live for a period of time at educational centers. The Inner London Education Authority maintains a rural center for urban children. Extended field trips are usually well organized and are led by teachers who know how to make the most of the educational potential of such trips, since many have taken similar study tours during college courses.

14. Realistic Activities

Young children learn through play, but older children enjoy activities which closely approximate adult functions. Young children engage in spontaneous drama and are satisfied with play money and household toys, but older children prefer more realistic dramatizations and projects. They cook dishes that they eat. They construct working weather stations. They publish their own newspapers. They manage their own stores, selling anything from sweets to school supplies.

One head teacher was asked why, in view of the dental dangers, he allowed children to sell sweets to other children. He replied that he would just as soon have the school make a profit, since children would otherwise run to the neighborhood sweet shop. No school seems very far from a candy store; the significance of sweets in child-rearing is a subject yet to be adequately documented!

15. Family Grouping

Junior schools, particularly those anxious to break away from total class teaching, are beginning to adopt family grouping. Since junior schools cater to a four-year age span, some modify the scheme to cover age spans of only two or three years. A few organize family groups to cut across the complete age range (Ridgway and Lawton, 1969).

Family groups in junior schools serve the same functions as they do in infant schools. Older children develop a sense of responsibility by helping younger children, who in turn are provided with older models with whom they can identify. Younger, able children can work with older ones, while slower children need not feel themselves unfavorably compared with their age mates. Activities cater to a broad spectrum of aptitudes and interests, without regard to age level expectations or the limitations of arbitrarily graded materials.

A liability from the American perspective is that it becomes more difficult to organize sequential or spiral schemes in elementary science or social studies. There are great gaps in content while children can conceivably go over the same ground on different occasions during the four years. However, the content areas are so differently treated in England and the curriculum is so loosely structured that vertical grouping does little more than confirm the accepted anarchy.

For the older age span, family grouping in England is spreading more rapidly than the corresponding nongrading schemes in the United States. Nongrading in its limited American conception is by and large confined to primary cycles covering the first three grades. There are few later elementary cycles. Nongrading is not spreading into the middle grades because the most frequently reiterated rationale behind it, smoother induction into developmental reading, becomes less convincing to parents and teachers. The American school system is far too age-graded in terms of textbooks, state curriculum frameworks, and local courses of study to provide much scope for multi-age group interaction.

16. The Integrated Day

"The integrated day" is one of the most popular current catch phrases among progressive junior schools. It might just as well be called "the integrated week" or "the integrated six years," expressing the ultimate extension of the conception described by Brown and Precious, the authors of a popular book on the integrated day (Brown and Precious, 1969).

Once the break from subject matter distinctions and a time-tabled schedule becomes complete, the integrated day combines a whole network of informal school practices. Many junior teachers select an integrating theme which is supposed to give some focus to various school activities. An integrating theme is not unlike the American idea of a unit of work, where related content and skills are drawn from a number of subject matter areas. English integrating themes, however, are much looser in conception than American units and may have a refreshingly nonacademic slant. For instance, a class may take movement as its theme. The pupils explore the potential for movement in dance, in mathematical shapes, in poetry, in three-dimensional construction, in mechanical and technological advances, in color, in sound—indeed, in any medium or manifestation. The theme may arise from an interest of the children or may be sparked by a field trip or represent one of the teacher's previous successful endeavors. Some themes are historical, set in earlier times. A practice teacher will often launch his own integrating theme, and the regular class teacher will happily oblige by turning the class over to him.

The integrated day allows children to work for long, uninterrupted periods and to pursue interests in depth. Children carry out intensive, detailed investigations that culminate in impressive reports, murals, model villages, or dramatic productions. They are at liberty to go off on tangents and are encouraged to do so by the rather loose conception of integration. Sometimes the children become so involved that they may continue to develop a single project for weeks. The three terms of the school year serve as convenient time limits for the development of integrating themes, culminating in the displays which almost invariably are arranged to signal their conclusion.

Some writers have distinguished between this curriculum format and the earlier project or topic teaching, which became popular in junior schools after the Second World War (Marsh, 1970a). Topic work was also based on activity methods, but the children tended to produce masses of similar products. They would do reams of writing, piles of art work, copious maps, massive scrapbooks—all on topics conceived and largely directed by the teacher. In the integrated day children work on many different projects which may be only loosely connected. The teacher encourages children to follow their own unique styles and to set off on their own explorations.

Without a timetable to follow children find their own work rhythms. Some schools have even dropped the long-hallowed midmorning break, when children are turned loose to run off steam outside while the teachers escape to the staff room for morning coffee. In the ideal integrated day children go outside whenever they feel like it, while teachers have their coffee whenever they are so inclined (Brown and Precious, 1969). In schools that retain the morning break, a number of children stay inside to continue their work, so engrossed do they become in what they are doing.

It is doubtful whether the abolition of the morning break will ever extend much beyond the fanatical fringe, for it is the teachers, rather than the children, who need it. All of the teachers assemble in the staff lounge to have coffee or tea and to chat, relax, and unwind. The break often stretches for half an hour, although fifteen minutes is a more accepted time limit. Such a complete work stoppage would be of real benefit to American elementary teachers. Rituals which develop in the staff room become hallowed by tradition. So much emphasis is placed on the morning break, along with the importance of showing proper hospitality, that the size of the staff room and the number of coffee cups are sometimes the most important factors in determining the number of practice teachers which a school is willing to accommodate. English teachers are courteous to visitors and usually welcome help from college students, but if there are not enough facilities in the staff room, then the teachers begin to show signs of acute distress.

In the integrated day the need for record-keeping by the teacher and by the children becomes crucial. With children carrying on their own work, the teacher needs to keep track of what is happening so that some children do not get lost in the shuffle.

While schools have developed a variety of means of recording anecdotes and other evidences of growth, there are few systematic schemes to provide continuity should children transfer from one school to another. The English place more weight on getting to know the children well in a small school setting than on objective evidence.

It is necessary for the head teacher to help young teachers and teachers who are used to more traditional ways to overcome their insecurities about working within such an unstructured format. Children also need help in developing appropriate work habits, since some children may also be insecure when asked to respond in new ways. Children who have become accustomed to being told what to do are ill prepared for so much freedom, so much independence, so much leeway to exercise their own initiative.

17. Cooperative or Team Teaching

Team teaching is an American idea which the English have borrowed and reformulated. The preferred English term is "cooperative teaching," for team teaching in the American sense often serves as an excuse to break up the integrated curriculum through departmentalized teaching. Team teaching tends to be organized on less hierarchical lines in England and is less lavishly augmented by teaching aids and special instructional equipment (Warwick, 1971). It often accompanies vertical grouping, an integrated day, and a generally positive attitude toward newer methods.

As in the United States, there are a great many different forms of team teaching. Some teams consist of two teachers and eighty children; others are more elaborate, involving a larger group of children and three or four teachers aided by part-time teachers, practice teachers, and volunteers. But because English teachers seem unconcerned about precise definitions and often use terms interchangeably, one has to visit a school before one can be sure that a school is doing team teaching. The staff may be doing something else which is even more intriguing.

Newly constructed open-planned schools do away with classroom walls, but they also tend inadvertently to encourage specialization. One teacher takes responsibility for the arts and crafts section; another will direct the language teaching; another may be responsible for the mathematics area. Part-time teachers may be brought in for music or foreign languages. This danger of departmentalization, inherent in American team teaching arrangements, works against other English developments which cut across subject matter distinctions. To guard against a departmentalized curriculum, some schools have designated one teacher as the lead teacher in, say, mathematics, but the other teachers are expected to provide mathematical experiences as well. The lead teacher may be one who has just returned from a Nuffield Foundation or a college course and who has become familiar with some of the newer equipment and instructional strategies. Team teaching thus allows for the development of special professional interests and offers the talents of a few adults to large numbers of children in the school.

As the children move about the school, they make use of a number of teachers. Again, there is a danger that some children will become lost or neglected, and many schools assign children to a home base with a homeroom teacher for at least part of the day. Each school seems to work out its own team teaching pattern, and no two are identical. The English tend to take a concept like team teaching and adapt it to the particular building and the particular staff, not the other way around. The plan changes from year to year as the staff changes or as a new wall is knocked down or a new Terrapin hut is erected.

18. The Middle School

The Plowden Report recommended middle schools for children from the age of eight or nine to the age of twelve or thirteen (Plowden, 1967). Whether the middle school will be more like the English junior school or more like the American junior high school is as yet undetermined (Schools Council, 1969a). The reorganization has hardly begun, particularly since new schools for a new age range require more money, either for new construction or the expansion of existing sites (Christmas, 1970). In addition, the development of middle schools may have been arrested by delays in secondary school reorganization and the raising of the school-leaving age from fifteen to sixteen.

One of the chief arguments in favor of the middle school is that the large comprehensive secondary school, taking children from the ages of eleven to eighteen, is at odds with the English ideal of a small school providing for a limited age span, where children are well known to the head and the staff. Large secondary schools have attempted to meet this objection by breaking the school into subunits which cover only two or three forms, sometimes in separate sections of the building.

The concept of the middle school arouses misgivings among some primary teachers and college lecturers. They grant that it is difficult for eleven-year-olds to enter the more formal structure of the English secondary school, and that eleven-, twelve-, and thirteen-year-olds might well benefit from continuing under informal junior school teaching arrangements after some modifications have been made for the older age span, but they fear that increasing departmentalization and more traditional objectives will be imposed on the younger children in the school.

The term "middle school" was coined in the United States to deal with approximately the same age range for some of the same reasons—the failure of the American junior high school to provide a specific educational program suitable to younger adolescents. The junior high school in the United States has been plagued by staff turnover; many subject specialists take posts in junior high schools as a steppingstone to a secondary school position. Junior high school youngsters have a reputation for being a difficult age group; many subject specialists are ill prepared to work with them.

One hope in England is to prepare teachers specifically for the age group represented in the middle school. The trouble is that no matter how specific a preparatory program a student has followed, he is just as likely to be assigned to a different age group, depending on the job market. The English teaching certificate is the same for every level.

Some primary school educators fear that the middle school will become more like the secondary school than like the junior school. The key man in any English school is the head teacher. If middle school heads are expected to be university graduates, they will most likely have had secondary school experience. Head and class teachers with secondary school backgrounds can influence the direction of the middle school away from the currently popular informality of the junior school. The middle school in this case would undermine rather than reinforce the influence of primary school practices. The prevailing hope, however, is that middle schools will rescue pupils previously assigned to large secondary schools for the continuing influence of primary education. Even if middle schools represent only a halfway house, they would certainly ease the shock which so often takes place when children accustomed to integrated learning under informal teachers are subjected to a rapid reeducation process in compartmentalized, formally structured secondary classrooms.

19. Teachers' Centres

The Schools Council recognized that to acquaint selected teachers with new curriculum programs would be useless unless sufficient follow-up work was organized. So Teachers' Centres, financed by Local Education Authorities, were required by the Schools Council for the diffusion of new programs. Staffed by wardens who have responsibility for overseeing the facilities and organizing the curriculum development work in them, one purpose of the centers is to train teacher leaders who will spread Schools Council projects among other interested teachers at local meetings and workshops conducted at the centers.

The Teachers' Centres are also conceived as in-service bases for curriculum development (Corstan, 1969). By no means is work to be limited to Schools Council diffusion projects; more important, they are to be used for all kinds of continuing programs in teacher education. Teachers' Centres have had a varied reception, depending in part on facilities, staff, financial support, and other available avenues for in-service education that may exist in the vicinity.

They are used extensively on afternoons, evenings, and weekends when open; they could as well be used during the day if teachers had more free time. They provide social as well as professional interaction, but facilities in many areas are still rather meager. In the meantime, the Colleges of Education stand ready to provide well-equipped laboratories, tutors as consultants, and recreational facilities, but they are not widely utilized by experienced teachers unless they are enrolled in specific college courses.

JUNIOR SCHOOL PROBLEMS

1. Financial Neglect

A chapter in Razzell's book *Juniors* is titled "The Primaries—Last in the Queue" (Razzell, 1968). Financial neglect has already been discussed in relation to infant schools, but in many ways conditions are even more desperate among the juniors. Many of the buildings are old, hand-me-down former senior schools dating back to Victorian times. The size of a great many classrooms is smaller even than the minimum space recommended by parsimonious government standards.

Financial regulations tend to penalize junior teachers. The salary structure provides more money for career teachers in secondary schools, where more higher-paid posts of special responsibility have been designated. The secondary pupil-teacher ratio is lighter, there are more free periods, teaching facilities are better, and the social status is higher. One secondary sixth-form pupil counts as the equivalent of ten primary pupils in tables for financial reimbursement. Financial neglect and lack of opportunity has led to the problem of teacher turnover.

2. Teacher Turnover

English junior schools have attracted a higher proportion of men than American elementary schools—approximately two out of five junior school teachers are male (Blyth, 1965). The Colleges of Education have continued to supply men prepared and eager to work with preadolescents. From this group most junior head teachers and deputy heads are appointed.

Unfortunately, many men leave junior schools. Some drop out of teaching altogether because of low salaries. Some move into secondary schools, attracted by higher status or greater financial rewards. When men remain with the junior level, they often transfer from school to school, apparently the accepted career pattern. It is less common to earn promotion within one's own school; a young man interested in advancement applies for positions elsewhere.

The turnover hampers program continuity. It takes time for a school staff to develop allegiance to informal methods. By the time teachers learn to function comfortably within the setting and with one another, they begin to move on, requiring new teachers to be inducted into unfamiliar patterns. There continues to be a teacher shortage in junior schools, although the worst shortage is among infant schools, where pregnancy is more likely to increase the turnover. The worst-hit areas are the working-class sections of industrial cities where part-time teachers, supply teachers, and probationers force hard-pressed heads to engage in a continuous process of shoring up the dikes.

3. Religious Education

It is most difficult for an American to assess religious education in English schools. In contrast to the American ban on religious instruction through the enforced separation of church and state, religious education is the one subject legally required in all English schools. Even the Plowden Committee, so amenable to change in other areas of the curriculum, came out in favor of continuing the requirement for religious education even though notes of reservation were appended to the document (Plowden, 1967).

No doubt the majority of English parents want the schools to continue to provide religious instruction, largely because England thinks of itself as a Christian country, but possibly because neither the homes nor the churches provide very much religious education on their own. The schools provide daily religious observance, according to fundamentally orthodox Christian doctrine. The curriculum for religious education is governed by an agreed-on syllabus, endorsed by the various church bodies. A conscience clause gives parents the opportunity to withdraw children from religious education, but, as might be expected, very few do. Church schools, primarily those run by the Church of England and the Roman Catholic Church, receive state money and supply their own brand of religious education, but regular state-maintained county and borough primary schools teach Christian theology in almost as undiluted a form.

This may have been all very well when England had a relatively homogeneous religious culture, but the influx of over 200,000 immigrant children, the majority of whom are Indian Hindus and Sikhs and Pakistani Moslems, into state schools is beginning to involve England in some agonizing afterthoughts. Do the schools have a right to Christianize Hindus, Moslems, Sikhs, Jews, and nonbelievers? Does the provision of a conscience clause lead to social discrimination against the children who are withdrawn? Moslem leaders are demanding equal time for Moslem religious instruction (Wigg, 1970), even though the English historically have not been particularly sensitive to the claims or sensibilities of religious minorities (Devlin, 1970).

The major criticism of religious education in English schools comes from nominal Christians who claim that over the years the schools have not been doing their job. Formal observance of prayers, hymns, and religious celebrations is now giving way to or being supplemented by dramatic productions and assemblies which deal with broader moral and social problems. Much leeway exists for imaginative interpretations of the agreed-on syllabus (Wainwright, 1970).

Practice, however, depends entirely on the head, and he may emphasize whatever interpretation he wishes. Typically, the children gather in the morning for an assembly in the hall. They sing hymns and songs and have a short religiously inspired program. This morning assembly allows the school to function as a corporate body, fostering the symbolic celebration of school spirit. A number of heads use this opportunity to offer a moral lesson. English heads do not shy away from dealing with moral issues, but these are too often dealt with in moralistic terms, with more attention to preaching than practice. Some educators recognize that religious concepts are often too abstract for children to assimilate (Goldman, 1963, 1964). The religious messages of hymns and Bible stories, unless taken in a literal sense, become relatively meaningless.

The basic issue is the right of a state institution to offer religious instruction in an increasingly pluralistic society. Attempts at providing watered-down doses of comparative religion do not satisfy the demands of either the nonbeliever or the confirmed believer. The conscience clause does not protect a parent's religious conscience.

The United States, with its more obviously pluralistic historical antecedents, has banned religious observance in tax-supported institutions to protect the rights of minorities. England, with a state religion, cannot resort to the principle of the constitutional separation of church and state, for there is no written constitution and church and state are intimately intertwined.

Religious education in its present form is likely to become a center of increasing controversy. Many primary teachers and heads are questioning its validity, even though powerful vested interests for its preservation remain.

Perhaps the greatest criticism from religionists is that the churches are relatively empty and the secular spirit is increasing in a country with a state religion, a required school religion syllabus, and over eight thousand state-aided religious schools. Either religious education is ineffective, or it has been so overdone that by the time children leave school they feel that they have had enough.

4. Spasmodic Curriculum Development

With so much individual school and teacher autonomy, there has been very little national or even local curriculum development. The English system of gradual curriculum reform may well be more effective in the long run, but right now it is possible in many localities for no curriculum development to take place at all. Very little does take place in thousands of schools, where heads and staff rely on traditions and the individualistic idiosyncracies of independent teachers.

The piecemeal nature of curriculum reform led to the formation of the Schools Council, which built on earlier efforts of the Nuffield Foundation. The Schools Council is anxious to preserve the autonomy and is sensitive to the independence of English teachers. Despite safeguards, the materials offered by the Schools Council suffer from two main weaknesses. The first is that with no other sponsorship than the not always acknowledged prestige of the newly formed Schools Council, many of the materials are hardly used at all. This leads to the second drawback—to get widespread distribution, many projects use packaged materials, which are distributed by commercial firms who naturally are inspired by the profit motive. Packaged materials are deplored by some head teachers, who worry that these will foster conformity on a wide scale rather than the diversity which the Schools Council hopes to encourage. Some of the most imaginative Schools Council projects never get off the ground, because to use them successfully, teachers must rethink their methods of operation. If Schools Council projects are used indiscriminately in nonintended ways, or if they are used hardly at all, the wide discrepancy related to curriculum development will remain and will probably increase.

Some junior schools are changing in many ways at once; others have scarcely changed at all. Some junior schools offer a curriculum with little or no coordination that ultimately boils down to the individual prerogative of the teacher; others have a curriculum which reflects the heavy hand of the head. Some schools are bound by tradition; others appear to have cast tradition aside.

5. How Much Guidance? How Much Freedom?

Children need independence, yet they also want models. At one time the charge against teachers was that they were offering too much direction; today some teachers are accused of providing too little. How far can a school move as it fosters freedom for pupils?

Infant schools deal with younger children, who generally respond positively to informal methods. Infant teachers provide a great deal of indirect guidance by the very ways in which they relate to children. Yet while there are more informal infant schools than informal junior schools, few infant schools have moved as far toward pupil independence as some junior schools are moving. This is one of the reasons that the junior stage is so exciting at the current time.

What is the role of the junior school teacher in regard to adult guidance and expertness in content fields? To teach informally is difficult, and the older the children, the more difficult it becomes. It is not that older children find freedom more demanding than infants; their greater maturity implies greater potential for self-direction with a more imaginative grasp of the potentials for problem-solving. But the teacher cannot abdicate his role as a leader of instruction; he needs to work out procedures which make free inquiry both effective and efficient.

6. Is There Too Much Diversity?

Americans may admire the lack of conformity and the autonomy of English schools, but Englishmen themselves are beginning to wonder if the diversity is not too chaotic. In no other country are there likely to be such marked contrasts between any one school and another. A child can move a few miles from a relatively formal school to a relatively informal school, from a tightly structured curriculum to an unstructured one, from one developmental reading scheme to an entirely different one. There is no accepted framework of content in either primary school science or social studies. A teacher can learn to function within one set of expectations, only to discover that new expectations are required when he changes jobs. The only threads which run through English schools are those which customary usage maintains. Many customs had been relatively pervasive from school to school, but now the weight of authority supporting them is rapidly eroding.

English children and teachers are moving much more frequently now than they ever have. Most children adapt quickly enough to new expectations, perhaps more easily than the teachers.

This kind of flexibility may be necessary in an increasingly mobile society, but when even those Englishmen devoted to teacher autonomy begin to question the widespread diversity in practice, then the problems must be becoming more acute.

7. Criticisms of the Integrated Day

The integrated day has not been well defended in print. Just how integrated can an integrated day be? Is everything to be integrated? Are children to be allowed to go off on any tangents which please them? Are the themes really integrated, or are they so loosely conceived that they merely allow each person to "do his own thing"? Can systematic mathematical development be left to chance or must special provisions be made to promote mathematical conceptualization? Many junior schools have responded to the criticisms implied in these questions by offering a partially integrated day. They take time out for certain studies, like mathematics and instrumental music, but they integrate everything else.

While a few teaching teams are developing cooperative integrated plans, each teacher tends to run his own integrated day, and he uses whatever facets happen to fit his own conceptions. The term tends to be used very loosely and can mean different things to different people. Too often it is used as a slogan, a rallying cry to attack arbitrary subject-based divisions. Some who defend the integrated day imply that it can serve as a total curriculum for junior-age children.

One test of how successful the integrated day is will be to see whether or not it produces self-directed learners who can function in the more highly structured secondary schools. What happens to children who leave the integrated junior schools for the separated secondary school? A commonly expressed agreement among secondary school teachers is that children who enter from informal schools which stress discovery approaches to problem-solving tend to be noisier, more difficult to manage, more insistent on asking questions, more resistant to teacher domination. The secondary teachers soon "sort out" the troublesome, but they have to expend a considerable amount of energy inducting them into changed expectations.

8. Neglect of Social Studies Objectives

To Americans familiar with having periods set aside for social studies and elementary science, the treatment of the content fields in English junior schools may seem superficial and in some cases neglected. The term "social studies" has only recently come into common usage in England. Junior school children have in the past studied history and geography, sometimes separately but sometimes in close association during topic teaching or integrated studies. History and geography are for the most part separated in the secondary school and are usually taught by different specialists; the other social sciences are virtually neglected.

In informal junior schools the formal study of either history or geography has been deemphasized. Many integrated topics are set in historical periods and are enriched by historical references, while environmental studies draw on geographical concepts and research methods. But the renewed interest in elementary school social studies which has developed in the United States with new teaching strategies, curriculum packages, model programs, reform groups, introductions to the disciplines in the early grades, revised scope and sequence charts, increasing influence of professional associations, and the plethora of available publications is largely absent. One Schools Council project is concerned with developing a greater degree of sophistication in the statement of social studies objectives (Schools Council, 1970e), but this is a far cry from the depth of concern expressed by American educators.

It is too easy to jump to the conclusion that because social studies is an undeveloped field in English primary schools that the content fields are ignored. The English have not become caught up in social studies reform because primary teachers do not use the disciplines to give structure to the curriculum. Like progressive educators in America during the 1920's and 1930's, English primary teachers use content for means rather than ends. Learning how to learn is more important than what is learned. Where English schools are much more vulnerable is in the lack of attention given to helping children to acquire social skills, develop group processes of learning, clarify social values, or reflect on social issues. Children spend a considerable amount of time engaged in group work, but English junior teachers miss many opportunities to help children clarify social attitudes, social concerns, and social skills—goals which many teachers in America use the social studies to illuminate.

9. Lack of Attention to Mental Health Needs

Although many sensitive teachers function intuitively from sound mental health perspectives, the science of psychology, with the exception of the work of Piaget, has scarcely influenced practices in English primary schools. The free atmosphere of English schools is conducive to less repressive measures of social control, but the prevention of mental illness is seldom a recognized goal, and provisions for disturbed children are inadequate. Most teachers express concern about the importance of mental health, but there are too few facilities available for distressed children and too little recognition of the symptoms of disturbance. Teachers who should know better often wrongly label children as backward, upset, "peculiar," or lazy.

Teachers themselves need to learn how to deal with their own emotional problems. There is still a widespread disdain for and fear of psychotherapy, and the stigma attached to mental illness is even more pronounced than in the United States. Too frequently teachers offer simplistic explanations for "queer" behavior.

Few teachers have had any training in group dynamics, and few children emerge with developed skills in social interaction. The skills involved in group work are just not taught; it is assumed that it is satisfactory merely to allow children to work together.

There is a related lack of skill among many teachers and College of Education students in cooperative interaction. In-service meetings often end up with teachers arguing with one another; communication is on an excessively verbal level. There is little recognition of the affective realm in human relationships, and a self-protective shying away from getting too close to one another results.

10. Poor Articulation

The transfer from infant schools to junior schools is usually achieved without much difficulty. The prevailing ethos at the two stages is generally similar, although some junior schools are much more formal than infant schools and some place heavier stress on competition. Since both stages tend to be organized with one teacher responsible for one group of children for most of the day, the transition from infant to junior status often means little more than a step across the playground.

It is the transition from junior schools to secondary schools that creates problems. There are comprehensive secondary schools which make halfhearted attempts to contact the older junior classes in order to inform the children of opportunities which will become available, but in some cases there is virtually no contact between the secondary school and the junior schools that feed into it. This is largely a carry-over from the time when there was less need for such articulation because junior children went to different kinds of schools on the basis of the eleven-plus examination.

The real problem of articulation is not between school and school but between stage and stage. Primary teachers and secondary teachers hardly speak the same language. Only recently have some county education advisers tried to bring primary and secondary head teachers together. When they do get together at infrequent conferences or meetings, they often make accusations. Why do secondary teachers sacrifice individuals to subjects? Why do primary teachers neglect the fundamentals? Why do secondary teachers rely so heavily on an examination syllabus? Why do primary teachers talk so smugly about their progressive values? Who is responsible for the increasing disrespect for authority?

During the eleven-plus era, the selective examination for grammar school entry tended to dictate the junior school curriculum and organization. Where selective examinations have disappeared or have been deemphasized, there is now a greater need for two-way communication. Without such articulation, work of the junior school may be antithetical to the educational provisions which follow.

11. What Comes After?

This is the heart of the matter: What happens when the children leave the junior school? Will the winds of freedom reach the secondary school, at least in its comprehensive form? Some secondary schools have attempted to introduce modified junior school practices with the lower forms—that is, with adolescents of twelve, thirteen, and fourteen. A few secondary schools have retreated from streaming and have organized mixed ability classes. The Schools Council Humanities Curriculum Project was designed to encourage studies of social problems for average and below-average students through class discussion and nondirective teaching (Schools Council, Nuffield Foundation, 1970). But the examination emphasis, the almost universal practice of ability streaming, the subject matter divisions of the curriculum, and the social distance between teachers and pupils all negate the openness encouraged by many English primary schools.

Those features of English primary education which intrigue

educators from abroad may have less long-range potential in England itself. England has traditionally been proud of its selective secondary schools. Despite the move toward comprehensive education, England is still stuck with the principle of selectivity, even while many other democratic countries are moving toward more open educational opportunities (Vaigo, 1970). English comprehensive secondary schools are by no means open, and of course independent public and grammar schools are closed, at the very least on the basis of social class and academic qualifications. Comprehensive schools vary greatly, but even the more flexible ones have only provided greater access of transfer from one stream to another. Pupils are still categorized as early school leavers, C.S.E. examination applicants, and G.C.E. examination applicants, first at O-level and then at A-level. The secondary examination system may be reformed, but no one talks seriously about abolishing examinations. Selectivity seems so ingrained within the teaching profession and so institutionalized in entry requirements for higher education that, sociologically, the single most important function of the English secondary school system continues to be to select the best from the rest.

9

The Preparation of
Primary School Teachers

Almost all English primary school teachers have been prepared at small, single-purpose institutions known as Colleges of Education. This is in contrast to the United States, where most elementary teachers attended multipurpose liberal arts colleges or universities. Since preparation for primary teachers in England is clearly vocational, many of the strengths and some of the limitations of the colleges can be traced to this emphasis.

Teacher education in England is due for a major reassessment in the 1970's. Pressures from outside the colleges, along with demands from within, have prepared the way for a national inquiry into teacher training (Church, 1970b; Hewett, 1970; James, 1972). Some educators are looking to developments in the United States for direction (Maclure, 1970), but it is highly unlikely that organizational changes in England can follow such models. Changes will take place slowly as traditional practices are carefully modified— this is the English way. But these changes will eventually affect the entire process of teacher certification.

At one time teachers' colleges were common in the United States, but the vast majority have evolved into large, regional, multipurpose colleges and universities. Is it possible to re-create important English practices within a large American university? Can a self-contained, English-style teachers' college be developed within a multipurpose American institution? How can common charges against the American university—that it treats students impersonally, lacks consistent direction, and relies on mass methods of teaching—be overcome? English Colleges of Education have a clearly defined purpose, rely largely on tutorial methods of teaching and keep in close contact with the progress of individual students. On the other hand, the superior physical facilities, more lavish financial provisions, heterogeneous student body, more varied cultural opportunities and scholarly resources of the American university can certainly enhance the preparation of teachers. Some universities are organizing subunits, such as residential or experimental colleges, but none has attempted to introduce the vocational clarity of the English College of Education.

A SINGLE–PURPOSE INSTITUTION

At an English College of Education all the students are preparing to become teachers. Since all colleges are affiliated with a university through Area Training Organisations or Institutes, it is possible to remain in college for four years and earn a university degree, but most students leave at the end of three years without a degree. The English pattern is more similar to European than to American practices. Historically, graduates of European universities have taught only in secondary schools or in independent private schools. Very few European primary school teachers have been educated at universities or have had the opportunity to earn a degree.

At a single-purpose institution, goals are reasonably clear. The students know why they have been accepted. The tutors are continually aware of their main function—to prepare broadly educated, vocationally equipped teachers for the schools of England.

Colleges of Education are lower in the prestige hierarchy than English universities. The qualifications of the staff and the students in the two institutions overlap, but this overlap is seldom recognized. Instead, the differences in minimum qualifications for admission are frequently mentioned to reinforce status differences. College lecturers are not as well paid as university lecturers, and they teach many more hours per week. College students often feel inferior to university students. Some enter the colleges as a second choice when they are not admitted to the more highly selective universities. Differences are accentuated by the fact that after three years university students receive degrees that have market value in a large number of occupations, while most College of Education students after three years receive only a teaching certificate, which has no transfer value to occupations outside the schools.

The curriculum of a single-purpose institution can be planned to meet reasonably clear-cut objectives. While there are vested departmental interests competing for the students' time, curriculum changes seldom reflect the American pattern of low-level compromise which is justified by hazy rhetoric about the proper combination of courses that will provide a sound "liberal" education. In a College of Education the curriculum is designed to produce better-educated teachers.

A single-purpose college can also promote staff communication. In contrast to the United States, members of a number of departments actually talk with each other about students. Tutors meet daily for morning coffee and afternoon tea in the senior common room, where they exchange ideas and impressions as well as quips and gripes. English staff members enjoy relaxing conversation, and communication among members of various departments is a refreshing contrast to American departmental isolation.

Will the single-purpose institution survive in England? The odds are not strongly in favor of it. Too many restrictions on the development of the colleges, tied as they are to D.E.S. projections about the supply and demand of teachers, have lessened their appeal, especially to men. The discussion in this chapter, based on two years of experience at one of the larger colleges, may one day have little more than historical interest. Even so, the strengths of the single-purpose institution should not be lost in whatever provisions will follow.

VOCATIONAL EMPHASIS

The English College of Education is a vocational institution. While there are differences from one English college to another, the curriculum is traditionally divided into three major strands. About one-third of the work consists of professional education courses under the jurisdiction of the Education Departments. Another third of the work is taken as a main subject or, in some cases, as a main subject and a second, subsidiary subject. The remaining third, a category loosely labeled "curriculum courses," consists of background study to teach the various areas of the school curriculum.

The work organized by the Education Departments includes the foundation disciplines of introductory psychology and sociology, generally taught in separate departments in the United States. The more academic education courses include educational psychology, educational sociology, the philosophy of education, and, sometimes, the history of British education. Other professional education courses are based on overlapping age bands, either at nursery-infant, primary, junior-secondary, or secondary level. These courses often include school-based components, sometimes requiring as much as one morning a week to be spent in the schools.

The second third of the work is devoted to a main subject. The student is expected to study the main subject in depth, ostensibly for his own personal development rather than for professional background. Some colleges offer the student a second main subject to study as a subsidiary interest. All students, including those who are preparing to teach nursery and infant children, must major in a main subject, and it is often one that they have studied during their seven years at secondary school.

In many colleges the main subject tutors interview candidates to decide who will be admitted to the college. They assess the prospective student's potential to study a discipline in depth, basing their judgment in part on his past performance. English students come to college much better prepared in a main subject than do most American students. Usually they have studied the subject for O- and A-level examinations in the fifth and sixth forms, the final three years of secondary education. They build on this background by spending at least one-third of their time with main subject tutors from the very beginning of college.

Despite the rationale in terms of personal development, in a College of Education a main subject is not studied for its own sake. Main subject tutors are expected to have had at least five years of teaching experience in the schools. Since students expect subject matter to be relevant to teaching, there can develop a strong vocational interest even in main subject work. Some departments make a concerted effort to point out teaching implications, often by carrying out projects in local schools.

The third strand consists of curriculum courses. Primary school teachers take a multitude of short courses, which are taught largely by the main subject tutors for students who are not specializing in their departments. These include courses in mathematics, history, geography, English, drama, dance, physical education, religion, and science. Such courses deal with subject matter background for teachers as well as with teaching methods. In this sense they are similar to American educational methods courses.

Without stretching the point too far, but admittedly stretching it a bit, a case can be made that approximately two-thirds of the course work in English Colleges of Education is directly vocational, and even this does not include practice teaching, which is offered on a full-time basis during each of the three years. Professional education courses are obviously vocational. Most main subject courses deal in part with curriculum implications for main subject students. And at least parts of the curriculum or methods courses deal with teaching implications. This contrasts with the United States, where more than three-quarters of the curriculum for prospective teachers is completely unrelated to schools, where practice teaching accounts for a large proportion of the education units, and where education courses suffer considerable academic disrepute.

Another important contrast between English Colleges of Education and American universities is the muting of the dichotomy between education departments and the rest of the academic community. In England disagreements about a proper balance in teacher education exist, but dialogue regularly takes place with a number of commonly accepted points of agreement. In the United States it is not uncommon for a prospective teacher to take ten courses in his major field of concentration without ever having a single application to teaching the subject in the schools mentioned. Indeed, it would be rare for an instructor in his major subject to have had any teaching experience in the schools at all. This cannot happen in an English College of Education, where all main subject tutors supervise practice teaching and have taught in the schools. Furthermore, main subject department members are expected to keep abreast of school curriculum projects involving the subject matter with which they deal.

Learning How to Learn

Some students (often those who do not really want to teach) are critical of the heavy vocational emphasis. Others, particularly some of the men, become disillusioned with the evangelistic ethos surrounding modern teaching methods, especially when the ethos seems to conflict with the heavy demands involved in teaching and the low remuneration and status accorded to English primary teachers.

Yet, when contrasting the English vocational emphasis with the American deemphasis in favor of the vagaries of "general" or "liberal" education, it is not too difficult to make a choice. American university practices are not easy to defend. How can a convincing defense be made of American students spending most of their first two years being "liberally" educated through introductory courses in which they have almost no background and which are taught at a factual level through mass lectures? Add to this the high American dropout rate during the first two years, the distaste of most American professors for teaching introductory courses, the domination of textbooks and lecture notes, the lack of student participation and discussion, and one is inclined to agree with the commonly held English stereotypes about American higher education.

In England general introductory courses are offered for the last time at O- (Ordinary) level, when the student is fifteen or sixteen; English students specialize, perhaps too narrowly, from that time on. In the United States the equivalent of O-level courses are offered to university students of nineteen and twenty. This seems to confirm the belief that the United States is a rich country wasting its resources, teaching low-level courses to too many students. It fortifies the English claim that sixth-form teaching in the last two years of the secondary school is more advanced than American college teaching in the freshman and sophomore years. Even though comparisons are difficult to document, in some very real senses this is true if courses are compared by levels of achievement demanded and if instructional strategies are considered. The English wonder what it is that Americans teach in secondary schools, if students seemingly start all over again in college. The English often ignore the differences between the highly selective English system and the more open opportunities within the American tradition, but English accusations are not easy to ignore.

THE SMALL, INTIMATE COMMUNITY

For many years most teacher training colleges were small, self-contained institutions with only a few hundred students each. After the Second World War enrollments rose steadily, especially after the increase in the length of the course from two to three years. A few of the approximately 160 colleges in the country have reached enrollments of between 1200 and 1500 students, but the majority serve 500 to 1000. In the early 1970's enrollments leveled off and even threatened to decline, reflecting some of the ambivalence about the role of the colleges that led to the national inquiry into teacher training (Burgess, 1971).

Many tutors look back with longing to the old days, when smaller numbers made for a closer sense of belonging to a college community. But even with the growth of colleges, students are still surprisingly well known to one another and to the staff. There is still a very real sense of belonging. Tutors and students participate together in such organizations as school choirs and orchestras. Even for those students who reside in lodgings in the surrounding towns, the college campus remains the chief center of social activities. Students take tutorials, share common rooms, eat the noon meal, and participate in a multitude of clubs, teams, organizations, and societies on the campus. It is difficult for a student to be overlooked or neglected. Students with particular talents are given special encouragement. Students whose academic performance indicates difficulty are treated with special concern. The wastage (dropout) rate is very low compared with American figures. Marginal students are salvaged through individual attention, extra teaching practices, staff conferences, and the direct intervention of administrative officers.

Contrast this with the situation in American universities. More than half of American students "drop out" before graduation, and academic failure is only one of the causes. It is likely that most students drop out because they are faced with financial difficulties, have decided to get married, or no longer feel any sense of purpose. Students who drop out complain that nobody seems to care whether they remain or leave. Unfortunately, this too often is the truth. In a commercial enterprise where students buy their education, there has always been another customer to replace a student who leaves. In the United States students simply disappear. One semester they are in attendance; the next semester they are gone. Few people know what happened to them, and seemingly no one cares.

The familiar accusation is that the American multipurpose university has become an impersonal knowledge factory. Students complain that they are treated like I.B.M. numbers, particularly during the first two years. There is hardly an instructor with whom a beginning student can talk for any length of time. Despite professional counseling services, there are few people who are readily available to offer personal communication.

The students complain that American instructors appear to be too busy following their own professional interests to devote much time to talking with students outside of class, even about the subject matter which they teach. American professors teach twelve semester hours per week or less; many consider this to be the extent of their commitment to the student body.

An English student may resent the excess of "pastoral" care that some English tutors give to their tutorial groups. American students, after all, do enjoy the privacy of anonymity, which may be more in keeping with the ethos of the current student culture. In a large, impersonal university a student is left alone to mind his own business. He may prefer it this way, but he might appreciate at least being given the choice of being known or being left alone.

The development of residential colleges within American universities is an attempt to create conditions more conducive to interpersonal relationships among students and between students and staff. Members of the residential community make the decisions about their instructional program and residential concerns. One does not have to form a residential subcollege in England, for the College of Education is already a residential unit; its small size contributes to a sense of membership, and its purpose is also clear. The traditions of tutorial teaching, the low staff-student ratio, and the physical compactness of a small campus reinforce the sense of community.

TUTORIAL TEACHING

The average ratio of staff to students in a College of Education is one to ten. These generous staffing provisions allow for the basic unit of instruction, the tutorial group. There are some large lecture classes, and some other class sections have fifteen or twenty members, but these are balanced by tutorials, which can include only a handful of students. Although the number of students in higher education has greatly increased, the tutorial tradition is still considered viable. The tutorial is considered to be the main bulwark of English higher education. It is the setting in which the values of English academic life flourish.

Tutorials can be traced to the Oxford-Cambridge tradition, later transplanted to the red-brick universities and carried over into the training colleges for primary teachers. A representative tutorial group at a College of Education has about ten members, which equates roughly to the staff-student ratio. The principal means of instruction is the structured discussion. Those who practice tutorial teaching well see it as a way to bring out the analytical thinking powers of students.

In a well-planned tutorial the students come prepared to discuss issues. The tutorial may be devoted to issues arising from a recent large lecture, to a specific reading assignment, to an essay topic, or to a series of questions agreed on in advance. The tutor's role is to structure the discussion initially, to challenge students' opinions, to clarify differences, to summarize when needed, and to help draw out implications. Some tutors are very skillful in taking a back seat, talking very little, but yet challenging students to explore the deeper implications of the issues under discussion.

The tutorial style blends with what the English consider to be the mark of an educated person, the ability to communicate succinctly in speech and in prose. An effective tutor helps students to think critically, to reason effectively, to defend a position convincingly, and to express his thoughts with clarity and precision.

In contrast to these positive qualities, English college students show little skill in group work or in mutually supportive discussion. They prize the ability to argue with one another and with tutors, but they seldom defend each other or help the less verbal to express themselves. Consequently, some tutorials degenerate into battle-grounds for the most vocal students, with a number of participants remaining silent most of the time for fear of exposing their "ignorance" or having their feelings hurt. It becomes the tutor's obligation rather than the students' concern to draw out quieter members of the group.

Learning How to Learn

Tutorial teaching can break down in a number of other ways. Some tutors spend too much time lecturing, either explaining a position or presenting background information. Where a large proportion of the tutorial group consists of women, members may be hesitant to disagree with one another or to challenge the tutor. Where students have not taken the time to prepare adequately for the tutorial, the discussion may be lively but consist largely of "waffling."

Many English students who come to the United States on exchange programs complain that they miss tutorial teaching. Similar tutorials, if available in America, are offered only in advanced seminars. English exchange students cannot see the value of large lecture courses, furious note-taking, textbook cramming, and multiple-choice or brief paragraph examinations. Even if not verbally adept themselves, English college students want the opportunity to hear other students express points of view. They also have difficulty deferring to the mantle of unapproachable authority within which some American professors tend to cloak themselves.

In some respects tutorials contribute to the continuation of the elitist tradition. Because it is too expensive to extend the virtues of tutorial teaching to great masses of students, a broad base for post-secondary education becomes virtually impossible. But though tutorials are an expensive, time-consuming, demanding form of instruction, it would be difficult to conceive of British higher education without them.

PRACTICE TEACHING PROVISIONS

By far the most impressive features of English Colleges of Education are the provisions for practice teaching. These are so obviously superior to those available to most American students that it is a wonder that more American universities have not adopted them. Some American universities have introduced innovations in pre-student-teaching laboratory experiences, have placed students in two different locations for practice teaching, or have experimented with partially paid internships. However, variety in practice teaching opportunities is not considered innovative in England; it is more or less the stable pattern throughout the country to provide full-time teaching practice during each of the three years, although there is great variety in the specific provisions among the colleges.

During each of the three years of the certificate course every student spends from four to ten weeks in full-time teaching practice. At Berkshire College of Education the pattern consists of four weeks of practice in a junior school in the first year; six weeks in a nursery, infant, or secondary school in the second year; and a full term with the age level of one's choice in the third year. The students do not attend college classes during these periods.

A student who has completed a three-year course at a College of Education feels better equipped than an American graduate to assume teaching responsibilities during his initial, probationary year. Indeed, English students are at times disillusioned about teaching even before they leave college, for they have early experienced the tests of reality and know more about what they have to face. In the United States, however, overprotection of student teachers is all too common. Americans are not given three years in which to mature professionally and to assess their teaching tactics in actual classroom situations; therefore the demands of full-time teaching cause reality shock for many beginning teachers.

Particularly impressive to a visiting American is the responsibility assumed by practice teachers from the very beginning. The first teaching practice during the first year at college is real, not an observation period, a pre-student-teaching assignment, or a chance to "wet the feet" in gradual stages. Students are expected to assume responsibility for teaching small groups of children from almost the first day. They usually take over the entire class for at least part of each day. They prepare elaborate teaching plans and teaching aids and are asked to evaluate each day's experience in writing. Class teachers leave students alone with groups of children and may even go away on a week's travel tour with half of the class, leaving the practice teacher with the remainder.

If the involvement during the first year seems heavy, it increases during the second and third years. During the final practice the student tends to take over major responsibility for instruction.

Not only do the students in England have more responsibility, but the college staffs have a much heavier commitment to supervision than in America. One of the unique features of a College of Education is that every staff member, including all members of academic departments, participates in the supervision of practice teaching. By contrast, in the United States only a minority of education department members supervise student teachers. Even many of the education professors do not wish to sully their reputations (or expose their ignorance) by participating in the field-assessment of the products of educational courses. And to find American professors of English, history, or mathematics engaged in school-related work is, of course, a rarity.

The heavy demands on college tutors engaged in school supervision are staggering. Supervision is not considered a part of the normal teaching load; it is done above and beyond it. Tutors have to fit their visits into the little spare time in the week that is not scheduled for tutorials. At Berkshire College of Education a tutor is expected to visit each student on teaching practice at least twice each week. In addition, regular conferences or tutorials with practice teachers are scheduled on a weekly basis, either on the school site or at the college. Each tutor is paired with a second tutor, and each will visit his partner's students to provide a second judgment. For the final teaching practice a third judgment may come from external examiners who visit a cross section of the students to help maintain national standards. English students expect tutors to be available for regular consultations and to provide specific help and critical appraisal.

Initial teaching experiences can be emotionally draining, and practice teachers work very hard. Students are expected to take preparation seriously. They compile notebooks with long-range and short-range teaching plans, and they evaluate the results of their work daily. Plan books, or teaching files, often assume book-length proportions and are expected always to be available for inspection by class teachers, head teachers, college tutors, and external examiners. Some of the lesson plans and record-keeping may be a form of "busy work," but a good deal of the preparation, particularly under a flexible college tutor, is pertinent to the process of self-evaluation and professional growth. Students object, however, to the teaching file being weighted too heavily by tutors or external examiners in arriving at grades for final teaching practice.

In addition to the three scheduled teaching practices, students are given many other opportunities to visit and work in schools. A number of the professional education courses are given in the schools for one morning a week. Children are often brought into the college to illustrate work in main subject or curriculum courses. Many of the curriculum courses develop projects for students to try out with children. There are school observation weeks, opportunities to work with children in clubs, projects to involve students with immigrant or handicapped children, opportunities to attend school camps and week-long field trips. Students are quick to complain if they are not given sufficient opportunity to try out what they are learning in a school setting. In fact, although English students have much more time to work in schools than Americans, they would like to have far more. An increasingly popular recommendation is that college students spend one-third of their time in schools over the three-year period. This would amount to twice the number of weeks currently set aside for school-based work.

A number of other reforms related to teaching practice are under discussion (Cambridge Institute of Education, 1970). One is to make greater use of class teachers in evaluation and supervision (Church, 1970a; *Times Educ. Supp.*, 1970). Many schools used for practice are located twenty or thirty miles from the college. Visits of college tutors, no matter how frequent, are no substitute for the day-to-day, specific communication which is possible between students and class teachers. Such communication takes place naturally, but it does not officially count in the formal assessment, nor are class teachers paid for their contributions.

Another suggestion is to build a relationship between the college course and the probationary first year of full-time teaching. First employment is seldom tied to preservice training, even though it is at this point that beginning teachers are more receptive to the suggestions of college staff members. The first year is officially a probationary year, but aside from informal help from the head teacher and an occasional visit from a Local Education Authority adviser, the teacher is on probation in name only. Some have suggested that the probationary year be sandwiched between years of academic study.

It is enlightening to contrast the extensive preservice opportunities in England with American patterns. While there are hundreds of different patterns in America, only a few come close to providing full-time practice teaching during each of the three years of the professional sequence. Instead of doing practice teaching each year, many American students have to wait until their final year to take student teaching. Instead of full-time practice, many American students are attached to schools for only part of the day, while they continue to take academic courses on the campus. Probably the worst feature of American student teaching is the aura of overprotection. Too often students are very gradually inducted into taking responsibility, in deference to the obvious insecurity that many of them show. Some spend as much as three or four weeks doing little more than observing the class teacher. English students, on the other hand, are thrown right into the water. Some, indeed, are used virtually as supply, or substitute, teachers, a practice which would be illegal in America and is highly suspect in England.

But while the English teacher is better prepared than his American counterpart to begin teaching, after initial certification has been obtained he has insufficient opportunities to continue with formal study. There is no obligation for certified teachers to return to college, and there is little salary incentive for them to do so. The American practice is to encourage graduate study, to provide salary and career incentives, and to encourage career teachers to take advanced courses. The English invest almost all their financial resources in preservice teacher education, despite the fact that the majority of students are young women, many of whom will not continue in teaching. The government provides only a trickle of money to support the advanced education of career teachers.

THE LIFE OF A COLLEGE STUDENT

To American exchange students their English counterparts seem to have an incredibly "good deal." They are provided room, board, and tuition at government expense. They are given a grant based on parental income to cover additional living expenses. English students have what Americans call a "free ride" scholarship, and they do not have to be outstanding college athletic prospects to receive one! It is not necessary for English students to earn their way; in fact, it is a matter of principle that they do not. The heavy schedule of classes, which often amounts to twenty or more class hours per week, hardly allows for an outside job. Besides, wages are too low for part-time jobs to make much of a financial difference. Many students take jobs to earn money during the four-week breaks between terms and during the ten weeks of summer, but if they do this, it is on top of assignments which they are expected to complete during "holidays."

A large proportion of American students work at jobs during the school year as well as during vacation periods. Many American students are also provided with a considerable amount of financial support from their parents. Consequently, there are wide differences in the amount of spending money available among Americans. A number of American students drive their own cars, maintain fairly elaborate wardrobes, and have enough money to pay for expensive commercial entertainment, while others barely eke out an existence.

In England most of the students exist near the poverty line. Tuition and living expenses usually are provided by the government, and a little extra money is given in grants, which students use to buy books and pay for inexpensive college entertainment. An equalitarian culture has developed, based partly on financial necessity. Women pay their own way on dates, but dates are not the prevailing form of socialization. Students drift into the college pub, dances, club meetings, and common rooms. They dress in a kind of popularized "uniform" based on the prevailing student fashion. In recent years clothes have become scruffier, hair is longer, and beards are more common.

The students know that they have a good deal. They know that when compared with their peers who did not secure places in higher education they are the favored few, not so much in economic terms but because of the three years of sheltered living and the more secure career opportunities. Since few live within commuting distance of parental homes, they turn the college campus into their home. In college hostels, or dormitories, they live without the restrictions from which American students have only recently won relief. They often feel guilty about being so privileged. They blame themselves for apathetic responses to student causes or for meager attendance at the multitude of events sponsored by college clubs and societies.

Life at a College of Education is not too taxing, and this too is cause for student guilt, as well as for snide remarks on the part of tutors. Although they generally work very hard during teaching practice, at other times many English students seem to work in spurts. One can observe students reading in the library a few days before essays are due, and most students "revise," or review, for final examinations. The pace is relatively relaxed, and few of the demands are arbitrary. The certificate course lasts three years, and the crucial point for evaluation does not take place each term or semester, but rather near the end of the three years. Unlike the

United States, the sleepless nights and semester ritual of cramming during final examination week occur not eight times in four years but only once in three. Students who stay on for the B.Ed. degree are examined again at the end of the fourth year.

One is impressed with the many talents that find outlets in college-sponsored activities. There are a great many options available, and students participate in musical activities, dramatic productions, informal sports, clubs, societies, and a variety of special events. Participation tends to be more casual than in the United States, particularly in athletics, where the coaches often turn out to be other students.

The student culture is not too different from student cultures around the world. There is a growing degree of alienation from middle-class, materialistic values, some retreat into peer-group identification with the accompanying rejection of the over-thirties, and considerable social distance between staff and students; but there is surprising deference to the authority of tutors. More than politeness is involved when students knock at a tutor's door before intruding or wait until acknowledged before speaking. Tutors begin and end most conversations. Staff and students talk more frequently about more matters in England, but they communicate with less equality than in America.

Still, students cannot complain that nobody cares, for in English Colleges of Education there is a remarkable concern shown for the welfare and potential of each student. Marginal students are salvaged. Where American students would be failed or suspended, English students are given second and third chances. Many are casual about completing assignments on time; they often arrive at tutorials five or ten minutes late, for which they invariably provide polite apologies.

Compared with students in America, France, Japan, or Mexico, English students seem to be a calm, nonviolent, almost casual lot. They have taken part in some political demonstrations, and, like students throughout the world, they suffer from an unfavorable public image. But power confrontations between students and either college or civil authorities have been surprisingly peaceful, limited to matters like protests over South African rugby and cricket tours, a few sit-ins, and periodic strike threats by the National Union of Students. Violence by or against students is almost nonexistent. The common American newspaper and television shots of clubbings, rock-throwing, tear gas attacks and mutual vilification and hatred between police and students are not yet a part of the English scene. Matters may get worse as alienation increases, but relationships between college administrators and students are never so distant that a complete rupture in communication takes place. Even revolutionary students need not resort to violent protest to deliver their message.

STUDENT CRITICISM

The National Union of Students represents 95 percent of the British students in universities, Colleges of Education, polytechnics, art schools, and other branches of higher education. It employs a professional staff of 140 engaged in research, publicity, student services, and advice to member unions. The N.U.S. has established itself as an important channel of communication with government authorities at national and local levels (Binyon, 1970; Straw, 1970). It campaigns for increased student grants, greater student protection in disciplinary procedures, student representation on governing bodies, and the protection of civil rights, while it provides student services such as insurance, employment advice, and travel reductions (N.U.S., 1970).

It is no easy task to be Student Union officer at a College of Education. While a few local unions have won a "sabbatical" leave for the student president so that he may function as a full-time executive, most student presidents have to fit demanding organizational responsibilities into a heavy class schedule. When practice teaching begins, most of the members of the executive council become immobilized.

Executive council members usually take a militant, anti-administration stand before the student body, while they present an image of responsibility before the tutors. Moderates are subject to attacks by revolutionary students on one side and indifference on the other. If they are outmanipulated by the college administration, they quickly lose support; unless they achieve clear-cut concessions their leadership image becomes tarnished. Unless student leaders are viewed by the rest of the student body as catalysts for change, their bargaining power among the college staff is decreased. While faced with these conflicting expectations, student leaders accuse the colleges of many shortcomings.

Student Objections

1. Students are manipulated. Students have recently won representation in many colleges on academic councils, boards, and committees. Not being as experienced as the college staff in working within the complex decision-making process, they are often outmaneuvered. They lack access to the seats of power where many decisions originate. The interlocking committees are designed in part to slow down decision-making as well as to delegate responsibility. Parliamentary tacticians frequently put off decisions to future meetings. The students find that their voices go unheeded or that they have to sit through another round of formal motions.

2. Apathy is a result, not a cause. College students are constantly accusing themselves of apathy. They describe themselves as apathetic about their union, about the college political machinery, about student causes and campaigns. Perspicacious students describe this apathy as the natural responses to the runaround they receive. No wonder that student participation in college communities is halfhearted, when token representation is seldom matched by even token power.

3. Colleges provide an inferior education. The magazine *Black Bored* presented an astute historical overview of the initial purpose of training colleges in an article entitled "Colleges of Education, 2nd Class?" Training colleges were formed to offer a cheap, academically diluted, conservatively oriented training for the future teachers of the poor. The article claims that the colleges still provide a watered-down academic training, giving relatively shallow treatment to a wide range of subjects. And since College of Education students generally go out to teach in primary schools and in the lower streams of secondary schools, they still teach children who are primarily from working-class backgrounds (*Black Bored*, 1970).

4. The College of Education restricts vocational choice. Students are trapped within a single-purpose institution. They may have accepted a place in college after failing to gain a university place, or they may have changed their minds during the three years. They may not want to teach, but no other career is open to them. Men students, in particular, are among those attempting to push the colleges toward a broader intake of students and toward a wider definition of purpose.

5. *Rebellious students are threatened or victimized.* Colleges that have long been administered on authoritarian lines expect students, most of whom are women, to comply docilely with regulations. Tutors long accustomed to such traditions have considerable difficulty adjusting to a newer breed of students who threaten demonstrations and press demands. Because college authorities recommend students for future jobs through confidential reports to employing authorities, rebellious students can easily be singled out for indirect reprisals. Even in more liberal colleges, students can usually be controlled through ridicule—tutors are seldom gentle when putting students in their place. The fear of ridicule is often stronger than the fear of persecution.

Tactics of Students

To counter these limitations, students have developed a number of tactics. These tend to be employed more frequently at those colleges with a large proportion of male students. Predominantly female colleges still follow the genteel submissive relationships, although Women's Liberation may one day change this.

1. *The use of regular channels.* Representation within the internal political structure of some colleges was won rapidly in the late 1960's, often without a fight, sometimes by invitation of the principal. This in itself is enough to arouse student suspicion. Furthermore, students soon realize that committee deliberations result in very few decisions and that students as well as dissident faculty members are skillfully outmaneuvered by those who can master procedural machinery. Student representatives sit on college committees and boards to express student views on the issues under discussion. At times they raise extraneous issues, often simply to propagandize, but they know full well that they are out of order and will be effectively put down.

2. *Withdrawal of representation and noninvolvement.* When they do not suspect that the democratic process is going to be used merely to control them, students welcome the invitation to sit on committees. Arbitrary dismissal or suspension is not likely when universities and colleges establish disciplinary committees with student representatives. However, if the students are allotted only a minority of the votes, they may refrain from selecting representatives. In this way no student can be caught in the bind of being

asked to sit in judgment of another student when his influence can be negated by a majority of lecturers and governors.

3. *The threat of strike action.* The students' most effective weapon is the threat of a strike. They know that they must make this threat with care and only in connection with issues over which students have become thoroughly aroused. Only when the injustice is sufficiently blatant can leaders count on widespread student support and at least a moderate amount of backing from tutors. Students know that solidarity is the only protection against being singled out for reprisals. Very few college unions have learned to use the strike or the threat of a strike to develop this solidarity. On the few occasions that they have attempted to close the college temporarily, they have succeeded in bringing more favorable counterproposals from the authorities.

4. *Cooperation with other groups and the N.U.S.* Student unions at several colleges supported local strikes of the National Union of Teachers in 1970. Unlike the teachers, who are split among many unions, the students belong to only one. Because they can count on widespread student support across the country, they can more quickly develop unity of purpose in a national campaign dealing with a bread-and-butter issue, such as a proposed basic national scale for student grants (Venning, 1971).

5. *Appearance at inquiries.* The English are fond of holding inquiries by parliamentary committees, advisory councils, or special bodies set up for specific purposes (Robbins, 1963; Select Committee, 1969; Church, 1970b; Hewett, 1970). How students will testify is a cause of grave concern to college authorities. When not intimidated, college students speak out openly as individuals and as representatives of student organizations. The National Union of Students campaigned for two years to bring about a national inquiry into teacher training, which was ultimately announced by the Conservative Party after its election in 1970.

THE HARD WORK OF THE STAFF

Compared with American university professors, College of Education lecturers carry a very heavy load. Whereas American professors exploit graduate assistants, English lecturers exploit themselves. In English Colleges of Education lecturers teach fifteen hours a week or more. They supervise students on teaching practice three times a year. They are involved in various departmental and college committees. They meet students in individual tutorials. They serve as "general tutors" for groups whose members stay together over the three-year period. They do most of their own clerical work, write their own letters, and spend a great deal of time reading and commenting on innumerable essays. Many take part in college clubs, musical societies, and musical productions. At the same time they engage in their own professional study and writing.

While English tutors frequently grumble, they work under different pressures from those of their American counterparts. Perhaps the pressure is more constant in England; one has to plan ahead simply to find a free period. Coffee breaks and tea breaks provide a safety valve. The senior common room is the meeting place for morning coffee, again for coffee after the noon meal and, of course, between 3:30 and 4 o'clock for afternoon tea. It is difficult to envision American professors stopping work three times a day to gather together.

An American professor has little contact with students outside of his teaching commitments; he is supposed to have his time free to engage in research, scholarship, and professional leadership. The English College of Education tutor has virtually no free time to devote to research during the academic term. He is overcommitted, with multiple demands on his energies, yet his career opportunities are based on some of the same criteria that govern advancement in American and British universities.

There is very little freedom in England for each instructor to plan his own course. If a course has multiple sections, then all of the sections work toward the same objectives according to a commonly agreed-on syllabus. Examinations are not based on individual classes but on the three-year course considered as a whole. In this more centralized curriculum the multiple sections of each specific course must be closely coordinated.

In England, the higher the rank, the less time available for working on one's own private, professional interests. In the United States conditions are reversed. The higher the rank, the greater the amount of personal freedom, the fewer the students, the greater the privileges, the higher the status, and, of course, the larger the salary. If an American professor is clever enough, he can help himself to a teaching assignment in which he scarcely teaches and in

Learning How to Learn

which he is responsible only for special studies related to his own particular interests. He can become an educational entrepreneur, acquiring independence through government grants, influential positions in professional bodies, and by building a coterie of admiring graduate students to collaborate with him on his research interests. English university lecturers are not as effective in the entrepreneurial role, but they are no strangers to the good life or the prerogatives of high status.

There is a curious, somewhat ecclesiastical term used to explain why some college tutors put up with the heavy demands. Tutors describe it as a "sense of vocation," that is, a sense of calling, the satisfaction that one is giving of oneself. A number of tutors, particularly women staff members, accept this calling, but it can lead to overwork. Including attendance at jointly staffed classes and tutorials, some tutors spend twenty-five contact hours a week with students during heavily scheduled terms. Many of the men rebel against overloads but are trapped by college traditions and the commitment to meet tutorials according to a low staff-student ratio.

Granting that overloads are inadmissible, which ideal is *least* appropriate, the university ideal of research or the English college ideal of service? The question is deliberately stated in the negative, since neither model is particularly consistent with reality. Many American professors neglect students in the cause of scholarship, yet only a small fraction have the skills or the resources to conduct meaningful research. Many English college tutors are denied time to engage in reflective scholarship and feel harried in carrying out the service function. But the sense of service at least offers students guidance, opportunities to communicate, and the feeling that tutors are concerned about their welfare. Too often such assurance is absent in the American setting.

10

High Standards

Englishmen commonly insist that they uphold standards in education while Americans do not. The English talk so much about "high standards" and their concerns seem so foreign to Americans that at first this apparent ethnocentric prejudice blocks communication. Many Englishmen genuinely feel, for instance, that they have little to learn from American higher education practices because American universities are unconcerned about standards. After a period of mutual vilification, often in the form of good-natured bantering, the American begins to receive the message.

SIX MEANINGS OF THE TERM

Though the English place a great deal of weight on educational achievement, the term "standards" is used in so many different senses that these first have to be disentangled. Six different meanings will be developed, although these by no means exhaust the senses in which the term is used.

First there are minimum standards, which may appear as minimum entry levels for advanced educational or occupational opportunities. Five O-level passes are required for entry into a number of clerical and professional training programs, including teacher training. This minimum standard for admission to a College of Education has been severely criticized (A.T.C.D.E., 1970). A second usage refers to elite standards. High-prestige institutions such as Oxford colleges will accept only the most highly qualified applicants. A third usage concerns the teacher as standard-bearer—he is expected to act as a model for the children by demonstrating high standards in his professional life. The fourth meaning deals with encouraging high standards in the efforts of the pupils themselves, as when the teacher expects the children to submit their best products for classroom display. A fifth use of the word has to do with the quality of craftsmanship of a particular piece of work. Finally, there is the use of the term in reference to behavioral norms, or ideals that tend to influence actual behavior.

Minimum Standards

Minimum educational standards in England are often enforced by external bodies. English teachers do not trust themselves to establish their own minimum standards; they submit pupils to outside evaluators who supposedly have wider contacts and more objective criteria. Secondary school examinations are good examples of externally controlled standards. The examinations are set and marked by regional boards according to nationally established norms with a fixed distribution among the various categories of passing grades (Pedley, 1969). The lowest passing grades become the minimum standards; the highest passing grades help to identify the potential elite.

The contrast between the United States and England with regard to minimum standards is exemplified in attitudes toward driver education. American expectations differ from state to state and often depend partially on written responses. In England, Ministry of Transport examiners serve as the external authority. The test is common throughout the country; learners must prove to examiners that they meet a minimum standard of driving proficiency through rigid adherence to the Driving Code in twenty-one different situations. Thousands of private driving schools coach the learners, charging heavy fees for extensive lessons. A number of applicants repeatedly fail the examination. Upon failure the examiner invariably remarks, "I am sorry; you have not reached the appropriate standard."

Some minimum standards are well within reach, so that most people eventually achieve a passing mark. If one keeps going back month after month, for example, he will eventually pass the driving test (although one lady had to take it thirty-eight times!). A common expectation is that children should read independently by the time they leave the junior school. Obviously, some children are unable to meet this standard, and this has become cause for grave professional concern (Tansey and Unwin, 1969). Other minimum standards are achieved by only a minority of applicants. Most students "fail" the eleven-plus. Most students fail to remain in school long enough to enroll in the sixth form. In some respects the English have become a nation of failures, at least in the light of their self-concepts, because crucial minimum educational standards condemn the majority to be rejected.

American education in this sense obviously has no minimum standards, which greatly disturbs English defenders of the principle of selectivity. These are some quotations from interviews with English teachers:

> "Any American student can receive a senior high school diploma if he remains in school."
> "With no national examinations, no ready way exists to compare attainments at one secondary school with another."
> "Anyone with enough money or sufficient perseverance can be accepted at some kind of university."
> "Anyone can graduate from an American university if he piles up sufficient credits."
> "Without an externally evaluated final examination, what does an American degree mean?"

Elite Standards

The English boast that their leading institutions maintain very high standards, properly setting an example of excellence for the rest. The elitist tradition has been justified by the belief that the allocation of scarce intellectual resources should be concentrated on the very few who are born or bred to lead. The public schools defend their right to exist on their tradition of character-building for leadership (Snow, 1959; Wilkinson, 1964; Kalton, 1966; Weinberg, 1967).

Standards for admission to the schools with the highest prestige are very high indeed. There is such a pool of talent waiting to enter certain university departments that the faculties accept only those students with the very highest grades on three A-level examinations. In addition, students must prove to be "the right sort" of people through personal admission interviews. To earn a first-class honours degree is a mark of distinction that retains its value throughout the recipient's career.

In each field there are a few colleges that have achieved a commonly recognized leading position. A member of an American university drama department interviewed the principal of a famous English drama college which had one thousand candidates competing for twenty admission places.

Q. Did you have trouble selecting from so much eager talent?

A. Yes, it was difficult. Eight candidates were clearly superior, but there was difficulty in choosing the other twelve.

Q. Was that because there were so many other good ones?

A. No, it was because we could not select twelve others who obviously were good enough.

Many sixth-form teachers determine their success by the number of university scholarships their students win. The prestige of the independent public schools and the semi-independent direct-grant grammar schools is based on their reputation in gaining university places, particularly to Oxford and Cambridge (Robbins, 1963).

The tradition of elitism is dying slowly, if it is dying at all (Bottomore, 1964). At the apex of the secondary education pyramid are the ancient and respected public schools, followed by the minor public schools, the direct-grant grammar schools, the well-established state-maintained grammar schools, those comprehensive schools that have good A-level results, and so forth. Unfortunately, the schools at the bottom of the secondary school prestige pyramid, the secondary modern schools, often pattern school organization (including the customs of interhouse competition and pupil prefects) on the heavily endowed public boarding schools. Where secondary modern schools might have succeeded in advancing educational innovations, they increasingly turned to streaming and a selective examination system of their own. This reinforces the low self-images of many pupils.

Recently I discussed the concept of intelligence with a class of school leavers, the bottom stream of a secondary modern school in Nottingham. "We're not intelligent," I was told, "the intelligent ones go to grammar school, the next go to the bilaterals— and then there's us, we're the dustbin, sir!" And then the question: "If we're the dustbin, why do they stream us here?"

[Williams, 1970, p. 161]

The Teacher as Standard-Bearer

Because the teacher provides an example of desirable patterns, his personal standards help to raise aspirations among the pupils. His aesthetic appreciations and sensitivities influence them. His lettering on the board, his arrangement of displays, his pottery and woodblocks, all serve as models for imitation. If he reads widely, he communicates this value to the children. They naturally acquire some of his attitudes toward problem-solving, withholding judgment, and scientific skepticism.

Children learn to take pride in what they do from a teacher who takes pride in his own work. When he makes demands on himself, the children appreciate this extra effort and are inclined to strive harder themselves. The greatest source of pride for a conscientious teacher is the growing independence he sees in the children he teaches.

Encouraging Children to Do Their Best

Another sense in which teachers speak about standards is in relation to the children's work habits. They hope that the children will continually aim for a high standard, that their intellectual potential will be "stretched" in the same way that muscles are stretched. Children who work diligently and take pride in their accomplishments are not likely to fall into a rut. When the teacher has high expectations and is not satisfied with second-rate work, the child, in his desire to please the teacher, attempts to live up to increasing expectations.

The trick for the adult is to encourage children to do their best without exerting undue pressure. With the decline of competition as a motivating force in the primary school, it becomes increasingly evident that different standards must be set for different children. Children aim to achieve better work not through comparisons with one another but by seeking improvement in relation to their own previous efforts.

The Element of Craftsmanship

To emphasize the craft element of a product is to raise standards of workmanship. As a child takes pride in mastering detail or painstakingly adhering to authentic forms, he assumes the attitudes of the medieval craftsman (Marsh, 1970a).

Craftsmanship is appropriate not only within the crafts as such. It implies deeper, more intimate exploration of materials and the appreciation of artistic values in everyday activities. A child strives to improve the craft of writing. He exercises the craft of the scientist when, during an experiment, he records detailed observations according to commonly accepted classification systems.

A tradition of careful craftsmanship has developed in the Oxfordshire schools, thanks to the influence of Robin Tanner, who built on the ideals of William Morris (Van der Eyken and Turner, 1969). There has been an attempt to re-create the authentic patterns of early English artisans, who, though they worked more slowly than modern factory employees, worked with loving care.

Largely replaced by mass production, craftsmanship struggles to survive as modern artists return to historical sources, seeking out village thatchers, hedgers, weavers, potters, masons, woodworkers, and printmakers. At the end of his long career Robin Tanner served as H.M.I. for arts, crafts, and handwriting in Oxfordshire, where he inspired teachers through visits, courses, conferences, correspondence, and meetings with practicing artists (Van der Eyken and Turner, 1969). The work of children in Oxford village schools continues to reflect Tanner's influence even after his retirement.

Since earlier craftsmen drew inspiration from natural materials and motifs, Tanner urged teachers to help children to observe nature carefully, pay close attention to detail, and approach their work with the pride of true artisans. Block prints are constructed according to authentic processes. Textiles are printed with natural dyes. Wool is carded, spun, and then woven on handmade looms. Displays are described in fine italic script, drawing on the medieval art of calligraphy. By taking pride in workmanship and maintaining fidelity to traditional forms, children continue within an unbroken national heritage while infusing their products with the freshness of youthful creativity.

Standards of Behavior

Standards of behavior extend beyond matters of classroom management, even though expectations about attitudes and values are seldom made explicit in English primary schools. Many of the norms are idealized and are seldom fully attained in practice, but they serve as expectations nonetheless. Although many of the values are middle-class, most children are able to conform to them, at least within the confines of the school. For instance, there is a courtesy present in many English classrooms that is seldom found in the more brash American culture. Children are courteous not only to visitors, to the class teacher, and to the head (toward whom many are markedly deferential), they are even polite to one another. Another common expectation is that children will grow in the ability to be self-directive. As they learn to assume more and more responsibility for themselves, they develop greater respect for the rights of other class members. Self-direction enhances mutual respect, which in turn improves classroom discipline. Perhaps such standards of behavior grow out of the total culture, but they certainly make teaching in England a less harrowing experience than it might otherwise be.

ARE STANDARDS DECLINING?

English college lecturers can talk for hours about the threat to standards. Are they deteriorating or will they remain high? "Will more mean worse?" is a controversial topic related to the increasing enrollment in institutions of higher education (Cox and Dyson, 1969a, 1969b). Will the decrease of streaming and competition, increased use of modern teaching methods, and disappearance of the eleven-plus make primary schools less invigorating intellectually? Can comprehensive schools ever reach the level of the good grammar schools? If more secondary pupils are achieving passing grades on O-levels and A-levels, have the marking criteria become less rigorous?

To an American these arguments may seem relatively pointless. They serve as convenient charges for traditionalists and anti-traditionalists to hurl at one another. Since more and more pupils are staying on in the secondary schools, more and more are earning qualifications for entry into higher education, and greater pressures are being exerted to transform an elitist system into a more open, equalitarian one. What is going to happen to English standards? About all that is certain is that the English will continue to talk about them!

In some senses standards will decline, for the same kind of higher education is not possible with masses of students as was once possible for an intellectual and social elite. In some respects standards will rise, since a greater number of qualified students now have opportunities open to them that were formerly reserved for the very few.

STANDARDS IN THE UNITED STATES

Of the six interpretations of standards, the first two make very little sense in the United States. There is little sympathy for examinations to determine minimum qualifications, especially those which serve to reinforce self-concepts of failure or inadequacy. In the United States it is felt that schools, not learners, should meet minimum standards. The current trend to hold school systems accountable for progress in learning for all pupils has forced the schools to become more concerned with raising the literacy levels of poor children (Beavan, 1970).

Likewise, elitist standards arouse very little sympathy. There are elitist universities in the United States with relatively high standards of admission, both in terms of ability to pay the very high fees and ability to score well on the S.A.T. or the College Board admission tests. In contrast to England, the open-door enrollment policies of hundreds of degree-granting institutions in the United States dilutes widespread public acknowledgment of the prestige of elitist universities, at least at the undergraduate level. Furthermore, Americans do not really believe in the necessity for elitist standards in the same way that the English do. There is almost an antipathy to the notion that a social or intellectual elite is inherently more qualified to govern or sit in the seats of institutional power.

It is in the third, fourth, and fifth senses in which American schools might pay attention to England's preoccupation with standards. The idea of the teacher as a model, exemplifying high personal standards in his work and relationships, might be more widely acknowledged in the United States. The American teacher works under much more favorable conditions than the English teacher does, yet he does not seem to take nearly as much pride in his work. If Americans were attaining greater personal satisfactions along with a sense of pride in the achievements of children, they

Learning How to Learn

would demonstrate greater professional maturity. Instead of feeling that his job is to impart knowledge and skills to the immature, the English teacher often feels that he sets an example by studying with them. Not only does he try to extend the children; the conscientious English teacher extends himself.

American teachers might well show more concern about helping children to submit their best work. This does not mean constantly correcting the papers of children with a heavy red pencil. In fact, English infant teachers tend to do less correcting than Americans. It does mean expecting the children not to be satisfied with their first attempts. It means having confidence in children's potential to demonstrate improvement. It is gratifying to talk with English teachers who have formerly taught streamed classes and to hear them express pleasure in achieving high standards of work in classes of mixed ability. Many children who formerly would have been placed in lower streams have raised their levels of aspiration to conform with raised expectations.

More American concern for qualitative standards of craftsmanship would encourage children to slow down long enough to learn to imitate the craftsman. Attention to quality might serve as one antidote to twentieth-century surroundings, which exemplify shoddy, aesthetically sterile products and planned obsolescence.

THE HIGH EXPECTATIONS THAT
ACCOMPANY INFORMAL METHODS

Concern for standards might be regarded merely as an educational curiosity, except that it represents something basic, without which English informal methods might well be less successful. The combination of high expectations with informal controls represents the English genius for retaining many old values when introducing new ideas. High expectations go back a long way in English tradition. H.M.I.'s enforced standards nationally through annual inspections in the early days of state education. The closest approximations to American grade-level expectations were the old English examination standards that were spelled out at progressively higher levels for reading, writing, and arithmetic (Razzell, 1968). National standards were withdrawn by 1926, but the concern for reaching higher levels of achievement has never disappeared.

Much that is considered new in English education is not new

at all. Individualization, concern for children's interests, topic teaching, and the activity curriculum have gone through long gestation periods. English primary schools have progressively encouraged more informality, more openness, and greater freedom of choice, but rejection of the past has not accompanied the introduction of newer goals and methods. There is little sympathy for utopian prescriptions—suspicion of educational panaceas is deeply ingrained.

When Americans talk about transplanting England's open schools, they need to appreciate in how many ways high expectations accompany English informality. There is something so old-fashioned about the concept of standards that it does not sit well with educational radicals. It involves expectations by the teacher and, in essence, depends on the extrinsic reward of teacher approval and the implied punishment of approval withheld. At the same time, English children must contend with approval or disdain for their efforts by peers. They learn either to work with sufficient care the first time around or to do it over again until they feel they have reached an acceptable standard. In a very real sense, then, the concern for raising standards is antithetical to a thoroughly permissive atmosphere. Even A. S. Neill, who is no defender of extrinsic rewards, has warned against license for children to do as they please (Neill, 1966).

In another sense concern for standards denies one implication of child-centered theory—that the child, rather than the teacher, should set the learning goals. Through the intervention of the teacher, children are taught to avoid playing about, disturbing others, performing poorly, working in a slipshod manner, restricting themselves to peripheral interests, or flitting from activity to activity. Sanctions, though often unspoken, are present nonetheless and gently and informally enforced. Disruption by newcomers may be temporarily allowed, and exuberance by high-strung children is occasionally accommodated, but unacceptable behavior is consistently discouraged. The teacher makes his presence felt. Messages of approval and disapproval are transmitted, even though these messages may not often be verbalized. Self-discipline consists of behavior that is learned slowly over a period of years through numerous opportunities to practice it and through the examples set for children by others.

CAN AMERICAN SCHOOLS BECOME FREE?

American admiration for English openness is expressed within two educational sectors which tend to be panacea-prone and where many children may be ill prepared for the English form of slowly developing self-discipline.

English openness is attractive to American parents and teachers who are either educational revolutionaries or idealistic reformers and are thoroughly disenchanted with American school bureaucracy. A growing number of free schools cater to liberal or radical upper-middle-class whites who look to Summerhill as a model. A. S. Neill has no truck with standards or teacher expectations or extrinsic motivation of any kind. His primary concern is children's happiness (Neill, 1960, 1967). To him, education is a form of therapy; over the years he has worked with many disturbed children who have been placed in his school because they have not been able to cope with rigidity (Neill, 1960). In hopes of creating a radically different form of education, some affluent American parents are willing to pay their way out of state-supported schools, even willing to put up with temporary, makeshift facilities. The second dissatisfied sector is found within experimental schools for the urban poor, where the failure of restrictive education and debilitating environmental influences are all too obvious and where anything might be better than repression and neglect. The question is, will schools based on freedom, openness, and loving pupil-teacher relationships work in the United States?

It is doubtful that some of the interpretations by Americans of English openness would function effectively even in England. What does work in England is a combination of the open and the closed, the free and the restricted. There is a great deal of freedom, but it is exercised within the limits and constraints of traditional attitudes toward the processes and the products of education. English primary teachers tend to be highly pragmatic and essentially conservative. English children are not angels. Even under an environment reflecting calm cultural conditioning, without controls they become noisy, careless, and slipshod, and they can easily flit about. But they are not left to do so; after a few weeks or, at the most, within a term or two, children are expected to settle in.

The settling-in process involves all sorts of constraints. At work are two apparently conflicting emphases, which often exist side by side. Controls are relatively relaxed, but expectations are relatively structured. Those American teachers who are emotionally disposed toward freedom and relaxation often miss this duality. Because effective English teachers are very relaxed about allowing children to work out their own learning patterns, it does not mean they hold laissez-faire attitudes toward work or behavior.

Would American children in either experimental working-class public schools or experimental upper-middle-class private schools settle in as quickly? American working-class children have much to rebel against. They are caught in a cycle of poverty, often combined with racism, where the restrictions of crowded, substandard housing are compounded by discrimination and the threat of violence. Well-to-do children of liberal parents often appear more hyperactive than the English. Nondirective child-rearing practices in America hardly reinforce habits of self-control. American teachers who are emotionally drawn to English concepts of freedom are seldom equally concerned about standards of work or behavior. Freedom in American schools without a concern for high standards might develop self-discipline and high achievement for some children, but it might just as easily compound the tension and result in slipshod, low-level work for others. Even if English openness might work in America with many, there would always be a minority of disturbed children in the slum schools or the private, affluent schools to create considerable havoc. Neglect, hostility toward authority, and the inappropriateness of deferred gratification as a motivating force block many working-class children from acquiring that degree of self-control which is appropriate for free methods.

If teachers do not care about achievement, middle-class parents, even highly liberal ones, by the ethos of their culture cannot help but care, and black parents with aspirations for their children care as strongly. Blacks want to equip the next generation to fight racism more effectively. Parents are highly critical of the inferior education of the slum school. They are tired of the runaround they and their children receive when lowered expectations result in substandard performance. Black teachers are not the ones talking about greater freedom and relaxation for black children. They tend to talk about a tougher education, one that is more academically successful.

Here is where one needs to be cautious about literally transplanting English primary education to the United States, even when it is well understood, which it frequently is not. English education appeals to many radical reformers who mistakenly see Summerhill as its embodiment. Neill's success is based on putting happiness and therapy first; he cares very little about high standards, effective work habits or achievement goals. His greatest contribution to English state education has been to remain outside and attack its basic premises (Neill, 1936, 1953).

Openness without an accompanying concern for standards would produce conditions quite different from those that exist in the majority of English primary schools so greatly admired. Without a long tradition of expecting children and teachers to put forth their best efforts, it is doubtful that English schools would be as successful as they are. Standards without openness can degenerate into teacher domination and competitiveness. Openness without standards can degenerate into teacher withdrawal and an excess of confusion. The English live comfortably with both high standards and freedom, with two values which seem to have divergent emotional appeals.

11

Class Bias: England's Number One Educational Problem

EDUCATION ON THE CHEAP

Many developments in English primary schools can best be interpreted in terms of economics. The suggestions that have the best chance of getting off the ground are those which can be implemented most cheaply. English primary education for the masses has been, is now, and will continue to be education on the cheap.

Expressing this judgment brings immediate agreement from English class teachers, head teachers, and College of Education lecturers. It angers, however, those responsible for making financial recommendations. It is a damning conclusion and probably ought not to be openly asserted by a visiting American who has enjoyed English hospitality. The blow can only be softened by acknowledging that funds are severely limited.

England cannot escape from the heritage of the past. Processes long ago set in motion can hardly be halted, for it is most difficult to counter priority decisions made by previous generations. Present state-maintained educational institutions developed from terminal elementary education for the children of the poor

(Blackie, 1971). The children are still packed into overcrowded, underfinanced educational facilities.

A number of college students preparing to become primary teachers become cynical when they grasp the full implications of their educational history. The discussion below reflects some of this cynicism, but there is no desire to underestimate the contributions of educational reformers of the past or of current leaders struggling to improve conditions.

What were some of the priority decisions of previous generations? First, that independent private schools would enjoy greater esteem and more upper-middle-class loyalty than state schools. Second, that secondary schools, which until recently were organized on the basis of selectivity, would be more generously financed than primary schools. Third, that benefits would be more accessible to the middle-class minority than to the working-class majority. Too many English state primary schools, the *only* sector completely open to all children, are overcrowded and understaffed. They originated in poverty, were impelled by sentiments of charity, and have never been adequately financed. The following six basic cost factors all penalize the primary sector to the advantage of the other sectors. In each case continuing decisions keep primary education in a deprived state.

1. Salaries of teachers (Blyth, 1965).
2. Construction of school buildings (Plowden, 1967).
3. Amount of floor space allocated for each pupil (Razzell, 1968).
4. Pupil-teacher ratio (D.E.S., 1970).
5. Capitation allowances for supplies, equipment, and books (Plowden, 1967).
6. Education of teachers (A.T.C.D.E., 1970).

The gap between primary and secondary education cannot be closed completely. To rectify all inequalities would involve prohibitive costs. Many of the inequities could be at least partially corrected if heavy expenditures were allocated, but it is extremely doubtful that this will be done. Many of these issues are debated at the local authority level. Attending a meeting of the Education Committee of a county governing authority can be a sobering experience. Committees may have as many as forty members and meetings are well attended, but the handful of people pleading for more equitable allowances for primary schools are outnumbered by "realists," apologists, or cost-conscious guardians of the rates (local taxes). The sentiments of most Education Committee members traditionally place secondary and tertiary education first, instead of the other way around, and improving disbursements for primary schools at the county level would necessitate increasing or radically shifting the educational budget. Since most members are older, prominent citizens, it is very unlikely that many attended state-maintained primary schools themselves. If sentiments cannot be shifted on an Education Committee, it is extremely doubtful that arguments in favor of more money for primary schools can budge members of the county Finance Committee, which is the more powerful arbiter of how local authority funds will be allocated.

Matters are hardly better at the national level. At a conference one speaker facetiously quipped that D.E.S. statisticians understand only two mathematical processes, how to divide projections by forty and by thirty. The two figures are the maximum, and in urban areas apparently the expected, recommended sizes for primary and secondary classes.

In many cases teachers have adopted highly admired practices to save money or to cope with large classes. The positive aspects of these practices have been presented in other chapters; the following listing, however, offers a somewhat more cynical interpretation of some educational innovations.

1. English teachers show great ingenuity in developing their own teaching materials and learning aids, but how else would they have acquired them?

2. Individualized teaching has gained momentum, but how can mass teaching be effectively organized with forty or more children and inadequate textbooks?

3. Small-group work is spreading, but with so many children and so little space, how else are currently endorsed practices of grouping for instruction to be organized?

4. Open-planned buildings for team teaching are being constructed, but a major justification may be that savings in building costs occur when more of the covered area is designated as teaching space.

5. Adventure playgrounds make creative use of natural surroundings, but they depend largely on voluntary labor and the collection of scrap wood and discarded products.

6. The autonomy of the head in the individual school is most commendable, but it certainly saves central authorities money by allowing them to provide less in the way of supervision, coordination, and advisory services.

7. The Schools Council is an admirable example of an educational partnership between Local Education Authorities and the national government. However, L.E.A.'s find it far cheaper to rely on central development teams, teacher leaders and teacher centers (which are usually refurnished obsolete classrooms in old buildings) than to organize curriculum development programs on their own.

8. Colleges of Education prepare primary teachers with practical, vocational training, but the less rigorous standards of admission, lower academic reputations, and lower level of financial support when compared with universities remind students of the origins of the colleges—the poorly endowed teacher training schools for the children of the poor.

9. Englishmen are suspicious of educational hardware, which they claim will never replace the personal response of living teachers, but since modern educational technology has become increasingly expensive, it is cheaper to rationalize and do without.

10. The Open University promises a second chance to those who have never had an opportunity to earn a degree, but cost-conscious governments are well aware that it is far cheaper to instruct by radio and television, correspondence, modest provisions for tutorials, and a negligible capital outlay for university buildings, than it is to expand full-time higher education.

The point hardly needs further reiteration: many current reforms, admirable as they are, result from economic necessities or decisions which become convincing only on the basis of cost.

There are four major reforms urgently needed which would be very expensive. Despite modest starts on a limited basis, there is little hope that they will be extended widely enough to relieve current problems. These four needs are:

1. Expansion of nursery school education (Van der Eyken, 1969).
2. Improvement of school and community services in Educational Priority Areas (Plowden, 1967).
3. Equalization of educational opportunities in secondary and higher education (Mauger, 1970).

4. Increase in professional competence of teachers through:
   a. higher initial salaries which can competitively attract better qualified entrants (Sproule, 1970c);
   b. higher salary increments to make teaching more attractive as a long-term career (N.A.S., 1970);
   c. the establishment of a profession staffed by graduates through preservice requirements and, equally important, through wider opportunities for career teachers to earn in-service degrees (A.T.C.D.E., 1970).

The United States shares some of these problems, but there is less fatalism about dealing with them, despite the financial burden. The four major reforms listed above have fared better in the United States. (1) Publicly supported preschool education in America may become common within a decade. (2) Had not funds been diverted to the Vietnam war and had not the War on Poverty encountered a more stubborn enemy than originally anticipated, the national commitment to alleviate conditions in disadvantaged neighborhoods might have produced more favorable results. At least the United States is beginning to recognize the full dimensions of the problems. (3) Greater equality of educational opportunity is available in secondary and higher education, although success within the educational system is still related to social class. A much higher proportion of working-class youth are now completing secondary school and going on to college. (4) The professional status of American teachers has been enhanced through rising salary scales and opportunities for advanced study. Finally, there is not the same disregard for primary education. When money is allocated, it is not taken from one age group in order to provide for another.

Why is so little money spent on primary schools in England? The most frequent answer is that the money is not available. The country has made a valiant effort since the end of the Second World War to increase the percentage of the national budget devoted to education; England is now spending more of its gross national product on education than on defense. The rate of growth of expenditures exceeded 10 percent for a period of close to twenty-five years after the war, and during this time England had to cope with war damage, fluctuations in the birth rate, an increase in the school-leaving age, rising aspirations of youth to stay on in school, currency devaluation, and inflation. The main beneficiaries

Learning How to Learn

of national efforts have been secondary and tertiary education, largely in response to the need to provide facilities for the increasing numbers of pupils staying on in secondary schools and those entering higher education.

With England having one of the slowest overall economic growth rates of any advanced industrial country, this kind of educational expansion could not proceed indefinitely. The crunch came about 1968; only by taking money away from defense appropriations and subsidies to industry was a drastic reduction of educational expenditures avoided. Primary school construction was not given a higher priority until the rate of expansion had to be cut. One goal for the 1970's is to replace all primary schools built prior to 1903, but even this may prove to be inadequate—some of the schools built since 1903 are not exactly modern learning laboratories! A great many of the outdated schools cater to poor children in rural areas and the older sections of the cities. An inescapable conclusion points to class-based discrimination against primary schools, punishing most heavily the children of the working class.

DISCRIMINATION AGAINST THE MAJORITY

America's major problem is not class discrimination but racism in the form of race prejudice against all blacks, whatever their social class. When racial discrimination is added to social class discrimination—that is, where a large number of blacks are counted within the lowest income levels in the rural South and in the segregated ghettos of large cities—the failure of American education is compounded. Segregated schools in both the North and South become even more debilitating where many of the people affected are also suffering the hardships of poverty.

But it is still a minority of the population who become the victims of poor schools. American education utterly fails only with the economically depressed. Educational opportunities remain relatively open to the majority. Black students of middle-class backgrounds, for instance, are well represented in higher education, and a growing number of working-class blacks have taken advantage of scholarships, loans, and federally subsidized work-study programs. Middle-class families may be better equipped than working-class families to take advantage of educational opportunities, but first-generation college students who come from working-class backgrounds are well represented at many state-supported universities.

While in America it is the minority, in England it is the *majority* of children who are deprived of equal educational opportunity. In England a somewhat smaller middle class (Raynor, 1970) has far greater relative advantage, while a less affluent working class (Rose, 1970), despite recent advances among skilled craftsmen and members of the automotive industry, suffers far greater disadvantage. The scarcity of selective educational opportunities means that middle-class parents strive much more vigorously to prepare their children to use education for social mobility. For working-class families in England, social mobility is less a by-product of increased education than the result of occupational advancement and the economic power of the labor movement.

SECONDARY SCHOOL DIVISIONS

Independent public schools have traditionally catered to the upper middle class, while grammar schools have been largely reserved for the lower middle class and some of the more successful members of the working class. Secondary modern schools (formerly senior elementary schools) have been allocated to the working class. Regional modifications and organizational offshoots complicate a strict classification according to class divisions, but the core of the clientele for the three largest categories of secondary schools has remained stable since the 1920's.

The independent schools are the schools of privilege (J. Wilson, 1961; Glennerster and Pryke, 1964; Dancy, 1966; Kalton, 1966; Wakeford, 1969; Glennerster and Wilson, 1970). The independent public schools acquired their name, which has caused much confusion for twentieth-century Americans, from their origin as charitable institutions for poor scholars, which served as a kind of public recruiting program for the clergy. They cater to the upper middle class, which has faith in their historically tested reputation for providing the right sort of education for the right sort of people in the right sort of atmosphere. Less highly placed middle-class parents are often willing to pay the high fees for the added chance of entry into higher education. Preparatory schools prepare for entry into public schools, which prepare for entry into universities, which prepare for entry into the more prestigious occupations.

Selective state schools are the province of the lower middle class. The grammar schools and the high streams of the comprehensive schools are heavily populated by middle-class pupils (Campbell, 1956; Floud, 1957; Stevens, 1960; Davis, 1967; Ford, 1968, 1970; Hewitson, 1970; Lacey, 1970). Streaming by ability, when it was practiced in the state junior schools, helped the middle class win a good share of places within the selective system.

The nonselective schools, which include the secondary modern schools and the lower streams of the comprehensive schools (Schools Council, 1970a), are left to the working class (W. Taylor, 1963; Partridge, 1968). These are the schools that cater to the majority of English youth. To judge by the recognized English criterion, examination results, the nonselective state schools have not had an impressive record.

There are exceptions. Ambitious or talented working-class youth can be sponsored for mobility through placement in selective streams. A few even win scholarships to the public schools. Working-class youth who do jump all the hurdles and finally make it to the university seem to do just as well as middle-class students. However, according to the Robbins Report, based on percentages of the national population, middle-class youth had twenty times the opportunity to attend university as working-class youth (Robbins, 1963). It is not that able working-class youth have not been fit for the universities; the university admission policies simply have not been receptive to them.

As presently constituted, the academic system that carries a student from a selective secondary school to a university or College of Education has little appeal to working-class youth. Colleges of Further Education and polytechnics offer a more vocationally oriented education, which can be taken on a part-time basis through apprenticeship training and industry-sponsored, government-supported, released-time arrangements. This alternative, while lower in prestige and too frequently ignored by educational research, has greater appeal to the young man from the working class. Academic education in England rejects the practically minded and is in turn rejected by them.

THE FAILURE OF THE 1944 EDUCATION ACT

When it was passed, the 1944 Education Act seemed like a genuine step toward the more efficient allocation of talent with a corresponding equalization of opportunity. No longer were fees to be charged at the grammar schools. The new technical and secondary modern schools were to carry parity of esteem. Now the able children of the poor could earn their way through merit. Assisted by a grant system to defray the costs of higher education, the talented sons of laborers could rise to educational heights, untroubled by fees and no longer penalized by lack of inherited privilege. The English took pride in the fact that higher education was free to anyone who could prove his ability to meet entrance requirements.

Few people still believe in the myth of equality based on merit. The system breaks down in two easily predictable ways. The class bias of the schools puts working-class children at a disadvantage, while middle-class parents select schools that serve their children's best interests. Unless one is convinced that all the potential merit resides within the middle class, this situation makes a farce of equality based on merit. Some apologists seem to subscribe to the belief that middle-class children do so well because they are more intelligent and more ambitious, and that these characteristics may be partly or even largely inherited.

No matter which party is in power, English governments largely reflect middle-class interests (Raynor, 1970). Middle-class representatives sit on the decision-making bodies affecting education at both national and local levels. In particular, they control the purse strings. The English teaching force is socioeconomically homogeneous to a surprising degree and overwhelmingly middle-class.

BLINDNESS TO THE MAGNITUDE OF THE PROBLEM

Until very recently the teaching profession has given little recognition to the magnitude of class differentials. Even though every major government educational report published in the last twenty years overwhelmingly demonstrated inequalities of opportunity (Central Advisory Council, 1954; Crowther, 1959; Robbins, 1963; Newsom, 1963), conclusions and implied recommendations never attacked the problems directly. Some examples of widely publicized findings illustrate this tendency toward understatement of the basic issue. A minority of children were shown to be wrongly placed in higher streams, and incorrect placements were largely influenced by social class membership (Barker Lunn, 1970). Intelligence test scores tended to favor middle-class children, but intelligent working-class children were not realizing their potential (Douglas, 1967). Early school-leavers from grammar school were more likely to be working-class (Central Advisory Council, 1954; Dale and Griffith, 1965). Working-class pupils in grammar schools were less likely to take advantage of higher education (Jackson and Marsden, 1962). By implication, if the selective system were functioning more efficiently, it might right itself in time. With minor modifications working-class youth would receive a fairer deal.

Sociological theory and research has scarcely influenced government recommendations. The work of Basil Bernstein on restricted and elaborated codes of language has been well disseminated (Bernstein, 1960, 1961a, 1961b, 1965), but there is seldom any attempt to radically recast educational methods or community approaches to counteract prevailing conditions.

Teachers hold stereotyped views of the working class, and the lower the working-class level, the more stereotyped the judgments become (Goodacre, 1968). These range from sympathetic, paternalistic concern for the detrimental effects of cultural deprivation (no books in the home, little play space, overharassed mothers, inadequate diet, too much unsupervised television-watching) to hostile accusations of immorality (sexual license, parental neglect, child-beating, willful ignorance, drunkenness). When the subject under discussion is West Indian colored immigrants, the remarks often border on the offensive.

With few exceptions English teachers are all white and all English. Though there has been some movement into the teaching profession by the children of manual workers (Glass, 1963), educational leaders as well as the vast majority of the teaching force are solidly middle-class, even in schools where the student body is predominantly working-class. Most teachers have little understanding of the subcultures with which they deal and very little access to the families of the children they teach, so there are few opportunities to rectify misconceptions. Generally speaking, primary teachers do accept the children, but because they lack identification with their culture they miss opportunities to utilize the experience, language, and values that the children bring from home. Instead, they try to change all these by attempting to instill middle-class behavior.

In the United States, on the other hand, large numbers of teachers come from working-class backgrounds. They are black and white, from many ethnic groups, and from a wide spectrum of social origins. Though many adopt middle-class values, they retain familiarity with the cultures in which they were raised. The American Federation of Teachers has derived part of its strength by drawing on union loyalties of teachers whose fathers were active in the labor movement. The growing heterogeneity of the profession is reflected in teachers' attitudes toward strike action, modes of dress, language patterns, and interpersonal communication.

CLASS SEGREGATION

The secondary modern school was doomed from the start. In the larger cities it became essentially a working-class school for working-class children, yet it was staffed by middle-class teachers trying to present a middle-class curriculum. Segregating the remainder of the working class within their schools, by creaming off the more academic middle-class and working-class youth to the grammar schools, left a student body without many candidates for the highest ability groups. Still, what was left could be more precisely streamed and the C.S.E. examination system was designed to reflect ability and motivational differences. Higher ability groups have over the years gradually been presented for the more generally recognized G.C.E. O-level examinations, and a few secondary modern schools have developed sixth forms. If the cream is removed, it is still possible to separate the best of what is left.

Many examples in the literature of educational sociology deal with conflicts between teachers and pupils arising from the unrealistic expectations of an inappropriate curriculum for the lower ability streams (Hargreaves, 1967; Rose, 1970). Secondary teachers often express open hostility or despair about lower-stream classes, which is in turn met by resentment from the pupils. Other teachers give up, content to keep expectations at a minimum in return for a semblance of order. A popular television comedy series, "Please Sir," deals with the trials of a young teacher facing the good-humored insolence of potential school-leavers in Form Five C. The teacher and the peer leaders avoid open confrontations because, naturally, they are all endowed with hearts of gold, but the humor is based upon clear recognition by the viewing audience that this

Learning How to Learn

lot will never amount to much because typical school expectations are completely alien to them.

THE ANXIETY OF MIDDLE–CLASS PARENTS

Advanced educational qualifications are becoming a prerequisite for an increasing number of middle-class occupations. Children who are expected to rise within the status hierarchy or merely to hold their own must enter the selective sectors of education.

Middle-class occupational positions are expanding at a slow rate (Raynor, 1970), but aspiring members of the working class are increasingly competing for them. At the same time the number of places in higher education is severely limited. To middle-class parents the odds appear less favorable than they actually are.

If the parents are sufficiently well-to-do, they do not take chances. The English upper middle class is somewhat smaller than it is in the United States (Raynor, 1970), and it is the major source of support for the independent schools. It is almost an essential prerequisite for boys to be sent away to boarding school, sometimes at an early age. Girls may spend some of the primary school years in a local county or church-aided school, if a good one is accessible. Parental choice for the upper middle class, then, is a matter of which independent school will be selected. Family traditions, institutional reputations, differences in fees, academic qualifications, athletic opportunities, and many other factors which might be important to the headmaster and parents are considered. In some of the better-known boarding schools, housemasters also have some say as to who will be accepted. An effort is made to match the school and the boy. It is by no means a one-way decision. Parents cannot buy their way into a public school; the students are carefully selected. Private schools with less well-established reputations, however, cannot afford to be too choosy.

The process begins early. In the independent sector preparatory schools prepare youngsters from the age of eight to enter the public schools, which tend to admit by examination at the age of thirteen. Some prep schools have pre-prep departments and even nursery classes. It is possible, then, to avoid the state system completely, if parents have enough money to make a substantial annual investment for twelve to fifteen years for each of their children.

For lower-middle-class parents the choice is somewhat more

difficult. School fees, especially those for boarding schools, can be very expensive; if no scholarship help is available, they may amount to a third or more of a parent's income. Many plans exist, aptly sponsored by insurance companies, to put aside money for future school fees. A decade ago, if a boy did not pass the eleven-plus his parents might have withdrawn him from the state to the private sector in hopes that with coaching and a better pupil-teacher ratio the necessary academic requirements could still be met.

Most of the lower middle class take their chances with the state system, but they must prepare their children from a very early age for the anticipated competition. Parents begin preparing children shortly after birth through careful attention, explanations and conversation, educational games, attendance in a play group, selection of the best available infant school, and active support for the school program.

Although English middle-class parents are not fully aware of it, their position in the competitive struggle is strong. The language, the conceptual patterns, and the thinking processes fostered by the schools are all middle-class. Motivation is based on middle-class work patterns and reward systems. The teachers, by and large, hold middle-class points of view. And the children bring wider backgrounds of experience and can count on the reinforcement provided by parental support and interest. They even have their grooming and manners working for them. In addition, middle-class parents learn to manipulate the system for the benefit of their offspring. Parental choice is thought to be an important factor in English education (Ayerst, 1967; White, 1970). Parents can choose the independent or the state sector, a single-sex or a coeducational school, a boarding or a day school, a church-aided or a county-maintained school. Although choice would seem to be a fundamental right of all parents, it is mostly middle-class parents who exercise choice, carefully shopping around for the school with the best reputation. Some will change their place of residence if attendance areas are strictly enforced, but this is seldom necessary, because they can usually find a well-established Church of England primary school within close commuting distance. Working-class children, however, walk to whatever school is closest.

An element of class competition does creep in. The middle-class screening system is not perfectly successful; it does not select all middle-class children nor deny entry to all working-class chil-

Learning How to Learn

dren. Some able working-class children overcome the handicaps and are placed in the higher ability streams. During the time when the eleven-plus examination was in wide use, middle-class parents whose children were denied entry into the grammar schools were among its major critics. Anxiety reached a peak prior to the announcement of test results. Middle-class parents whose children failed to gain entry could either assume the financial burden of paying for private education or suffer the disgrace of having their children attend secondary modern schools. Before selective secondary schools became an ideological symbol, the eleven-plus was unpopular both with working-class parents who recognized the screening intent and with middle-class parents who recognized the danger of being screened out. Curiously, in schools that placed less emphasis on the eleven-plus examination as the basis for selection and relied more on head teachers' judgments, class distinctions became even more pronounced (Barker Lunn, 1970). Middle-class teachers and heads were much more likely to choose middle-class children than was the class-biased, but at least objective, examination, which could not take into account appearance, manners, or parental influence.

Today England lives with a system of semiselection. Many different arrangements exist side by side. Some L.E.A.'s retain selective maintained and direct-grant grammar schools and call all others comprehensive schools, which is in part a contradiction in terms. How can a school be comprehensive if its student body does not represent all segments (Berg, 1968)? Even where reorganization has been thoroughgoing, merely designating all schools, whether grammar or secondary modern, as "comprehensive" does not make them identical. Staff and reputation do not change all that quickly. Most parents still know which school is which, and knowledgeable parents can still manipulate the system to their own advantage.

Middle-class parents in England have genuine cause for anxiety. Though there is a great deal of status-seeking in America, the middle classes do not face the same threats they do in England. The less able middle-class children in America attend comprehensive high schools along with everyone else, and they can always find *some* institution of higher education that will accept them. The less able children of the English middle class have no such protection; the more able have to struggle merely to hold their own.

SCHOOLS FOR THE WORKING CLASS

England's educational system is dualistic—by and large, separate provisions exist for the more academic and the less academic, the more affluent and the less affluent. It is not thoroughly class-related, because superior performance on examinations is rewarded, and lip service is paid to the democratic ideal of equal opportunity. However, the percentage of working-class students in universities today is as low as it was two generations ago (Robbins, 1963).

Formerly, working-class children were herded into the elementary schools, which were thoroughly avoided by even borderline clerical workers just a cut above the working class (Blackie, 1971). Today lower streams in secondary schools are practically the exclusive province of the working class. Middle-class parents shun the secondary modern school with almost as much fervor as their grandparents shunned the elementary school.

Though English state education has become moderately disassociated from class at the primary stage, it is highly class-oriented beyond it. Even at the primary level, neighborhood schools still reflect neighborhood housing patterns, and upper-middle-class families by-pass the state system. Yet the primary schools today are no longer the exclusive province of the poor. English primary schools represent the only nonselective sector in which the working class can benefit from newer developments and improved conditions.

To extend this degree of opportunity into secondary and higher education has become a political goal of the Labour Party (D.E.S., 1965a), and to effectively resist comprehensive schooling has become a political objective of the Conservative Party (Devlin, 1970). Truly comprehensive, unstreamed secondary schools, if they ever become the norm, will extend equalitarian principles, allowing the working class to benefit as they already have with regard to primary education (Simon and Rubinstein, 1969; Batley *et al.*, 1970; Burgess, 1970; Conway, 1970; Simon and Benn, 1970).

Jackson and Marsden's study of class discrimination in English education is the most damning so far published, for it implies that the few working-class youths who do succeed at school are either from former middle-class families who have become temporarily depressed socially or from homes that have adopted middle-class values and motivation (Jackson and Marsden, 1962). What happens to able working-class children whose families retain traditional working-class values? A few accounts of the utter failure of secondary modern schools are available in fiction and in research, but no one has yet discovered *why* English education has been so inhospitable to the working-class majority. While Basil Bernstein's explanations (among them that the language patterns the working-class child hears and uses at home are ignored in school) are convincing, they do not go far enough. They simply help to explain why present learning expectations are so foreign to the working-class child.

What is shocking is the acknowledgment of Bernstein's findings without any accompanying willingness to radically modify schools or teacher education. One is reminded of the Victorian complacency about the poor "always being with us." English working-class children, even lower-working-class children, must have *some* abilities, *some* motivational drives, *some* useful language, *some* valuable experiences which might serve as the basis for a more successful education. There is very little attempt, even in the primary school, to build on existing strengths. Bernstein himself has decried the fact that his research findings have been accepted with little attempt to draw forth teaching implications (Bernstein, 1970). He has also criticized the use of the term "compensatory education." English educators have not even begun to come to grips with anything that might be considered compensatory. In addition, the term places the onus of neglect on the family culture rather than on the school. Should teachers try to compensate for the language of the children's families, or should they, more realistically, compensate for their own overly verbal curriculum and expectations?

New reading programs for children of immigrants based on structural linguistics represent one positive shift in teaching strategies (Schools Council, 1969c, 1970b; Stoker, 1970). However, it is not just the children of immigrants who cannot communicate in acceptable school language; most native-born English children cannot either. As long as most of the teachers do not speak the same language or identify with the cultures of most of the pupils, primary teachers will be frustrated in their efforts to fulfill very difficult expectations, while secondary teachers will be able only to determine the examination-taking abilities of the minority of pupils who are most like themselves.

12

What Can Americans Learn from English Primary Schools?

To try to re-create an English primary school in America without English children, English teachers, or English cultural traditions appears to be a somewhat dubious goal, but since many English practices embody more universal potential, there is good reason for analyzing them in detail. This concluding chapter will bring together one hundred features that have potential for transfer to the United States. Essential characteristics, which embody more fundamental principles than the currently popular descriptions of English "open" education, have been distilled from the longer list. These specific cross-cultural comparisons should prove more helpful to teachers than vague and unqualified praise for the attributes of openness.

The current mood in English primary schools is clearly opposed to the separation of subject areas. This book has rejected a format that conveniently divides the curriculum into familiar American subject matter components. At the same time, however, some of the most helpful English books concerned with primary teaching are devoted to special fields; this is particularly true with regard to artistic expression, including creative movement, creative drama, and creative writing—areas which have long been neglected in the United States. References included in the bibliography following this chapter will provide a wealth of examples for the teacher who is interested in further classroom applications of the principles summarized below.

ONE HUNDRED POTENTIALLY
TRANSFERABLE FEATURES

The Contributions of Change Agents (Chapter 2)

1. Teachers themselves are considered to be the critical agents of change. The gradual diffusion of newer practices in thousands of schools stems from the emphasis on teacher self-determination. A change becomes firmly established when it results from a teacher's voluntary decision based on personal commitment.

2. The individual school is considered to be the viable unit in which to promote curriculum reform. Authority over curricular decisions is delegated by governing bodies to the head teacher and his staff. The English primary school is much smaller than the typical American elementary school—it covers a more restricted age band, enrollments do not often grow beyond three hundred children, and the teaching staff seldom exceeds a dozen members.

3. Local Education Authority advisers and national inspectors defer to the autonomy of head teachers. They clearly recognize the teacher's prerogatives and show sensitivity to his professional integrity.

4. The Schools Council constitutes a national body, financed jointly by local authorities and the Department of Education and Science, which has been organized to stimulate curriculum change. The Schools Council remains independent of political influence and maintains safeguards to protect professional jurisdiction.

5. Most crucial among these safeguards is the control of the decision-making process at every level by the teaching profession. Projects are initiated as a result of requests from the field, and there is clear recognition that organizations representing teachers must control the determination and direction of curriculum innovation.

6. Teachers are being offered an increasingly wider range of choice among projects, teaching strategies, and curriculum materi-

als. The goal is not to reform, upgrade, or update the teachers but to increase the number of options available to them and to encourage diversity rather than conformity.

7. Teachers are involved at each stage in the development of a Schools Council project, from the determination of program objectives to testing in pilot centers to the process of diffusion. The most widespread method of diffusion is to equip teacher leaders with opportunities to spread new practices among other teachers.

8. A teacher may select at will from among parts of one project, combine aspects of two or more projects, or reject features that seem inappropriate to him. There are none of the pressures associated with American district-wide curriculum reform to coerce the teachers into accepting or adopting a particular strategy or new set of teaching materials.

9. From the time of its introduction, educational television has been conceived in terms of enrichment, not as a means of substituting the authority of experts for the shortcomings of teachers. Never has any attempt been made to undermine the autonomy of the class teacher by relegating him to the demeaning role of technical assistant to the master teacher on the television screen, which was the unspoken but clearly evident strategy of the Airborne Television Project sponsored by the Ford Foundation. Production standards for both Independent Television and B.B.C. programs for schools are extremely high. There are no competing adult programs during the daytime hours, and signals of the regular channels reach the entire country.

10. Teachers do not feel threatened by their clients as many American teachers appear to be. English teachers are not as fearful of parental interference nor as apprehensive about losing classroom control. Showing less anxiety, less hostility, and less concern about pleasing the public, teachers can afford to demonstrate greater initiative and more independent judgment.

11. This stems in part from a clear distinction between the responsibilities of the community and those of the school. British parents seldom assume that they have any right to offer teachers advice. Governing bodies in education that represent the public seldom interfere in professional matters. School governors and education committee members are appointed, not elected; political considerations are therefore secondary. Public authorities guard

public interests by acting as appeal boards and by controlling financial allotments.

12. Even in large cities bureaucratic controls are minimal. In contrast to the United States, metropolitan boroughs do not employ an extensive administrative machinery, require a complicated decision-making process, devise a surplus of red-tape barriers, or block the initiative of individual schools.

While there are implications for America in each of the features mentioned above, the most direct and self-evident modification would be to permit school faculties to function with the autonomy which the British system protects. American teachers need to feel greater freedom from administrative controls, school board interference, parental dictation, and the inflexibility of bureaucratic organization. American school district officials must convince school board members to give individual schools the power to make decisions and to protect the right of decision-making from outside interference.

The Head Teacher (Chapter 4)

13. The English head teacher acts with authority. His power rests in part on the conviction that he can help to bring about change, a conviction that acts as a self-fulfilling prophecy. Because he assumes that he is responsible for providing leadership, he exerts leadership, which in turn is acknowledged by others and further fortifies his conviction.

14. The head is first and foremost a teacher. He does not view himself as a bureaucrat, a personnel manager, or a public relations official. He teaches children himself, and he helps others to improve their teaching effectiveness by bringing to bear his many years of classroom experience.'

15. Because his daily contacts with them are extensive, the head knows the children well as unique individuals. He knows them both as their teacher and through anecdotal records which the class teachers share with him.

16. The head often sponsors innovation. He puts the weight of his authority and prestige behind projects he considers to be promising. He works with teachers to carry innovations forward. Head teachers have become the most influential figures in England in accelerating the pace and determining the extent of change.

17. The post of deputy head offers prospective administrators opportunities to assume additional commitments and to earn increased remuneration. The deputy, along with individuals holding other designated graded posts of responsibility, assists the head, encourages teacher initiative, and provides leadership to take over in the head's absence.

18. Increasingly, heads involve teachers in cooperative decision-making. The face-to-face, intimate communication among the small staff creates a primary group. Such a social climate is conducive to the diffusion of ideas, since daily staff room contacts and pressures for group approval often penetrate through resistance or insecurity.

19. Heads relate to the community with self-respect. While some keep parents at a distance, few find themselves in the much less dignified American position of expending too much energy trying to respond to parental criticism or community pressures. Heads have confidence in themselves as community leaders on school-related issues. Some even assume an educational function with parents, a role long ago abandoned by the more harassed American school officials. The head teacher of a village school may become a highly respected arbiter of community affairs.

20. Heads participate in teacher education. They make arrangements for school visitors, college projects, and practice teaching. They consult with practice teachers, supervise probationary teachers, and encourage professional growth among the staff. The National Association of Head Teachers has publicly called for a more definitive role in teacher education, with more time to be devoted to school-based experiences.

21. Heads assume responsibility for the entire school program. They do not hesitate about making decisions that might affect the children's welfare. Their hands are not tied by higher authorities, they need not clear decisions through a chain of command, and they are not immobilized by union contracts or parental interference. English heads believe that in schools the welfare of the children should come first.

While some differences between the American elementary school principal and the English head teacher result from differing traditions, one implication is overwhelmingly clear. The English head teacher exercises authority and exerts curriculum leadership, while the American elementary school principal is too often immobilized by unwarranted restrictions, conflicting pressures, and unrealistic expectations. In each country the status leader should be able to act as a catalyst for change, provided that the individual school is given power to determine its own priorities.

The Class Teacher (Chapter 5)

22. The degree of autonomy possessed by the English class teacher is unequaled anywhere else in the world. He not only has the opportunity to determine his own objectives, he is obligated to do so. No official hands the English teacher a curriculum guide or a course of study. There are no required textbooks or grade-level expectations. He cannot excuse himself by blaming administrators for blocking his initiative. The initiative is entirely his own.

23. The class teacher resists imposed expectations and outside controls. His independence is fortified by the realization that he must decide what he will attempt to do with the children. Many American teachers do not resist restrictions on academic freedom; they seldom claim the right of noninterference in professional matters.

24. The absence of any district-wide curriculum framework means that each teacher can adapt his own program to the particular children whom he teaches and to the particular neighborhood in which they reside. This flexibility takes on added significance when children or neighborhoods deviate from conventional norms.

25. Teachers are increasingly turning away from total class assignments to individualized expectations and informal communication with children, substituting indirect teaching for directive instruction. There are fewer class demonstrations, less class discussion, less talking at children, and much more informal conversation in small groups.

26. Teachers work alongside the children, carrying out investigations and devoting time to their own creative interests. Because they take less time to instruct in front of the total class, they have more time to participate in the learning process with the children.

27. Teachers respect children's ideas. They encourage the children's initiative, their problem-solving attempts, and the process of discovery. They allow children to make mistakes while seeking their own solutions. By showing greater respect for children's learning

potential, they encourage the development of self-discipline and independence.

28. Primary teachers frequently claim that they are more concerned with *how* children learn than with *what* they know. They are more concerned with favorable attitudes toward schoolwork than with measuring the amount of information acquired. They strive to build independent study skills that will decrease the children's reliance on adult direction.

29. Self-criticism and skepticism prevent English primary teachers from developing a sense of complacency. They are seldom defensive when discussing problems, somewhat humble when relating accomplishments, and strongly concerned about the need to improve conditions.

30. In contrast to American teachers, English teachers are not obsessed with discipline. Experienced teachers take classroom management problems in their stride. They recognize that effective discipline grows from curricular provisions and an atmosphere conducive to self-direction among pupils. While English informal methods do not eliminate discipline problems, they keep them within manageable proportions. The disciplinary problems that do exist are largely associated with children who lack sufficient maturity or the emotional stability to maintain self-control.

31. There seems to be far less coercion in English primary schools than in American elementary schools. Punishment is less frequently administered and is seldom harsh. Corporal punishment, degrading to punished and punisher alike, is fast disappearing in state primary schools.

32. Teachers improvise many of their own learning devices. They prepare workcards, puzzles, games, tape recordings, and experiments. They assume that they should prepare many of their own materials rather than expect them to be provided by commercial firms and publishers. The more inventive teachers devise learning aids for individual children.

33. Teachers are adaptable, meeting unexpected problems with ingenuity and often with good humor. They overcome shortages of space, supplies, and equipment that would defeat many American teachers, who are paid a great deal more money to work in buildings that are much more lavishly equipped.

34. Many teachers are talented in one or more of the creative

arts. They can offer examples for inspiration and are able to recognize and encourage the creative interests of children. Largely neglected in American elementary schools, and among the first provisions to be sacrificed in an economic squeeze, the arts are highly prized in English primary education.

35. When teachers talk about children, the English tend to be more positive than Americans and to complain less about behavior problems. Staff room conversation has a more professional tone; there are fewer complaints and less venting of hostilities.

Although many teachers are searching for new ideas in the United States, many American school systems tend not to treat creative teachers with dignity. Too many American teachers are forced to work their way around the bureaucratic machinery. A curriculum package prepared by "experts" implies a very low regard for the "average" teacher, for it reduces his job to opening packages for children. The American primary teacher needs to feel a greater sense of academic freedom; he does not need someone else to determine his priorities for him.

Nursery Education (Chapter 6)

36. The state-maintained nursery schools, considered the first stage of primary education, set the standards for all other preschool provisions. In America state responsibility for education does not begin until the child is five or six; in England it begins for some children at three. Since the Second World War each successive government has reiterated a pledge to expand state provisions for the nursery age group, and a modest expansion is at last taking place in Educational Priority Areas.

37. Nursery assistants, or nursery nurses, take training in Colleges of Further Education, which admit school-leavers at the age of sixteen. American secondary schools have done little to provide paraprofessional training for young people who wish to work with preschool children.

38. English nursery schools have long adhered to an orthodox tradition that conceives of play as the work of children and which relies heavily on active participation through inviting children to select activities in learning centers. Social interaction, physical development, creative expression, and natural language usage are com-

bined in a balanced program that does not overemphasize any single aspect of growth.

39. English nursery school practices have influenced the rest of the primary school curriculum. Many practices now common in infant and junior schools, such as self-selection of activities, centers of interest, informal communication, and spontaneous creative expression, were first widely accepted within English nursery schools.

40. Malting House, the school established by Susan Isaacs as a laboratory in child development, emphasized scientific discovery in the search for the origins of scientific thought. A variety of authentic scientific apparatus catered to children's interests and encouraged the expression of scientific curiosity.

41. At Malting House clinical insights drawn from the psychoanalytic study of childhood guided the free expression of feelings. In particular, allowing children openly to express aggression and sexuality has potential to unleash the learning abilities of verbally restricted working-class children.

42. Additional scientifically controlled studies in laboratory settings are needed in order to replicate with more diverse groups the approach pioneered by Susan Isaacs with bright children almost fifty years ago. Is unobtrusive teacher support combined with the encouragement of emotional release and intellectual curiosity applicable to a wider cross section of social classes and measured abilities?

Infant Schools (Chapter 7)

43. Since there are no grade levels in infant schools, there are no arbitrary norms to meet. The absence of grade-level expectations reduces pressures on children to achieve predetermined rates of progress in reading. There are no standardized annual tests to measure achievement. Reading or mathematical ages, when calculated, are determined largely for diagnostic purposes.

44. Unlike American children, who are expected to begin formal reading shortly after entering first grade at the age of six, children in England are not pressured to begin to read before they are ready. If they are ready to read at five, they begin then; if they are not ready until they are seven, they are not pushed to begin earlier.

45. Without the American dichotomy between the value of

play in the kindergarten and the importance of formal work in the first grade, it is considered entirely appropriate for older children to engage in play and for younger children to begin to acquire more structured learning skills.

46. All children attend a full day at school from the age of five, and a minority precede this with a half day at school from the age of three. Unless the spirit of the informal kindergarten philosophy extends upward, there are potential dangers in a full day at school for five-year-olds in the United States. If preceded by optional attendance for a half day at four and followed by greater informality in the succeeding years, there might be some merit in extending the length of the kindergarten day to challenge further the largely untapped learning potential of American five-year-olds.

47. At least three major benefits are derived from having a separate school for children of infant school age. A head teacher is released to offer instructional leadership; the children become better known because the school is small; the staff concentrates attention on the needs of a limited age band. If large American elementary schools were divided into two distinct but related units under two autonomous principals, more suitable provisions might be developed for each age band.

48. Since nearly all English infant heads are women, there are many career opportunities for experienced women infant teachers. The preponderance of women in leadership positions has probably advanced the development of informal methods in English infant schools.

49. A school day organized with few fixed points decreases the necessity for directive controls, total class teaching, or the division of the curriculum into separate periods. The non-timetabled day promotes integration of content and a more informal structure.

50. Young children who are allowed to work without a fixed sequence of separated periods can meet daily or weekly commitments in a flexible manner. Each child establishes his own rhythm of work, thus developing greater self-regulation in the use of his time.

51. Individualized teaching materials are designed as far as possible to be self-selective, self-explanatory, and self-correcting. Since expectations are set on an individual basis, children need not work their way through the same materials in a given sequence.

They may proceed at their own rate. Evaluation procedures are individualized as well. In this sense individualization becomes more than an instrumental teaching technique; it governs the process by which growth is evaluated.

52. Competition is seldom fostered by infant teachers. Evaluation tends to be more anecdotal than statistical, relying more on subjective judgments than on objective test data. The purpose of evaluation is not to measure performance but to help teachers better understand children.

53. Instead of being used for basal reading series and other textbooks, instructional funds are devoted to school and classroom libraries. The wide variety of information books, reference works, and storybooks purchased for these libraries help to promote independent reading.

54. Workbooks designed to consolidate reading or mathematical skills are generally not used. Instead, learning aids tend to be administered on an individualized basis. These take the form of either individualized workcards and games made by the teachers or commercially produced apparatus and skill-building kits.

55. The affective and the cognitive domains are much more evenly balanced in England than in America. Infant schools encourage dramatic play, construction, creative movement, story-telling, and the visual arts. To engage in the creative arts is always considered legitimate activity; the arts are not viewed as a time-filler or a special reward for good behavior at the end of the day.

56. Small groups for instruction tend to be temporarily constituted and heterogeneous in measured ability. Group projects are selected by children on the basis of interest or organized by teachers to reinforce particular skills. The American scheme of each day rotating three semipermanent developmental reading groups geared to achievement levels would be considered in England a shameful waste of time for teachers and children alike.

57. Centers of interest are separated by temporary bays and dividers, allowing children to work together with a degree of isolation from other groups and from the teacher. The teacher moves from group to group offering help and encouragement.

58. Removing some of the furniture from the classroom provides more space. Each child does not need his own private desk. Children stand at easels or workbenches, sit in library corners, at ta-

bles, and in study areas, or they spread out on the floor. Since they share furniture and facilities, they learn to move freely about the room without causing a commotion.

59. Open communication is encouraged. Children help one another, compare notes, conduct joint projects, and engage in spontaneous conversation. Such communication is an important feature of the informal atmosphere.

60. The teacher does not withdraw from the instructional role but instead substitutes indirect for direct guidance. Indirect teaching implies selective intervention with individuals and small groups in order to stimulate, extend, challenge, and support learning activities. The teacher arranges the environment, is readily available for consultation, and intervenes when appropriate.

61. Mathematics teaching in the infant schools has been heavily influenced by the research of Piaget. Based on manipulation of concrete materials, experimentation with structural apparatus, and direct application of first-hand sense impressions to real problems, it aims at gradually developing mathematical understanding. There is no rush to move children too quickly into dealing with symbolic abstractions.

62. Piaget's concern for concrete experience and vivid sense impressions is carried into story-telling, poetry, and other artistic endeavors. Helping children to become increasingly sensitive to a wide variety of sounds, sights, smells, and tactile sensations stimulates artistic interpretations.

63. There are a number of imaginative English approaches to reading, such as *Breakthrough to Literacy*, a Schools Council Project consisting of initial reading material derived from the science of structural linguistics. Each infant teacher retains the right to decide which scheme or combination of schemes to use.

64. The most far-reaching development in English infant schools is vertical, or family, grouping, a way to organize classes heterogeneously across the entire age distribution. Adherents cite some benefits of vertical grouping: it allows young children to become better known by one teacher over a period of years; it develops a sense of responsibility in older children, who induct new arrivals into established patterns; it provides older models for younger children to imitate; it promotes individualized instruction; it relieves disciplinary problems; and it promotes interstaff communication. It is essential that family grouping be applied to all areas of

the curriculum and not restricted to developmental reading; it is also essential that it bring together temporary, cross-age, heterogeneous, task-oriented groups. Unless fully implemented, family grouping will suffer the same fate in America as nongrading, a concept similar in intent but woefully undeveloped in application. It should not be allowed to degenerate into a disguised form of streaming by ability within an essentially unchanged age-graded school, the all too frequent fate of nongraded cycles in America.

Junior Schools (Chapter 8)

65. Older children who are capable of working for longer periods of time are encouraged to launch long-range projects at which they can work without being interrupted.

66. The workshop environment turns the classroom into a learning laboratory. Resource books, reference works, scientific apparatus, technical aids, construction materials, and human resources are available for children to draw on as they see fit.

67. The range of choices is extended as children increase in maturity. Children choose what they want to do, how they will do it, where they want to work, and for how long they wish to continue. They modify their plans as they proceed. The need to make a series of judicious choices helps to develop initiative.

68. Attention is focused on the process rather than the products of education. Methods to encourage further learning become more important than immediate results. Attitudes toward learning and habits of thought, such as persistence in the search for truth, become more important than the acquisition of specific information.

69. One of the most significant benefits of long-range time commitments is the more leisurely pace. When teachers deliberately encourage children to slow down, they promote a deeper exploration of materials, more careful habits of observation, and a concern for qualitative standards. This contrasts with the "hurry up and finish before the period is over" attitude of many American teachers who are bound by a segmented curriculum arranged in fixed time periods. The decrease in pressure allows children to relax, yet it may well increase their powers of concentration as they become more fully absorbed.

70. Teachers of older children learn to perform as catalytic agents. They engage children in dialogue by probing, challenging,

doubting, and raising aspirations. They judiciously withhold approval until children sense that they have earned such a response.

71. Drawing from the apprenticeship tradition, the teacher serves as an adult model of craftsmanship. He demonstrates such crafts as block printing, tie-dyeing, soap carving, or pottery-making, while the children "have a go" at it themselves.

72. When a child wishes to be left alone, his privacy is respected. There are quiet corners and out-of-the-way places where children who wish to work in solitude can do so. Inner-directedness and reticence are seldom viewed as signs of inadequate social adjustment.

73. Most impressive to visitors, and seldom found in America, are opportunities for older children to engage in creative movement. Stimulation is provided for children to express feelings and interpret situations through their bodies. Rather than being considered feminine or effete, as it might be considered by American boys, creative movement is an essential component of a balanced physical education program.

74. Closely linked to creative movement is creative drama. Dramatic productions integrate music, poetry, construction, and costume design with themes drawn from history and other social studies. Spontaneous creative drama relies on suggestions and a minimum of props—perhaps a tape recorder, physical education apparatus, and a few dinner tables from the school hall.

75. Creative writing is another means of fostering the development of imagination. In many classes children are expected to do some creative writing each day. This ranges from brief, descriptive accounts of learning experiences to sensitively conceived and imaginatively executed poetry.

76. Mathematics for older children is not necessarily treated as a separate subject, although many teachers set aside instructional corners for its sequential development. In accordance with the Nuffield School Mathematics Project, which stresses the application of mathematics to other curriculum areas, mathematics is frequently integrated with projects in other content fields. Children make graphs and illustrative charts; they keep records, conduct measurements, and functionally relate mathematics to scientific, geographic, and historical investigations.

77. The functional use of mathematics in projects helps develop favorable attitudes toward number work. Emotional blocking

associated with mathematical reasoning and computation need not arise when mathematics is used as a tool subject as well as a language by which mathematical abstractions are systematized.

78. Environmental studies encourage children to go outdoors to follow up scientific and geographic interests. Field trips into the countryside and surrounding towns enliven studies associated with the social sciences and transform the surrounding environment into an extended school laboratory.

79. Field trips to an outdoor camp or to continental Europe may be organized, sometimes lasting as long as a week. Intergroup living opportunities may be as valuable as the intellectual stimulation the trips offer. The trips provide a focus for preparatory study and enriched perceptions for the subsequent development of the theme.

80. Integrated themes are loosely conceived, allowing children to search out their own topics. Children are given sufficient time to carry investigations to considerable depth and to summarize results in displays, which frequently include elaborate three-dimensional constructions.

81. Construction tends to be given greater prominence in English junior schools than in American later elementary grades. Models, woodwork, craft objects, and sculpture are constructed at workbenches, in passageways, and outdoors. The noise or messiness of hammering, sawing, carving, and modeling does not upset teachers unduly, nor does it seem to bother the other children. Children who learn effectively by working with tools are given sufficient time to do so.

82. The morning break, though not always needed by the children, who frequently go right on with their work, seems beneficial to teachers. The break provides a welcome opportunity for teachers to share impressions over coffee in the staff room, away from the noise of the children. American teachers might do well to take a complete break and gather together for fifteen or twenty minutes each morning instead of trying to gulp a cup of coffee during recess.

83. Team teaching in England is adapted by each staff to the needs of a particular school. This freedom to adapt as necessary is a tribute to English organizational autonomy. The most recommended form of team teaching is cooperative teams in which teachers draw on specific interests to help one another provide a

common curriculum. This seems preferable to departmental organization according to subject specialization or a hierarchical arrangement with a team leader in command.

84. More men are found in junior schools in England than in America, providing more masculine models for children and more opportunities for men to serve in designated posts of responsibility. Graded posts offer class teachers additional remuneration for taking on additional commitments.

85. Middle schools, if they become more common, will extend to an older age range, including twelve- and thirteen-year-olds, the benefits of the informal philosophy more common in junior than in secondary schools. The competition of middle schools may stimulate changes among the lower forms of conventional secondary schools.

Preparation of Primary School Teachers (Chapter 9)

86. Colleges of Education provide many opportunities for students to apply what they learn to actual school situations. From the beginning of the three-year course, educational studies, curriculum (methods) courses, and main subject work are scheduled concurrently, and each segment includes school-based components.

87. In addition to informal school visits and class projects, college students engage in full-time teaching practice during each of the three years. By spacing teaching practice over three years, not only is experience gained in a variety of locations with different age groups, but, more important, students develop increasing self-confidence. Periods between teaching practices become periods of growth. First-hand impressions are solidified, further course work becomes more meaningful, the appraisal of teaching commitment becomes more realistic, and increasing maturity is brought to bear on successive assignments. After the third teaching practice most students are reasonably confident about meeting the demands of full-time employment, a frame of mind in marked contrast to the insecurities expressed by American graduates.

88. Practice teachers are given genuine responsibility from the start. They are expected to come to teaching practice well prepared, with extensive plan books and a wide variety of learning aids that they have made. Unlike American student teachers, they are seldom overprotected or prevented from taking full responsibility.

89. Higher education in England is distinguished by tutorial

teaching, which is arranged individually or in small groups. Typically, a tutorial consists of a structured discussion, in which participants are expected to challenge one another and the tutor, defend a position through rational argument, and communicate with clarity and precision. Tutorials are supplemented by lectures and classes, but they constitute the distinctive element in British higher education.

90. Tutors work closely with students. Tutorial relationships are given high priority in determining a college lecturer's commitments. Almost all tutors have had teaching experience in schools and all supervise teaching practice.

91. Study of a main subject (or academic major) begins when the student enters college and is structured as a continuous three-year course rather than as a series of separate credits. Most English students enter college much better prepared in a main subject than American students. They start from a higher level and pursue study in greater depth.

92. Students are well known to college authorities. Weak students are salvaged through careful attention and genuine concern. The wastage (dropout) rate is low, partly because students do not become lost or neglected as they often do in large, impersonal American institutions.

93. The grant system supplies students with a modest stipend, which enables them to devote all their time and energy to their education without having to take an outside job to pay their expenses. The size of the grant depends on the income of the parents; full grants are given to the less affluent.

94. Students in higher education belong to a single, powerful student union. Spokesmen for the National Union of Students are consulted regularly by the national government, by professional teachers' associations, and by the press. At the local college level, the union executive represents the student body in negotiations with the principal, the staff, and the board of governors. Students have voting representatives on the Academic Board and on major college committees.

High Standards (Chapter 10)

95. The teacher makes heavy demands on himself. He considers himself a model for children, hoping that in time they will internalize his work habits, cultural interests, and intellectual curiosity.

The teacher cannot expect the children to set high standards if he does not set high standards for himself.

96. Teachers take pride in the children's work. Using walls and any other available space to display finished work stimulates children to raise their aspirations, especially when the work represents the children's best efforts. Artistic creations and culminating reports provide impressive evidence that outstanding performance is expected.

97. When the teacher gradually but persistently raises standards, he prevents children from remaining satisfied with their first attempts. This in turn leads to greater freedom of creative expression. For instance, children need not feel restricted during the initial enthusiasm of creative writing by concern over spelling, handwriting, or grammar. If the work is not to be displayed or presented for the inspection of others it need not be redone, but if it is to be submitted children will carefully make a "fair" copy.

98. Concern for authentic craftsmanship encourages a deeper, more patient exploration of materials. Instilling in children the pride in workmanship associated with the village artisan helps to counteract the indifference to qualitative standards found in an economy based on mass production.

99. Standards of behavior stem from the expectation that children will grow in their ability to become self-directive. There is an ever-present expectation that children will gradually settle into patterns of interaction that are not disturbing to others.

100. Americans need to appreciate that high standards of workmanship and behavioral expectations that demonstrate a concern for others accompany English informal methods and the more relaxed English atmosphere. To miss this connection is to miss a key to the success of English primary schools.

A CRITIQUE OF THE CONCEPT OF
OPEN EDUCATION

"Open education," as a slogan or a catch-phrase, can serve as a rallying cry against the rigidities of American school systems. However, it is not a very useful term to describe English schools as they exist, for such a characterization leads to too much confusion. Many conceive of openness in the Summerhill sense, where rules are determined by the corporate community meeting in open council, and where children have the freedom to do as they please. It is easy to jump to the conclusion that the therapeutic objectives that have guided A. S. Neill at Summerhill apply to a large number of English schools. Such a misconception ignores the process and direction of change in English state-maintained schools and the multiplicity of roles performed by English primary teachers.

English schools are not as open as they first appear to be. For the most part, they retain (sometimes only in attenuated form) a number of traditional expectations and patterns, which supply a sense of continuity with the past. The increase in informality has been a slowly evolving process, not an overnight transformation.

It is true that most English primary schools are more open than most schools in the United States. Some, designed to facilitate team teaching and to provide access to a number of teachers and other children, are literally open-planned, without separating walls or doors. Few restraints are imposed on freedom of movement. Children are seldom expected to remain in their seats or to ask permission to sharpen their pencils or go to the toilet. The curriculum is more open in that children may shift from one activity to another on their own initiative. Teaching is more open, providing greater leeway for children to engage in independent problem-solving. In some ways expectations are more open—children are permitted to develop according to their own individual patterns of growth.

But as a descriptive term, "open education" can be relatively meaningless. What is to be defined as open and what is to be considered closed? When education becomes completely open, what remains? The answer might turn out to be—nothing. When the concept is carried to its logical extreme, it leaves little place for schools or teaching. Openness must be considered as a *relative* term describing a condition which can contribute to more tangible and more conclusive qualities.

ESSENTIAL FEATURES OF ENGLISH PRIMARY EDUCATION

The direction of change over the past twenty-five years cannot be subsumed under a catch-phrase like "the open classroom" or "the informal school." Instead, a number of features have become essential; without them English schools could hardly have evolved to their current state. In some respects they hold promise for more widespread applicability; they are among the features which might be transferred to a receptive American setting when made consistent with American traditions and values.

Crucial to any assessment of current developments are the ways in which teachers view themselves. Concept of self partially determines how one is viewed by others. Teachers in England, both head teachers and class teachers, take a more professional stance than do their American counterparts. They claim genuine professional autonomy and they are afforded this by others. Power and authority are vested in the head, who is considered above all a teacher. He is expected to exert curriculum leadership, but it is the class teachers who decide what will be taught. Teachers resist imposition from outside the school, and they expect to be consulted in matters that concern them. Productive relationships with children, parents, and governing bodies grow from this sense of self-respect. While innovations are publicized and suggestions are offered by advisers, no one would dream of trying to tell the head teacher or his staff what to do. In England decisions about curriculum matters are made by those professionals who are actively engaged in carrying them out. English head teachers and their staffs are shocked to learn that in America policy decisions about what to teach or how to teach it are determined by laymen elected by the public.

This leads to a correspondingly much clearer definition of relationships between home and school. Teachers are firmly convinced that parent-teacher relationships must be based on cooperative but clearly separated functions. Parents are responsible for children in the family setting, but teachers are responsible for the educational program of the school. Part of the resistance to closer home-school ties stems from the suspicions of English teachers that in America the blurring of functions between home and school has led to parents dictating to teachers and teachers fearful of making changes that might upset the public.

On a much more extensive scale than in the United States, teachers in England trust children to acquire increasing independence. The teacher-pupil relationship is based on mutual respect. This appears on the one hand in more relaxed discipline, less fear, and reduced hostility, and on the other in greater reliance on learning procedures that offer pupils ample opportunities to make

Learning How to Learn

choices. The ideal expression of the pupil-teacher relationship is captured in the title of Leonard Marsh's book, *Alongside the Child in the Primary School* (Marsh, 1970a). The teacher continues to learn alongside the child; his example provides a mature model, but he does not impose mature thought patterns or overly direct the learning process. Within such a relationship, greater student self-direction becomes an expectation. Pupils increasingly take on responsibility for themselves because they feel trusted by a teacher whose judgment they themselves trust.

A further essential feature is that the individual school is the key unit. This is related to the size of the school itself. In England it is firmly held that schools should not be allowed to become too large. It is vital that children be well known by the teachers and by the head. The age span within a nursery, infant, or junior school is restricted to a few years. From a bureaucratic standpoint this pattern of organization might be considered inefficient, since the size of each school is too small to allow for economical construction costs and since small units necessitate more money to be allocated for administrative salaries. In terms of human relationships, however, the size of the unit is far more functional than in America. It is possible for all of the teachers to gather daily in a small staff room. It is possible for the head to know the names, home backgrounds, and learning characteristics of every child in the school. It is possible for staff members to work in close cooperation; indeed, they cannot escape from one another. The faculty acts as a primary group within which intimate, face-to-face communication develops. This feature, when coupled with the autonomy afforded to each teacher, allows the individual school to serve as the unit for curriculum change. Under the leadership of a persuasive, imaginative head who believes that he has the responsibility to influence teachers and the obligation to encourage their initiative, each school has the freedom to shift its direction. The focus of change is not at the district level but in the school itself.

The single most far-reaching organizational pattern pioneered in England is family, or vertical, grouping. This creates classes of mixed age and achievement levels and encourages grouping practices that are temporary, heterogeneous, and concerned with the entire curriculum. In order to implement a version of family grouping in America, teachers would have to be willing to abandon reading groups, grade-level expectations, and a tightly structured curriculum. Family grouping embodies another essential characteristic—the view that learning among young children is integrated, need not be segmented, should not become overly concerned with reading as a skill subject, and is facilitated by multiple opportunities for heterogeneous group interaction.

In the race to intensify and systematize the content fields, American schools have neglected the ingredients of a balanced curriculum for children. While English primary schools might well need to become more systematic with regard to cognitive development, they have not forgotten the artistic realm. The English primary curriculum shows a much better balance between cognitive and affective objectives. A good deal of the school day is spent in exploring the creative arts. Sensitivity to artistic expression accompanies imaginative teaching of creative movement, creative drama, creative writing, three-dimensional crafts, visual arts, singing, and instrumental music.

English primary schools have made some remarkable changes over the past twenty years, and the extent of change has been spreading since the publication of the Plowden Report in 1967. The first steps in introducing essential English ingredients to the United States and transferring some of the more specific ideas discussed in the previous section are fairly obvious. It would be relatively simple to reduce the size of the large elementary school to two or three separate units, each of which would have a separate administrator and enroll only a few hundred children. Next it would be vital to select bold, imaginative elementary school principals, men and women challenged by the potential for leadership who are themselves expert teachers. It would then be necessary for the principal and his staff to feel sufficiently secure about making those modifications which in England are considered the rightful prerogatives of a teaching faculty.

Initiative is stifled in the United States by the concern with interference. An American school that wants to test the feasibility of English patterns needs protection from community restrictions. Should complaints be received from meddling parents, overbearing school board members, or frightened bureaucrats, members of the administration must steadfastly support experimental schools. Interference is such a threat, especially when proposed changes are in the informal English direction, that a statement would need to be made by the appropriate American policy-making body temporarily

Learning How to Learn

relinquishing control of the curriculum. The legally constituted school board needs to put aside for a specific period of time its right to determine the curriculum and, further, it must formally delegate authority to each individual school. This delegation must be made clear to the parents, the press, and other community watchdogs. To function in the English manner, an American school staff needs to be able to rely on the full backing of the central administration and the board of education.

American teachers will not understand how to function with professional autonomy until they have had opportunities to study themselves and the process of change through school-based, in-service meetings. They will need to reinforce one another and to learn what it means to make decisions without the threat of interference. For too long, American teachers have been told what to do or have blamed others for imposing restrictions; they need to be able to act forthrightly on the courage of their convictions. Professional autonomy carries obligations that can be far more challenging than conformity to regulations.

English teachers have learned to be increasingly sensitive in recognizing the proper occasions for selective intervention. They are convinced that informal teaching is very hard work. The awareness of appropriate circumstances for indirect teaching has been well expressed by Sybil Marshall. She warns that creative teaching, especially associated with the arts, depends on understanding the basic philosophy underlying modern methods, a sensitive appreciation of what constitutes the artistic process, and the adult's active participation in learning (Marshall, 1963, 1969, 1970).

Finally, the mistaken impression that American teachers can imitate the English simply by substituting nondirective for directive teaching, or by replacing rigidity with unplanned informality, must be corrected. English informal methods have evolved gradually. The apparent informality of English schools is the result of skillful indirect teaching, not of nondirective withdrawal from the teaching commitment.

BIBLIOGRAPHY

Bibliography

Asterisk (*) indicates British publication.

ABBOTT, J. *Student Life in a Class Society.* Pergamon Press, 1971.
* ADAMS, F.; MILLAR, E. M. M.; JEFFREYS, M.; and VAN DER EYKEN, W. *New Opportunities for Young Children.* Nursery Schools Association, 1968.
ALINGTON, A. F. *Drama and Education.* Dufour, 1961.
* ALLEN, B., ed. *Headship in the 1970s.* Blackwell, 1968.
* ALLEN, G., and others. *Scientific Interests in the Primary School.* National Froebel Foundation, 1958.
* ALLEN, J. *Drama.* Her Majesty's Stationery Office, 1968.
* ALLEN, T. N. "Wanted: More Coloured Teachers." *Times Educational Supplement,* April 24, 1970, p. 13.
ARCHAMBAULT, R. D., ed. *Philosophical Analysis and Education.* Humanities Press, 1965.
* ASH, B., and others. *Discovering with Young Children.* Elek Books, 1971.

Ashley, B. J.; Cohen, H. S.; and Slatter, R. G. *An Introduction to the Sociology of Education.* Macmillan, 1969.

Ashton-Warner, S. *Teacher.* Simon and Schuster, 1963.

* Association of Teachers in Colleges and Departments of Education. *Higher Education and Preparation for Training: A Policy for Colleges of Education.* A.T.C.D.E., 1970.

* ———. *Summary of Teacher Training Courses at Colleges and Departments of Education.* A.T.C.D.E., 1971.

* Association of Teachers of Mathematics. *Notes on Mathematics in Primary Schools.* Cambridge University Press, 1967.

* Association of Teachers in Technical Institutes. *Education for the Future.* A.T.T.I., 1970.

* Ayerst, D. *Understanding Schools.* Pelican Books, 1967.

* Bailey, E. *Discovering Music with Young Children.* Methuen, 1958.

* Banks, O. *Parity and Prestige in English Secondary Education.* Routledge, 1955.

* Bantock, G. H. *Freedom and Authority in Education,* 2nd ed. Faber & Faber, 1965. (a)

——— . *Education and Values: Essays in the Theory of Education.* Humanities Press, 1965. (b)

Baratz, S. S., and Baratz, J. C. "Early Childhood and Intervention: The Social Science Base of Institutional Racism." *Harvard Educational Review* 40 (1970): 29–50.

* Barr, E. *From Story into Drama.* Heinemann, 1964.

Barth, R. S. *Open Education: Assumptions About Learning and Knowledge.* Pergamon Press, 1969.

Barth, R. S., and Rathbone, C. H. "Readings on British Primary Education and Its American Counterparts: A Selected Bibliography." *The Center Forum,* July 1969.

Bassett, G. W. *Innovation in Primary Education.* Wiley-Interscience, 1970.

Batley, R.; O'Brien, O.; and Parris, H. *Going Comprehensive.* Humanities Press, 1970.

Beard, R. M. *An Outline of Piaget's Developmental Psychology.* Basic Books, 1969.

* Beavan, K. "United States: Accountability Octopus Gains New Territory." *Times Educational Supplement,* May 29, 1970, p. 11.

* Begefjord, B. *Summerhill Diary.* Gollancz, 1970.

BELL, P. *Basic Teaching for Slow Learners*. Transatlantic Arts, 1970.

BEREITER, C.; ENGELMANN, S.; OSBORN, J.; and REDFORD, P. "An Academically Oriented Pre-School for Culturally Deprived Children." In *Pre-School Education Today*, ed. by Fred M. Hechinger. Doubleday, 1966.

* BERG, L. *Risinghill: Death of a Comprehensive School*. Penguin Books, 1968.

* BERKSHIRE COLLEGE OF EDUCATION. *Your Curriculum A–Z*. Issued in connection with the *First School Course*, a coordinated curriculum course for second-year students. Mimeographed. Berkshire College of Education, 1971.

BERNARD, T. I. "The Brain Drain: Why Do They Come Here?" *Educational Forum*, March 1971, pp. 353–58.

* BERNSTEIN, B. "Language and Social Class." *British Journal of Sociology* 11 (1960): 271–76.

———. "Social Class and Linguistic Development." In *Education, Economy and Society*, ed. by A. H. Halsey, J. E. Floud, and C. A. Anderson. Free Press, 1961. (a)

———. "Social Structure, Language and Learning." In *Educational Research* 3 (1961): 163–76. (b)

* ———. "A Socio-Linguistic Approach to Social Learning." In *Penguin Social Sciences Survey*, ed. by J. Gould. Penguin Books, 1965.

* ———. "The Open School." In *Where*, Supplement No. 12. Advisory Centre for Education, Cambridge, 1967. (a)

* ———. "Open Schools, Open Society?" *New Society*, September 1967, pp. 351–53. (b)

* ———. "A Critique of the Concept of 'Compensatory Education.'" In *Education for Democracy*, ed. by D. Rubinstein and C. Stoneman. Penguin Books, 1970.

BERNSTEIN, B., and DAVIES, B. "Some Sociological Comments on Plowden." In *Perspectives on Plowden*, ed. by R. S. Peters. Humanities Press, 1969.

BETTELHEIM, B. *Love Is Not Enough: The Treatment of Emotionally Disturbed Children*. Free Press, 1950.

———. *The Children of the Dream*. Macmillan, 1969.

* BINYON, M. "Students Angry at Secret Service Methods, D.E.S. Has Individual Dossiers on 800,000." *Times Educational Supplement*, December 12, 1969, p. 9. (a)

* BINYON, M. "Immigrants Face Danger of Being Dubbed 'Sub-Normal.' " *Times Educational Supplement,* December 26, 1969, p. 3. (b)

* ———. "Head Tells of Confidential Letter to University." *Times Educational Supplement,* February 27, 1970, p. 6. (a)

* ———. "Mr. Straw Puts Five Questions." *Times Educational Supplement,* April 3, 1970, p. 5. (b)

* BLACK BORED. "Colleges of Education, 2nd Class?" *Black Bored,* No. 1, 1970, pp. 6–8.

* BLACKIE, J. *Good Enough for the Children?* Faber & Faber, 1963.

* ———. "The Character and Aims of British Primary Education." In *Children at School: Primary Education in Britain Today,* ed. by G. Howson, Centre for Curriculum Renewal and Development Overseas. Heinemann, 1969.

———. *Inside the Primary School.* Schocken Books, 1971.

* BLACKSTONE, T. "The Plowden Report." *British Journal of Sociology* 18 (1967): 291–301.

* ———. *A Fair Start: The Provision for Pre-School Education.* Lane, 1971.

* BLACKWELL, F. F. *Starting Points for Science.* Blackwell, 1968.

BLOOM, B. *Stability and Change in Human Characteristics.* Wiley, 1964.

BLYTH, W. A. C. *Schools.* Vol. 1 of *English Primary Education.* Humanities Press, 1965.

* BOLT, R., and others. *Fundamentals in the First School.* Blackwell, 1969.

BOTTOMORE, T. *Elites and Society.* Penguin Books, 1964.

———. *Classes in Modern Society.* Pantheon Books, 1966.

* BOUCHER, L., and STARKEY, P. C. "Curriculum Development and Evaluation in Education Courses." *Education for Teaching,* Summer 1970, pp. 25–27.

* BOURNE, R. "A Century of State Education." In *Horizons for Education,* ed. by B. MacArthur. Council for Educational Advance, 1970.

BOWKER, G. *Education of Coloured Immigrants.* Humanities Press, 1969.

BOWLBY, J., and FRY, M. *Child Care and the Growth of Love.* Penguin Books, 1965.

* BOWYER, R. "Individual Differences in Stress at the Eleven-plus Ex-

amination." *British Journal of Educational Psychology* 31 (1961): 268–80.

* BREARLEY, M. *First Years in School: The Practical Implications for the Teacher.* Evans, 1963.

BREARLEY, M., and HITCHFIELD, E. *A Teacher's Guide to Reading Piaget.* Schocken Books, 1969.

* BRITTON, J. *Talking and Writing.* Methuen, 1967.

* ———. "Expanding Nursery Schools." *Times Educational Supplement,* July 24, 1970, p. 14.

* BROSAN, G., and others. *Patterns and Policies in Higher Education.* Penguin Books, 1971.

BROSSARD, C. "A School Run by Children." *Look,* November 19, 1963.

BROWN, M., and PRECIOUS, N. *The Integrated Day in the Primary School.* Agathon Press, 1969.

BROWNE, J. D. "The Balance of Studies in Colleges of Education." In *Toward a Policy for the Education of Teachers,* ed. by W. Taylor. Colston Research Society Papers, No. 20. Shoe String Press, 1969.

BRUNER, J. S. *Studies in Cognitive Growth.* Wiley, 1966. (a)

———. *Towards a Theory of Instruction.* Harvard University Press, 1966. (b)

* BURGESS, T. "Obituary for 10/65." *Times Educational Supplement,* July 3, 1970, p. 75. (a)

* ———. *Inside Comprehensive Schools.* Her Majesty's Stationery Office, 1970. (b)

* ———. "School Building Programme." In *The Red Paper,* ed. by D. Gowan, R. Cuddihy, and C. Lindsey. Islander Publications, 1970. (c)

———, ed. *Dear Lord James: A Critique of Teacher Education.* Penguin Books, 1971.

BURGIN, T., and EDSON, P. *Spring Grove—The Education of Immigrant Children.* Oxford University Press, 1967.

* BURT, C. "Susan Isaacs (1885–1948)." *Times Educational Supplement,* May 8, 1970, p. 50.

CALDWELL, B. M. "A Timid Giant Grows Bolder." *Saturday Review,* February 20, 1971, pp. 47–49, 65–66.

* CAMBRIDGE INSTITUTE OF EDUCATION. *Conference on School Experience in a College of Education Course.* Discussion papers,

July 10–11, 1970. Mimeographed. Cambridge Institute of Education, 1970.

* CAMERON, W., and CAMERON, M. *Education in Movement in the Infant School.* Blackwell, 1969.

* CAMPBELL, F. C. *Eleven Plus and All That.* Watts, 1956.

* CANE, B. S. *In-Service Training.* National Foundation for Educational Research, 1969.

* Casciani, J. W., and WATT, J. *Drama in the Primary School.* Nelson, 1966.

CASS, J. *Literature and the Young Child.* Humanities Press, 1968.

* CATTY, N. *Learning and Teaching in the Junior School.* Methuen, 1956.

* CENTRAL ADVISORY COUNCIL FOR EDUCATION. *Early Leaving.* Her Majesty's Stationery Office, 1954.

* ———. *15–18* (The Crowther Report). Her Majesty's Stationery Office, 1959.

* ———. *Half Our Future* (The Newsom Report). Her Majesty's Stationery Office, 1963.

* ———. *Children and Their Primary Schools* (The Plowden Report). Her Majesty's Stationery Office, 1967.

* CHANAN, G. "Colleges of Education: Repression by Confusion." *Rank and File,* Autumn 1970, pp. 14–16.

* CHILD, H. A. T., ed. *The Independent Progressive School.* Hutchinson, 1962.

* CHRISTMAS, L. "Southampton Primary Sector Follows Plowden into New Era." *Times Educational Supplement,* January 2, 1970, p. 5. (a)

* ———. "Case for Comprehensive University." *Times Educational Supplement,* March 27, 1970, p. 9. (b)

* CHURCH, M. "Probationary Year a Hollow Mockery." *Times Educational Supplement,* December 4, 1970, p. 6. (a)

* ———. "Mrs. Thatcher Wants Report on Training Within 12 Months." *Times Educational Supplement,* December 11, 1970, p. 3. (b)

* ———. "Switch Training to Universities—Says N.U.T." *Times Educational Supplement,* March 19, 1971, p. 9.

CHURCHILL, E. *Counting and Measuring: An Approach to Number Education in the Infant School.* University of Toronto Press, 1961.

CLARK, K. *Dark Ghetto.* Harper & Row, 1965.

* CLARKE, M. "Success Before Six?" *Trends in Education*, October 1968, pp. 11–16.

CLEGG, A. B., ed. *The Excitement of Writing.* Fernhill House, 1966.

* ———. "This 'Sifting' Cannot Go On." *Times Educational Supplement*, March 27, 1970, p. 9.

CLELAND, D.; REES-DAVIES, B.; and HAM, D. *Exploring Science in the Primary Schools.* Macmillan, 1967.

* CLEMAN, M. "Not Just Half—All Our Future." *Trends in Education*, April 1968, pp. 8–13.

* COARD, B. *How the West Indian Child Is Made Educationally Subnormal in the British School System: The Scandal of the Black Child in Schools in Britain.* New Beacon Books, 1971.

COCKBURN, A., and BLACKBURN, R., eds. *Student Power: Problems, Diagnosis, Action.* Penguin Books, 1969.

* COHEN, A., and GARNER, N. A. *Student's Guide to Teaching Practice*, 2nd ed. University of London Press, 1970.

COHEN, D. K. "Children and Their Primary Schools: Volume II." *Harvard Educational Review* 38 (1968): 329–40.

COLE, G. D. H. *Studies in Class Structure*, rev. ed. Humanities Press, 1964.

COLEMAN, J. *Equality of Educational Opportunity.* U.S. Government Printing Office, 1966.

COLLINS, M. *Students into Teachers: Experiences of Probationers in Schools.* Humanities Press, 1969.

* COMMITTEE ON HIGHER EDUCATION. *Higher Education* (The Robbins Report). Her Majesty's Stationery Office, 1963.

* CONFEDERATION FOR THE ADVANCEMENT OF STATE EDUCATION. *Caseviews Two.* C.A.S.E., 1970.

* CONSULTATIVE COMMITTEE OF THE BOARD OF EDUCATION. *Education of the Adolescent* (The Hadow Report). His Majesty's Stationery Office, 1926.

* ———. *The Primary School* (The Hadow Report). His Majesty's Stationery Office, 1931.

* ———. *Infant and Nursery Schools* (The Hadow Report). His Majesty's Stationery Office, 1933.

* CONWAY, E. S. *Going Comprehensive.* Harrap, 1970.

* COOPER, G. *The Place of Play in an Infants and Junior School.* National Froebel Foundation, 1963.

* CORNWALL, P. *Creative Playmaking in the Primary School.* Chatto & Windus, 1970.

* CORSTAN, G. B. "Spreading the New Ideas." In *Children at School: Primary Education in Britain Today,* ed. by G. Howson, Centre for Curriculum Renewal and Educational Development Overseas. Heinemann, 1969.

COTGROVE, S. *The Science of Society: An Introduction to Sociology.* Barnes & Noble, 1968.

* Cox, C. B., and DYSON, A. E., eds. *Fight for Education: A Black Paper.* Critical Quarterly Society, 1969. (a)

* ———, eds. *Black Paper Two: Crisis in Education.* Critical Quarterly Society, 1969. (b)

* ———, eds. *Black Paper Three.* Critical Quarterly Society, 1970.

* CUSHEN, M. E. *Educational Aids in the Infant School.* Matthews, 1966.

* CUTFORTH, J. *English in the Primary School.* Blackwell, 1956.

DALE, R. R., and GRIFFITH, S. *Down Stream: Failure in the Grammar School.* Fernhill House, 1965.

DANCY, J. C. *The Public Schools and the Future,* 2nd ed. Fernhill House, 1966.

* DANIELS, J. C. "The Effects of Streaming in the Primary School. I: What Teachers Believe." *British Journal of Educational Psychology* 31 (1961): 69–78. (a)

* ———. "The Effects of Streaming in the Primary School. II: A Comparison of Streamed and Unstreamed Schools." *British Journal of Educational Psychology* 31 (1961): 119–27. (b)

* DAVIS, R. *The Grammar School.* Penguin Books, 1967.

* DEAN, J. *Reading, Writing and Talking.* Black, 1968.

DEARDEN, R. F. "Instruction and Learning by Discovery." In *The Concept of Education,* ed. by R. S. Peters. Humanities Press, 1967.

———. *The Philosophy of Primary Education: An Introduction.* Humanities Press, 1968.

———. "The Aims of Primary Education." In *Perspectives on Plowden,* ed. by R. S. Peters. Humanities Press, 1969.

DENNISON, G. *The Lives of Children: The Story of the First Street School.* Random House, 1969.

* DENT, H. *The Educational System of England and Wales,* 4th ed. University of London Press, 1969.

244

* DENT, H. "The Builders 1870–1970." *Times Educational Supplement*, May 8, 1970, pp. 43–54.
* DEPARTMENT OF EDUCATION AND SCIENCE. *Village Schools.* Her Majesty's Stationery Office, 1961.
* ———. *Organisation of Secondary Education.* Circular 10/65. Her Majesty's Stationery Office, 1965. (a)
* ———. *Mathematics in Primary Schools.* Curriculum Bulletin No. 1. Her Majesty's Stationery Office, 1965. (b)
* ———. *Eveline Lowe Primary School.* Building Bulletin No. 36. Her Majesty's Stationery Office, 1967.
* ———. *Parent/Teacher Relations in Primary Schools.* Education Survey No. 5. Her Majesty's Stationery Office, 1968.
* ———. *Schools and the Countryside.* Education Pamphlet No. 35. Her Majesty's Stationery Office, 1969.
* ———. *Education Statistics for the United Kingdom, 1967.* Her Majesty's Stationery Office, 1970. (a)
* ———. *Education and Science in 1969.* Her Majesty's Stationery Office, 1970. (b)
* ———. *Teacher Education and Training* (The James Report). Her Majesty's Stationery Office, 1972.
DERRICK, J. *Teaching English to Immigrants.* Humanities Press, 1967.
DEUTSCH, M. "The Disadvantaged Child and the Learning Process." In *Education in Depressed Areas*, ed. by A. H. Passow. Columbia University Press, 1963.
* DEVLIN, T. "440 Compete for 100 B.Ed. Places." *Times Educational Supplement*, October 24, 1969, p. 8.
* ———. "L.E.A.s Spend Too Little on School Books." *Times Educational Supplement*, February 6, 1970, p. 11. (a)
* ———. "Schools Must Not Be Mosques." *Times Educational Supplement*, February 13, 1970, p. 14. (b)
* ———. "Mrs. Thatcher Will Withdraw Circular." *Times Educational Supplement*, June 26, 1970, p. 3. (c)
* ———. "Training Report Could Be Ready by Autumn." *Times Educational Supplement*, January 22, 1971, p. 6. (a)
* ———. "Bottom of the Book League." *Times Educational Supplement*, March 5, 1971, p. 4. (b)
DEWEY, J. *Art as Experience.* Minton Balch, 1934.
———. *Experience and Education.* Collier Books, 1938.

DEWEY, J. *The Child and the Curriculum*. University of Chicago Press, 1959.

――――. *Democracy and Education*. Macmillan, 1961.

DIENES, Z. P. *Building Up Mathematics*. Humanities Press, 1960.

――――. *Modern Mathematics for Young Children*. Herder and Herder, 1966.

DIENES, Z. P., and GOLDING, E. W. *Exploration of Space and Practical Measurement*. Herder and Herder, 1966. (a)

――――. *Learning Logic, Logical Games*. Herder and Herder, 1966. (b)

――――. *Sets, Numbers and Powers*. Herder and Herder, 1966. (c)

* DOBINSON, C. H. *Jean-Jacques Rousseau*. Methuen, 1969.

DOTTRENS, R. *The Primary School Curriculum*. UNESCO, 1962.

* DOUGLAS, J. W. B. *The Home and the School*. Panther Books, 1967.

* ――――. "The Influence of Parents." In *New Horizons for Education*, ed. by B. MacArthur. Council for Educational Advance, 1970.

DOUGLAS, J. W. B., and Ross, J. M. "The Later Educational Progress and Emotional Adjustment of Children Who Went to Nursery School or Classes." *Educational Research* 7 (1964): 73–80.

* DOUGLAS, J. W. B.; Ross, J. M.; and SIMPSON, H. R. *All Our Future*. Davies, 1968.

DOWNING, J. A., ed. *The First International Reading Symposium, Oxford, 1964*. Day, 1966. (a)

* ――――. *Initial Teaching Alphabet*. Cassell, 1966. (b)

* ――――. *Evaluating the Initial Teaching Alphabet: A Study of the Influence of English Orthography in Learning to Read and Write*. Cassell, 1967.

* DREW, C. E. *Modern Mathematics in the Junior School*. Ward, Lock, 1970.

* DRYER, K. "Grand Gestures Not So Grand." *Times Educational Supplement*, March 5, 1971, p. 5.

* ELVIN, H. L. "When Should Teachers Strike?" *Times Educational Supplement*, November 21, 1969, p. 2.

ENTWISTLE, H. *Child Centred Education*. Barnes & Noble, 1970. (a)

――――. *Education, Work and Leisure*. Humanities Press, 1970. (b)

* ENTWISTLE, N. J. "11-plus: The Great Divide." *Times Educational Supplement*, September 4, 1970, p. 2.

EVANS, E. D. *Contemporary Issues in Early Childhood Education.* Holt, 1971.

* FARLEY, R. *Secondary Modern Discipline.* Black, 1960.

FEATHERSTONE, J. "Schools for Children: What's Happening in British Classrooms." *New Republic*, August 19, 1967, pp. 17–21. (a)

——. "How Children Learn." *New Republic*, September 2, 1967, pp. 17–21. (b)

——. "Teaching Children to Think." *New Republic*, September 9, 1967, pp. 15–19. (c)

——. "Primary Mathematics." *New Republic*, November 11, 1967, pp. 34–35. (d)

——. "Report Analysis: Children and Their Primary Schools." *Harvard Educational Review* 38 (1968): 317–28. (a)

——. "Experiments in Learning." *New Republic*, December 14, 1968, pp. 23–25. (b)

——. "Schools for Learning." *New Republic*, December 21, 1968, pp. 17–20. (c)

——. "The British and Us." *New Republic*, September 11, 1971, pp. 20–25. (a)

——. "Tempering a Fad." *New Republic*, September 25, 1971, pp. 17–21. (b)

FENTON, F. *The New Social Studies.* Holt, 1967.

FISHER, R. J. "An English Criticism—Too Many Textbooks." *Educational Forum*, May 1969, pp. 527–32.

* —— . "Mystery of the Missing Students." *Times Educational Supplement*, February 13, 1970, p. 4.

FISHER, R. J., and MUCKENHIRN, E. "Cultural Differences in an American-English Exchange Program." *Elan*, Spring 1969, pp. 12–15.

* FISHER, R. J., and PAISEY, A. "Exchange Programme—or Program." *Times Educational Supplement*, July 17, 1970, p. 78.

FISHER, R. J., and SMITH, W. *Schools in an Age of Crisis.* Van Nostrand Reinhold, 1972.

FLANDERS, N. *Teacher Influence, Pupil Attitudes and Achievement.* U.S. Government Printing Office, 1965.

FLAVELL, J. H. *The Developmental Psychology of Jean Piaget.* Van Nostrand, 1963.

* FLOUD, J. "Teaching in the Affluent Society." *British Journal of Sociology* 13 (1962): 299–308.

* FLOUD, J.; HALSEY, A. H.; and MARTIN, F. M., eds. *Social Class and Educational Opportunity.* Heinemann, 1957.

* FORD, J. "Comprehensive Schools as Social Dividers." *New Society,* October 10, 1968, pp. 515–17.

———. *Social Class and the Comprehensive School.* Humanities Press, 1970.

FOSS, B. "Other Aspects of Child Psychology." In *Perspectives on Plowden,* ed. by R. S. Peters. Humanities Press, 1969.

FRASER, D., ed. *Social Studies: Curriculum Development: Prospects and Problems.* Thirty-ninth Yearbook of the National Council for the Social Studies, 1968.

FRIEDENBERG, E. Z. *Coming of Age in America.* Random House, 1963.

FROMM, E. *Man for Himself: An Inquiry into the Psychology of Ethics.* Holt, 1947.

———. *The Art of Loving.* Harper & Row, 1956.

* FROOME, S. *Why Tommy Isn't Learning.* Stacey, 1970.

GABRIEL, J. *Children Growing Up: The Development of Children's Personalities,* 3rd ed. International Publications Service, 1970.

* GARDNER, D. E. M. *Testing Results in the Infant School.* Methuen, 1942.

* ———. *The Education of Young Children.* Methuen, 1956.

———. *Experiment and Tradition in the Primary School.* Barnes & Noble, 1966.

———. *Susan Isaacs: The First Biography.* Barnes & Noble, 1969.

GARDNER, D. E. M., and CASS, J. *The Role of the Teacher in the Infant and Nursery School.* Pergamon Press, 1965.

* GATTEGNO, C. *Words in Colour.* Educational Explorers, 1969.

* GAYFORD, O. M. *i.t.a. in Primary Education.* Initial Teaching Publications, 1970.

GLASS, D. V., ed. *Social Mobility in Britain.* Humanities Press, 1963.

* GLENNERSTER, H., and PRYKE, R. *The Public Schools.* Fabian Society, 1964.

* GLENNERSTER, H., and WILSON, G. *Paying for Private Schools.* Lane, 1970.

* GOLDMAN, R. J. *First Years in School: Children's Spiritual Development.* Evans, 1963.

GOLDMAN, R. J. *Religious Thinking from Childhood to Adolescence.* Humanities Press, 1964.

GOLDTHORPE, J. H., and LOCKWOOD, D. "Affluence and the British Class Structure." *Sociological Review* 11 (1963): 133–63.

* GOLDTHORPE, J. H.; LOCKWOOD, D.; BECHOFFER, F.; and PLATT, D. "The Affluent Worker and the Thesis of Embourgeoisement: Some Preliminary Research Findings." *Sociology* 1 (1967): 11–31.

* GOODACRE, E. J. *Reading in Infant Classes.* National Foundation for Educational Research, 1967.

* ———. *Teachers and Their Pupils' Home Backgrounds.* National Foundation for Educational Research, 1968.

* ———. *School and Home.* National Foundation for Educational Research, 1970.

———. *Children and Learning to Read.* Humanities Press, 1971.

GOODLAD, J. I., and ANDERSON, R. I. *The Non-graded Elementary School.* Harcourt, 1959.

GOODMAN, P. *Compulsory Mis-Education.* Horizon Press, 1964.

* GOODRIDGE, J. *Drama in the Primary School.* Heinemann, 1970.

* GOSTELOW, L. *Picture Story Approach to Infant Teaching.* Evans, 1968.

GRIBBLE, J. *An Introduction to the Philosophy of Education.* Allyn and Bacon, 1969.

GROSS, B., and GROSS, R. *Radical School Reform.* Simon and Schuster, 1969.

* HAAS, W. "From Look and Say to i.t.a." *Times Educational Supplement,* November 28, 1969, p. 4.

* HALSEY, A. H. "Education and Equality." *New Society,* June 17, 1965, pp. 13–15.

* ———. "Attacking Social Deprivation: The Educational Priority Area." In *New Horizons for Education,* ed. by B. MacArthur. Council for Educational Advance, 1970.

HALSEY, A. H.; FLOUD, J. E.; and ANDERSON, C. A., eds. *Education, Economy and Society.* Free Press, 1961.

HALSEY, A. H., and TROW, M. A. *The British Academics.* Harvard University Press, 1971.

HAPGOOD, M. "The Open Classroom: Protect It from Its Friends." *Saturday Review,* September 18, 1971, pp. 68–69, 75.

HARGREAVES, D. H. *Social Relations in a Secondary School.* Humanities Press, 1967.

* Hawkes, N. *Immigrant Children in British Schools.* Pall Mall Press, 1966.
* Haynes, J. *Educational Assessment of Immigrant Pupils.* National Foundation for Educational Research, 1971.

Hentoff, N. *Our Children Are Dying.* Viking Press, 1966.

Herndon, J. *The Way It Spozed to Be.* Simon and Schuster, 1968.

Hess, R. P., and Bear, R. *Early Education, Current Theory, Research and Practice.* Aldine-Atherton, 1968.

* Hewett, S. "Injustices Still Left in the B.Ed.—Success Rates Vary Between Universities." *Times Educational Supplement,* October 17, 1969, p. 4.

* ———. "The Job Ahead for James." *Times Educational Supplement,* December 11, 1970, p. 2.

Hewitson, J. N. *The Grammar School Tradition in a Comprehensive World.* Humanities Press, 1970.

* Hill, B. "Doing Things on the Cheap." *Times Educational Supplement,* March 5, 1971, p. 4.

* Hill, F. "London Plans to Reduce Size of Primary Classes to 35." *Times Educational Supplement,* June 12, 1970, p. 4.

Hilliard, F. H., ed. *Teaching the Teachers: Trends in Teacher Education.* Verry, 1971.

Hodgson, J., and Richards, E. *Improvisation: Discovery and Creativity in Drama.* Barnes & Noble, 1966.

Hoffman, J., and Tower, P. "A Bibliography for the Free School Movement." *Summerhill Society Bulletin,* October 1969.

* Hogan, J. M., and Willcock, J. B. "In-Service Training for Teachers." *Trends in Education,* October 1967, pp. 17–21.

* Hole, V. "Children's Play on Housing Estates." Ministry of Technology National Building Studies, Research Paper No. 39. Her Majesty's Stationery Office, 1966.

Hollingshead, A. B. *Elmtown's Youth.* Wiley, 1949.

Hollins, T. H. B. "The Problems of Values and John Dewey." In *Aims in Education,* ed. by T. H. B. Hollins. Humanities Press, 1966.

Holmes, B. *Problems in Education: A Comparative Approach.* Humanities Press, 1965.

Holt, J. *How Children Fail.* Pitman, 1964.

———. *How Children Learn.* Pitman, 1967.

———. *The Underachieving School.* Pitman, 1969.

* Hornsby-Smith, M. P. "Parents and Primary Schools." *New Society*, January 11, 1968, pp. 54–55.

Hoyle, E. *The Role of the Teacher*. Humanities Press, 1970.

* Hughes, W. "Teachers Split in Pay Deadlock." *The Sunday Times*, March 21, 1971, p. 4.

* Hull, W. P. "Leicestershire Revisited." Early Childhood Education Study, Occasional Paper No. 1, 1969. Newton, 1969.

Hunt, J. McV. "The Psychological Basis for Using Pre-School Enrichment as an Antidote for Cultural Deprivation." *Merrill-Palmer Quarterly* 10 (1964): 209–48.

Irwin, M., and Russell, W. *The Community Is the Classroom*. Pendell, 1971.

Isaacs, N. "Children's Why Questions." In *Intellectual Growth in Young Children*, by S. Isaacs. Humanities Press, 1930.

* ———. *New Light on Children's Ideas of Number*. Ward, Lock, 1960.

* ———. *The Growth of Understanding in the Young Child*. Ward, Lock, 1961.

Isaacs, S. *Intellectual Growth in Young Children*. Humanities Press, 1930.

* ———. "Some Notes on the Incidence of Neurotic Difficulties in Young Children." *British Journal of Educational Psychology* 2 (1932): 71–91, 184–95. (a)

* ———. *The Children We Teach*. University of London Press, 1932. (b)

* ———. *The Educational Value of the Nursery School*. Nursery School Association of Great Britain, 1937.

———. "A Special Mechanism in a Schizoid Boy." *International Journal of Psycho-Analysis* 20 (1939): 333–39.

———. "An Acute Psychotic Anxiety Occurring in a Boy of Four Years." *International Journal of Psycho-Analysis* 24 (1943): 13–32.

———. *Childhood and After*. Agathon Press, 1948. (a)

———. "The Nature and Function of Phantasy." *International Journal of Psycho-Analysis* 29 (1948): 73–97. (b)

———. *The Nursery Years*. Vanguard Press, 1950.

* ———. *Social Development in Young Children*, student's abridged ed. Abridged and edited by D. May. Routledge, 1951.

Isaacs, S. *Social Development in Young Children.* Humanities Press, 1964.

Jackson, B. "Teachers' Views on Primary School Streaming." *Educational Research* 4 (1961): 44–52.

———. *Streaming: An Education System in Miniature.* Humanities Press, 1964.

Jackson, B., and Marsden, D. *Education and the Working Class.* Humanities Press, 1962.

* James, C. *Young Lives at Stake: A Reappraisal of Secondary Schools.* Collins, 1968.

* ———. "Changing the Curriculum." In *New Horizons for Education,* ed. by B. MacArthur. Council for Educational Advance, 1970.

* James, R. *Infant Drama.* Nelson, 1967.

Jameson, K. *Art and the Young Child.* Viking Press, 1969.

Johnston, D. J. *Teachers' In-Service Training.* Pergamon Press, 1970.

* Jordan, D. *Childhood and Movement.* Blackwell, 1960.

* ———. *The Arts in Education: Movement and Dance.* Evans, 1963.

Judson, M. E. *Books of Interest Concerning Infant Primary and Elementary Schools in the United States and England.* School Services Group, Boston, 1969.

* Kahan, M.; Butler, D.; and Stokes, D. "On the Analytical Division of Social Class." *British Journal of Sociology* 17 (1966): 122–32.

Kallett, T. "Two Classrooms." *This Magazine Is About Schools,* April 1966.

Kalton, G. *The Public Schools: A Factual Survey.* Fernhill House, 1966.

* Keeley, B., ed. *1020 Playgroups.* Pre-School Playgroup Association, 1968.

Kelsall, R. F., and Kelsall, H. M. *The School Teacher in England and in the United States: Findings of Empirical Research.* Pergamon Press, 1970. (a)

———. "The Status, Role and Future of Teachers." In *The Teacher and the Needs of Society in Evolution,* by E. J. King. Pergamon Press, 1970. (b)

Kent, G. *Projects in the Primary School.* Verry, 1968.

Kenworthy, L. S. "Ferment in the Social Studies." In *Readings for*

Social Studies in Elementary Education, by J. Jarolimek and H. M. Walsh, Macmillan, 1965.

KING, E. J. Education and Social Change. Pergamon Press, 1966.

———. The Education of Teachers. Holt, 1970.

KING, R. Education. Humanities Press, 1969.

KLEIN, M. "Some Theoretical Conclusions Regarding the Emotional Life of the Infant." In Developments in Psycho-Analysis, by M. Klein and others. Hillary House, 1952.

KOHL, H. Thirty-six Children. Norton, 1967.

KOHLBERG, L. A. "Early Education: A Cognitive-Developmental View." Child Development 39 (1968): 1013–62.

KOZOL, J. Death at an Early Age: The Destruction of the Hearts and Minds of Negro Children in the Boston Public Schools. Houghton-Mifflin, 1967.

* LABAN, R. The Mastery of Movement on Stage. Macdonald & Evans, 1950.

* LACEY, C. Hightown Grammar: The School as a Social System. University of Manchester Press, 1970.

* LAMPE, D. Pyke: The Unknown Genius. Evans, 1959.

* LANE, S. M., and KEMP, M. An Approach to Creative Writing in the Primary School. Blackie, 1967.

* LANGDON, M. Let the Children Write. Longmans, 1961.

LANGFORD, G. Philosophy and Education: An Introduction. Shoe String Press, 1971.

* LAUWERYS, J. A. Teachers and Teaching. Evans, 1969.

LAWRENCE, E., ed. Friedrich Froebel and English Education. Schocken Books, 1969.

LAWTON, D. Social Class, Language and Education. Schocken Books, 1968.

* LAYARD, R.; KING, J.; and MOSER, C. The Impact of Robbins. Penguin Books, 1969.

LEONARD, G. B. Education and Ecstasy. Delacorte Press, 1968.

* LEWIS, R., and MAUDE, A. The English Middle Classes. Penguin Books, 1953.

* LIGHTWOOD, P. Creative Drama for Primary School. Blackie, 1970.

LILLEY, I. M. Friedrich Froebel. Cambridge University Press, 1967.

* LITTLE, A., and WESTGAARD, J. "The Trend in Class Differentials in Educational Opportunity in England and Wales." British Journal of Sociology 15 (1964): 301–16.

* LOCKWOOD, D. The Black-Coated Worker. Allen & Unwin, 1958.

* Lovell, K. *The Growth of Basic Mathematical and Scientific Concepts in Children.* University of London Press, 1961.

Lowenfeld, V. *Creative and Mental Growth,* 3rd ed. Macmillan, 1957.

* Luckin, B. "Baffled by the Head's Budget." *Times Educational Supplement,* March 5, 1971, p. 5.

* Lunn, J. C. B. *Streaming in the Primary School.* National Foundation for Educational Research, 1970.

* Lunzer, E. A. "Recent Studies in Britain Based on the Work of Jean Piaget." Occasional Paper No. 4. National Foundation for Educational Research, 1960.

* McCullough, M. "Therapeutic Playgroup." *New Society,* January 9, 1969, pp. 50–51.

* McIntyre, D.; Morrison, A.; and Sutherland, J. "Social and Educational Variables Relating to Teachers' Assessments of Primary School Children." *British Journal of Educational Psychology* 36 (1966): 272–79.

* MacKay, D., and Thompson, B. *The Initial Teaching of Reading and Writing.* Longmans, 1969.

* Mackenzie, R. F. *State School.* Penguin Books, 1970.

McLellan, J. *The Question of Play.* Pergamon Press, 1970.

* Maclure, S. "American Challenge—Can It Happen Here?" *Times Educational Supplement,* November 20, 1970, pp. 16, 57.

* McMillan, M. *The Life of Rachel McMillan.* Dent, 1927.

* Maden, M. "Teacher Training." In *The Red Paper,* ed. by D. Gowan, R. Cuddihy, and C. Lindsey. Islander Publications, 1970.

* Mann, B. F. *Learning Through Creative Work: The Under 8's in School,* rev. ed. National Froebel Foundation, 1966.

Mannheim, K., and Stewart, W. A. C. *Introduction to the Sociology of Education.* Humanities Press, 1970.

* Marsh, L. G. *Children Explore Mathematics.* Black, 1964.

* ———. "Plowden: Some Implications for the Training of Teachers." In *Bulletin of the University of London Institute of Education,* Summer 1967.

* ———. *Alongside the Child in the Primary School.* Black, 1970. (a)

* ———. *Approach to Mathematics.* Black, 1970. (b)

Marshall, S. *An Experiment in Education.* Cambridge University Press, 1963.

* MARSHALL, S. *Aspects of Art Work with 5–9-Year-Olds.* International Publications Service, 1970.

* ———. "Art." In *Children at School: Primary Education in Britain Today,* ed. by G. Howson, Curriculum Renewal and Educational Development Overseas. Heinemann, 1969.

* ———. "Books and Methods for the Infant School." *Times Educational Supplement,* January 30, 1970, p. 45. (a)

* ———. "Modern Methods in School." In *The Red Paper,* ed. by D. Gowan, R. Cuddihy, and C. Lindsey. Islander Publications, 1970. (b)

MASON, E. *Collaborative Learning.* Agathon Press, 1972.

* MASON, S. C. *The Leicestershire Experiment and Plan.* Councils and Education Press, 1963.

* MATTERSON, E. M. *Play with a Purpose for Under-Sevens.* Penguin Books, 1965.

* MAUGER, P. "Selection for Secondary Education." In *Education for Democracy,* ed. by D. Rubinstein and C. Stoneman. Penguin Books, 1970.

* MAY, D. E. *Children in the Nursery School: Studies in Personal Adjustment in Early Childhood.* University of London Press, 1963.

MEGSON, B., and CLEGG, A. *Children in Distress.* Penguin Books, 1970.

* MELLOR, E. *Education Through Experience in the Infant School Years.* Blackwell, 1950.

MELZI, K. *Art in the Primary School.* Hillary House, 1967.

MERTON, R. K. *Social Theory and Social Structure,* rev. ed. Free Press, 1957. (a)

* ———. "The Role-Set: Problems in Sociological Theory." *British Journal of Sociology* 8 (1957): 106–20. (b)

MILLS, C. W. *The Power Elite.* Oxford University Press, 1959.

* MINISTRY OF EDUCATION. *The Training of Teachers.* Pamphlet No. 34. Her Majesty's Stationery Office, 1957.

* ———. *Development Projects, Junior School, Amersham.* Building Bulletin No. 16. Her Majesty's stationery Office, 1958.

* MOCK, R. *Education and Imagination.* Chatto & Windus, 1970.

MONTESSORI, M. *The Montessori Method.* Schocken Books, 1964.

* MORRIS, J. *Reading in the Primary School.* National Foundation for Educational Research, 1959.

Bibliography

* Morris, J. *Standards and Progress in Reading.* National Foundation for Educational Research, 1966.

Moustakas, C. *The Authentic Teacher: Sensitivity and Awareness in the Classroom.* Doyle, 1966.

———. *Creativity and Conformity.* Van Nostrand, 1967.

Moyle, D. *The Teaching of Reading.* International Publications Service, 1971.

Murrow, C., and Murrow, L. *Children Come First: The Inspired Work of English Primary Schools.* American Heritage Press, 1971.

Musgrave, P. W. *The Sociology of Education.* Barnes & Noble, 1965.

Musgrove, F. *Patterns of Power and Authority in English Education.* Barnes & Noble, 1971.

Musgrove, F., and Taylor, P. H. *Society and the Teachers' Role.* Humanities Press, 1969.

Nash, P. *Authority and Freedom in Education.* Wiley, 1966.

* National Association of Schoolmasters. *Salaries in the Seventies.* N.A.S., 1970.

* National Association for the Teaching of English. *English in the Primary School.* N.A.T.E., 1964.

* National Foundation for Educational Research. *N.F.E.R. Publications, 1970.* N.F.E.R., 1970.

* National Union of Students. *Introducing N.U.S.* N.U.S., 1970.

* National Union of Teachers. *The State of Nursery Education.* N.U.T., 1964.

* Neill, A. S. *Is Scotland Educated?* Routledge, 1936.

* ———. *The Free Child.* Jenkins, 1953.

———. *Summerhill: A Radical Approach to Child Rearing.* Hart, 1960.

———. *Freedom—Not License!* Hart, 1966.

* ———. *Talking of Summerhill.* Gollancz, 1967.

Newson, J., and Newson, E. *Patterns of Infant Care in an Urban Community.* Aldine-Atherton, 1963.

———. *Four Years Old in an Urban Community.* Aldine-Atherton, 1968.

Newsweek. "Does School + Joy = Learning?" *Newsweek,* May 3, 1971, pp. 60–68.

* Nuffield Junior Mathematics Project. *I Do and I Understand; Pictorial Representation; Beginnings; Mathematics Begins;*

Shape and Size; Computation and Structure. Chambers & Murray, 1967.

* NUFFIELD JUNIOR SCIENCE PROJECT. *Source Book: Apparatus; Source Book: Animals and Plants.* Collins, 1967.

* NUNN, T. P. *Education, Its Data and First Principles.* Arnold, 1947.

* NUTTALL, K. *Let's Act.* 4 vols. Longmans, 1959.

* O'CONNOR, D. J. *An Introduction to the Philosophy of Education.* Routledge, 1957.

ORNSTEIN, A. C. "Urban Teachers and Schools: Fashionable Targets." *Educational Forum*, March 1971, pp. 359–66.

* PARKIN, F. "Working Class Conservatism." *British Journal of Sociology* 18 (1967): 278–90.

PARSONS, T. *The Social System.* Free Press, 1951.

———. "The School Class as a Social System." In *Education, Economy and Society*, ed. by A. H. Halsey, J. Floud, and C. A. Anderson. Free Press, 1961.

PARSONS, T., and SHILS, E., eds. *Toward a Theory of Social Action.* Harper & Row, 1961.

* PARTRIDGE, J. *Life in a Secondary Modern School.* Penguin Books, 1968.

* PAYNE, S. "Students Nose Out the 'Secret Files.'" *Times Educational Supplement*, February 27, 1970, p. 3.

* PEDLEY, R. *The Comprehensive School*, rev. ed. Pelican Books, 1969.

PEEL, M. *Seeing to the Heart.* Fernhill House, 1968.

PERRY, L., ed. *Bertrand Russell, A. S. Neill, Homer Lane, W. H. Kilpatrick: Four Progressive Educators.* Macmillan, 1968.

* PETERS, R. S. *Education as Initiation.* Evans, 1964.

* ———. *Ethics and Education.* Allen & Unwin, 1966.

———, ed. *The Concept of Education.* Humanities Press, 1967.

* ———. "Theory and Practice in Teacher Training." *Trends in Education*, January 1968, pp. 3–9.

———. "A Recognisable Philosophy of Education: A Constructive Critique." In *Perspectives on Plowden*, ed. by R. S. Peters. Humanities Press, 1969.

PETERS, R. S., and HIRST, P. *The Logic of Education.* Humanities Press, 1971.

* PHELPS, R. *Display in the Classroom.* Blackwell, 1969.

* PIAGET, J. *The Child's Conception of Geometry.* Routledge, 1960.

Piaget, J. *The Language and Thought of the Child,* 3rd ed. Humanities Press, 1962.

———. *The Child's Conception of Number.* Humanities Press, 1964.

* Pidgeon, D., and Wiseman, S. *Curriculum Evaluation.* National Foundation for Educational Research, 1970.

Pines, M. *Revolution in Learning: The Years from Birth to Six.* Harper & Row, 1967.

* Plaskow, M. "Sitting with Nellie." *Times Educational Supplement,* October 31, 1969, p. 2.

* Porter, J. F., ed. "Teachers for Tomorrow." *Education for Teaching,* Autumn 1968, pp. 55–64.

Postman, N., and Weingartner, C. *Teaching as a Subversive Activity.* Delacorte Press, 1969.

Pratt, C. *I Learn from Children—An Adventure in Progressive Education.* Simon and Schuster, 1948.

* Public Schools Commission. *First Report.* Her Majesty's Stationery Office, 1968.

* Pym, D. *Free Writing.* University of London Press, 1956.

* Rance, P. *Record Keeping in the Progressive Primary School.* Ward, Lock, 1971.

* Rank and File. *A Teacher's Charter.* Rank and File, 1970.

* Rathbone, C. H. "A Lesson from Loughborough." *Froebel Journal,* June 1969, pp. 10–17.

———, ed. *Open Education: A Selection of Readings.* Citation Press, 1971.

Ravenette, A. T. *Dimensions of Reading Difficulties.* Pergamon Press, 1968.

Raynor, J. *The Middle Class.* Humanities Press, 1970.

* Razzell, A. *Juniors: A Postscript to Plowden.* Penguin Books, 1968.

* Read, H. *Education Through Art,* 3rd ed. Faber & Faber, 1958.

Reid, L. A. *Philosophy and Education.* International Publications Service, 1962.

* Renshaw, P. "A Re-appraisal of the College of Education Curriculum." *Education for Teaching,* Spring 1968, pp. 28–33.

Resnik, H. S. "Promise of Change in North Dakota." *Saturday Review,* April 17, 1971, pp. 67–69, 79–80.

* RICHARDSON, M. *Art and the Child.* University of London Press, 1948.

RICHMOND, W. K. *The School Curriculum.* Barnes & Noble, 1971.

RIDGWAY, L., and LAWTON, I. *Family Grouping in the Primary School.* Agathon Press, 1969.

ROBERTS, G. R. *Reading in the Primary Schools.* Humanities Press, 1970.

ROBERTS, G. R., and SOUTHGATE, V. *Reading—Which Approach?* Verry, 1970.

* ROBINSON, E. "Further Education." In *The Red Paper,* ed. by D. Gowan, R. Cuddihy, and C. Lindsey. Islander Publications, 1970.

* ———. "Fears for Status Behind 'Scrap Colleges' Call." *Times Educational Supplement,* March 26, 1971, p. 6.

ROGERS, C. R. *On Becoming a Person.* Houghton Mifflin, 1961.

ROGERS, V. R. *Teaching in the British Primary Schools.* Macmillan, 1970.

ROSE, G. *The Working Class.* Humanities Press, 1970.

ROSENTHAL, R., and JACOBSON, L. F. *Pygmalion in the Classroom.* Holt, 1968.

* ROUSSEAU, J. J. *Émile.* Dent, 1911.

* RUBINSTEIN, D., and STONEMAN, C., eds. *Education for Democracy.* Penguin Books, 1970.

* RUDD, W. G. A., and WISEMAN, S. "Sources of Dissatisfaction Among a Group of Teachers." *British Journal of Educational Psychology* 32 (1962): 275–91.

RUSSELL, J. *Creative Dance in the Primary School.* Praeger, 1968.

* SADLER, J. E., and GILLETT, A. N. *Training for Teaching.* Allen & Unwin, 1962.

SANDSTROM, C. I. *The Psychology of Childhood and Adolescence.* Pelican Books, 1968.

SAWYER, W. W. *Vision in Elementary Mathematics.* Pelican Books, 1964.

SCHEFFLER, I., ed. *Philosophy and Education,* rev. ed. Allyn and Bacon, 1966.

* SCHOENCHEN, G. G. *The Activity School.* Longmans, 1940.

* SCHONELL, F. J. *Backwardness in the Basic Subjects.* Oliver & Boyd, 1948.

* SCHOOLS COUNCIL. *Curriculum Development, Teachers' Groups*

and Centres. Working Paper No. 10. Her Majesty's Stationery Office, 1967. (a)

* SCHOOLS COUNCIL. *Society and the Young School Leaver.* Working Paper No. 11. Her Majesty's Stationery Office, 1967. (b)

* ———. *The Middle Years of Schooling from 8 to 13.* Working Paper No. 22. Her Majesty's Stationery Office, 1969. (a)

* ———. *Report 1968/1969.* Evans/Methuen, 1969. (b)

* ———. *SCOPE: An Introductory Course for Immigrant Children, Stage I.* Longmans, 1969. (c)

* ———. *Report 1969/1970.* Evans/Methuen, 1970. (a)

* ———. *"Cross'd with Adversity": The Education of Socially Disadvantaged Children in the Secondary Schools.* Working Paper No. 27. Evans/Methuen, 1970. (b)

* ———. *Teaching English to West Indian Children: The Research Stage of the Project.* Working Paper No. 29. Evans/Methuen, 1970. (c)

* ———. *Immigrant Children in Infant Schools.* Working Paper No. 31. Evans/Methuen, 1970. (d)

* ———. *Breakthrough to Literacy.* Longmans, 1970. (e)

* SCHOOLS COUNCIL/NUFFIELD FOUNDATION. *The Humanities Project: An Introduction.* Heinemann, 1970.

* SCOTT, P. "New Council to Plan Training Urged." *Times Educational Supplement,* December 26, 1969, p. 6.

* ———. "Expand Through Colleges Say Vice-Chancellors." *Times Educational Supplement,* May 15, 1970, p. 3.

* SCOTTISH EDUCATION DEPARTMENT. *Primary Education in Scotland.* Her Majesty's Stationery Office, 1965.

* SEABROOK, J. *The Unprivileged.* Longmans, 1967.

SEALEY, L. G. W., and GIBBON, V. *Communication and Learning in the Primary School,* rev. ed. Humanities Press, 1963.

* SELECT COMMITTEE ON EDUCATION AND SCIENCE. *Student Relations,* Vol. 1. House of Commons Paper No. 499. Her Majesty's Stationery Office, 1969.

* SHIPMAN, M. "Education and College Culture." *British Journal of Sociology* 18 (1967): 425–34.

———. *The Sociology of the School.* Humanities Press, 1969.

SILBERMAN, C. E. *Crisis in the Classroom: The Remaking of American Education.* Random House, 1970.

SIMON, B., and BENN, C. *Half-Way There: Report on the British Comprehensive School Reform.* McGraw-Hill, 1970.

* SIMON, B., and RUBINSTEIN, D. *The Evolution of the Comprehensive School, 1926–1966.* Routledge, 1969.

* SIMPSON, D., and ALDERSON, D. *Creative Play in the Infants School.* Pitman, 1960.

SKIDELSKY, R. *English Progressive Schools.* Pelican Books, 1970.

SLADE, P. *Child Drama.* Verry, 1954.

———. *An Introduction to Child Drama.* Verry, 1958.

SNITZER, H. *Living at Summerhill.* Macmillan, 1968.

* SNOW, G. *The Public School in the New Age.* Bles, 1959.

SPIRO, M. *Children of the Kibbutz.* Schocken Books, 1967.

* SPROULE, A. "End Compulsory R.E. Call." *Times Educational Supplement,* April 24, 1970, p. 7. (a)

* ———. "Tribunal Finds That Cheshire Head Acted 'Improperly.'" *Times Educational Supplement,* August 21, 1970, p. 5. (b)

* ———. "Panel Considers 'Trial Offer.'" *Times Educational Supplement,* October 9, 1970, p. 3. (c)

* ———. "Heads Should Work to a Seven-Year Contract." *Times Educational Supplement,* November 13, 1970, p. 11. (d)

STERN, C., and STERN, M. B. *Children Discover Arithmetic,* rev. ed. Harper & Row, 1971.

* STEVENS, F. *The Living Tradition.* Hutchinson, 1960.

* STEWART, W. A. C. "The Progressive Schools and Their Future." *New Society,* February 12, 1964, pp. 16–17.

STEWART, W. A. C., and McCANN, W. P. *Progressive Schools, 1881–1967.* Vol. 2 of *The Educational Innovators.* Macmillan, 1968.

STODDART, J., and STODDART, F. *Teaching of English to Immigrant Children.* International Publications Service, 1970.

* STOKER, D. *Immigrant Children in Infant Schools.* Evans/Methuen, 1970.

* STONE, H. *Some Play Materials for Children Under Eight.* National Froebel Foundation, 1963.

* STRAW, J. "Never Any Room for Student Violence." *Times Educational Supplement,* March 30, 1970, p. 6.

* STRAW, J.; SLOMAN, A.; and DOTY, P. *Universities: Boundaries of Change.* Panther Books, 1970.

STURMEY, C., ed. *Activity Methods for Children Under Eight.* Humanities Press, 1965.

SUGERMAN, J. M. "Research Evaluation and Public Policy: An Invited Editorial." *Child Development* 41 (1970): 263–66.

* SUTTON, C. "Curriculum Development for Teacher Education." *Education for Teaching*, Summer 1970, pp. 13–18.

* SWEIG, F. *The Worker in an Affluent Society.* Heinemann, 1961.

* SWIFT, D. F. "Who Passes the Eleven-plus?" *New Society*, March 5, 1964, pp. 6–9.

* TANNER, R. "Creativeness in Education." *Froebel Journal*, June 1966, pp. 3–7.

TANSEY, P. J., and UNWIN, D. *Simulation in Gaming and Education.* Barnes & Noble, 1969.

———. "Teaching Reading to Older Children." In *Teaching in the British Primary School*, ed. by V. R. Rogers. Macmillan, 1970.

TANSLEY, A. E. *Reading and Remedial Reading.* Humanities Press, 1967.

* TAYLOR, G. "B.Ed.—A National Waste of Scarce Resources." *Times Educational Supplement*, October 31, 1969, p. 4.

* TAYLOR, J. *Organising and Integrating the Infant Day.* Allen & Unwin, 1971.

* TAYLOR, W. *The Secondary Modern School.* Faber & Faber, 1963.

* ———. "The Study of Education." *Trends in Education*, April 1968, pp. 26–33.

———, ed. *Toward a Policy for the Education of Teachers.* Colston Research Society Papers, No. 20. Shoe String Press, 1969.

———. *Society and the Education of Teachers.* Humanities Press, 1970.

* TAYLOR, W., and BARON, G. *Educational Administration and the Social Sciences.* University of London Press, 1969.

* TIMES EDUCATIONAL SUPPLEMENT. "To Stream or Not to Stream." Editorial, January 30, 1970, p. 1. (a)

* ———. "Banning the Cane." Editorial, April 17, 1970, p. 2. (b)

* ———. "Liberal Arts Colleges?" Editorial, June 12, 1970, p. 2. (c)

* ———. "Forward to 1964." Editorial, July 3, 1970, p. 2. (d)

* ———. "Teacher Militancy and the 11-plus." Editorial, July 10, 1970, p. 1. (e)

* ———. "Teacher Tutors." Editorial, December 4, 1970, p. 1. (f)

* TIZARD, J.; RUTTER, M.; and WHITMORE, K., eds. *Education, Health and Behavior.* Longmans, 1970.

* TRAUTTMANSDORF, A. "Streamed No Better Than Non-streamed." *Times Educational Supplement*, January 30, 1970, p. 5. (a)

* ———. "C.A.S.E. Demands More Say for Parents." *Times Educational Supplement*, February 20, 1970, p. 10. (b)

TURNER, R. H. "Modes of Social Ascent Through Education." In *Education, Economy and Society*, ed. by A. H. Halsey, J. Floud, and C. A. Anderson. Free Press, 1961.

ULIN, D. S. "What I Learned from the British Schools." *Grade Teacher*, February 1969, pp. 100–03, 194–97.

* UNION OF WOMEN TEACHERS. *Policies and Services*. U.W.T., 1970.

* VAIGO, A. C. "Scandinavia: Exams Are on the Way Out." *Times Educational Supplement*, June 26, 1970, p. 16.

VAIZEY, J. *Education for Tomorrow*. Penguin Books, 1962.

VAN DER EYKEN, W. *The Pre-School Years*, rev. ed. Penguin Books, 1969.

* VAN DER EYKEN, W., and TURNER, B. *Adventures in Education*. Lane, 1969.

* VENESS, T. *The School Leavers—Their Aspirations and Expectations*. Methuen, 1962.

* VENNING, P. "New Digs Charge Will Hit Student Grants." *Times Educational Supplement*, February 12, 1971, p. 6.

* VERNON, P. E., ed. *Secondary School Selection*. Methuen, 1957.

* WAINWRIGHT, J. A. "Morals or Religion: A Survey of Surveys." *Times Educational Supplement*, March 20, 1970, p. 4.

WAKEFORD, J. *The Cloistered Elite: A Sociological Analysis of the English Public Boarding School*. Praeger, 1969.

WALMSLEY, J. *Neill and Summerhill: A Man and His Work*. Penguin Books, 1969.

* WALTERS, E. H. *Activity and Experience in the Junior School*, 6th ed. National Froebel Foundation, 1965.

* WALTON, J., ed. *The Integrated Day in Theory and Practice*. Ward, Lock, 1971.

WALTROCK, M. C. "The Learning by Discovery Hypothesis." In *Learning by Discovery: A Critical Appraisal*, ed. by L. S. Shulman and E. R. Kinslar. Rand McNally, 1966.

WANN, K. D.; DORN, M. S.; and LIDDLE, E. A. *Fostering Intellectual Development in Young Children*. Columbia University Press, 1962.

* WANSELL, G. "178 Direct-Grant Schools To Be Integrated or Inde-

pendent." *Times Educational Supplement*, March 27, 1970, p. 6.

* WARBURTON, F. W., and SOUTHGATE, V. *i.t.a.—An Independent Evaluation.* Murray & Chambers, 1969.

* WARWICK, B. *Team Teaching.* University of London Press, 1971.

WAY, B. *Development Through Drama.* Humanities Press, 1966.

WEBB, L. *Children with Special Needs in the Infant School.* Transatlantic Arts, 1968.

* ———. *Modern Practice in the Infant School.* Blackwell, 1969.

WEBER, L. *The English Infant School: A Model for Informal Education.* Agathon Press, 1971.

WEBSTER, J. *Practical Reading: Some New Remedial Techniques.* Fernhill House, 1965.

WEINBERG, I. *The English Public Schools.* Aldine-Atherton, 1967.

* WHITE, L. F. W. "Do Parents Really Have Choice in Deciding Which Schools Their Children Should Attend?" *Times Educational Supplement*, July 10, 1970, p. 13.

* WHITELEY, J. "Nuffield Science 5/13." *Times Educational Supplement*, January 10, 1970, p. 19.

* WHITFIELD, R. C. "The Core of a Study of Education for Teachers." *Education for Teaching*, Summer 1970, pp. 19–24.

* WIGG, D. "Muslims Demand Equal Religious Opportunity." *Times Educational Supplement*, September 4, 1970, p. 10.

WILKINSON, R. *Gentlemanly Power: British Leadership and the Public School Tradition.* Oxford University Press, 1964.

* ———, ed. *Governing Elites: Studies in Training and Selection.* Oxford University Press, 1970.

* WILLIAMS, E. M., and SHUARD, H. *Primary Mathematics Today.* Longmans, 1970.

* WILLIAMS, W. "The Proper Concerns of Education." In *Education for Democracy*, ed. by D. Rubinstein and C. Stoneman. Penguin Books, 1970.

WILLIG, C. J. "Social Implications of Streaming in the Junior School." *Educational Research* 5 (1962): 151–54.

WILLMOTT, P. *The Evolution of a Community: A Study of Dagenham After 40 Years.* Humanities Press, 1963.

WILLMOTT, P., and YOUNG, M. *Family and Class in a London Suburb.* Humanities Press, 1960.

* WILSON, B. "The Teacher's Role—A Sociological Analysis." *British Journal of Sociology* 13 (1962): 15–32.

* WILSON, J. *Public Schools and Private Practice.* Allen & Unwin, 1961.

WINNICOTT, D. W. *The Child, the Family, and the Outside World.* Penguin Books, 1970.

* WRAGG, E. C. "Forum—Practical Training for Graduates." *Times Educational Supplement,* February 6, 1970, p. 15.

* YARDLEY, A. *Young Children Learning; Reaching Out; Exploration and Language; Discovering the Physical World; Senses and Sensitivity.* Evans, 1970.

* ———. *The Teacher of Young Children.* Evans, 1971.

YOUNG, M. *The Rise of the Meritocracy.* Penguin Books, 1958.

* YOUNG, M., and McGEENEY, P. *Learning Begins at Home.* Routledge, 1968.

YOUNG, M., and WILLMOTT, P. *Family and Kinship in East London.* Humanities Press, 1957.

* YUDKIN, S. *0–5: A Report on the Care of Pre-School Children.* National Society of Children's Nurseries. Allen & Unwin, 1967.

INDEX

Index

Blyth, W. A. C., 68, 73
Boards of Education, U.S., 18, 232–33
Body movement as creative expression, 135–36, 224
Breakthrough to Literacy, 222
British Broadcasting Corporation (B.B.C.), 16, 134, 213
Brown, Mary, 142
Bruner, Jerome, 39
Buildings and grounds, 139–40, 195, 196, 199

C

Change
agents of, 15–22, 47, 64
features transferable to U.S., 212–14
American approach to, 14
social conditions affecting, 22–26
units of, 26–27
Child-centered philosophy, 30–33, 43, 44, 93, 102, 121, 190
Children
American and English, compared, 23–24
gifted, 93
teacher relationships with, 8, 23, 33, 71–72, 216–17, 230
Children and Their Primary Schools. See Plowden Report
Church schools, 149
Class bias, 124, 199–200
blindness to, 202–04
financial, 194–99
middle-class anxiety, 205–08
1944 Education Act, failure of, 201–02
in secondary schools, 200–01
and segregation, 204–05, 208–10
Classroom freedom, England and U.S. compared, 8–9, 24–25
See also Informal teaching
Collective power, teachers', 66–67, 119
Colleges of Education, England, 5, 13, 15–16, 19, 30, 35–36,

47, 50, 67, 81, 85, 102, 120–21, 138, 147, 148, 158, 197, 226
American teachers' colleges, compared, 163
criticisms of, 174–77
features transferable to U.S., 226–27
lecturers, 177–79
practice teaching, 167–71, 226
small, intimate, 164–65
student life, 171–74
tutorial teaching, 165–67, 226–27
vocational emphasis, 159–63
Colour Factor rods, 114
Community control of schools, 18, 22, 232–33
See also Parent-school relationship
Competition, decline of, 185, 187, 221
Conservative Party, 129, 177, 208
Cooperative nurseries, in U.S., 84
Cooperative teaching. See Team teaching
Corporal punishment, 44, 217
Courtesy in English schools, 187
Craftsmanship, 186, 224, 225, 228
Creative arts, 116, 128, 135–36, 218, 221, 224, 225, 228, 232
Cross-age grouping. See Family grouping
Cuisenaire rods, 114
Curriculum
advisers, 19
control and change of
English schools, 16–18, 51, 63, 65–66, 99, 101, 121, 151, 197, 212–13, 231–33
U.S. schools, 2, 7–8, 20–22, 27, 52–53, 64, 218
research, 22

D

Davies, Brian, 33
Day care centers, 95
Dearden, Robert, 37–38

Full school day from age five, 98–99, 220
Furniture, versatile, 109–10

G

Gardner, Dorothy, 87, 91
Ghetto schools. *See* Poverty area schools; Working-class children
Gifted children, 93
Goodlad, John I., 104
Grade-level standards, absence of. *See* Family grouping; Nongrading

H

Hadow Report, 97, 128
Halsey, A. H., 80
Handicapped children, 119
Head teacher, English, 100, 121, 144, 150, 230
and American principal, compared, 7, 18–19, 47–49, 215–16
authority, power, and status of, 51, 53–54, 59–61, 197, 212
changes affecting, 58–59
features transferable to U.S., 214–16
parents, relationship to, 9, 55–56
role of, 9, 46, 49–52
salary of, 48
training of, 47
women, 100, 220
Her Majesty's Inspectors (H.M.I.), 16, 30, 67, 99, 120
Hierarchical tradition, English, 13, 57–58, 60, 66
High standards, and informal methods, 189–90, 227–28
See also Standards

I

Individualized teaching, 107–08, 128, 196, 220–21

Infant schools, 96–98
characteristics, 98–116
features transferable to U.S., 219–23
history of, 97
problems of, 116–24
Informal teaching, 4
demands of, 69–71
and high standards, 189–90, 227–28
transplanting, to U.S., 191–94
and working-class children, 92, 94
See also Classroom freedom
Initial teaching alphabet (i.t.a.), 115
Inner London Education Authority, 26, 50, 140
In-service teacher education, 120–22
Integrated day, 105–06, 142–44, 220, 225
criticism of, 153
Intellectual approach to teaching, 35
Intellectual Growth in Young Children, 87–90
Interaction Analysis, 134
Intervention, selective, 113–14
Irwin, Martha, 139
Isaacs, Nathan, 88
Isaacs, Susan, 79, 113, 219
contribution of, 91–92
influence of, 86–93
Intellectual Growth in Young Children, 88–90
Malting House School, 87–88
Social Development of Young Children, 90–91

J

Jackson, Brian, 129
John Birch Society, 22
Junior high schools, U.S., 146
Junior schools, England
characteristics of, 132–47
features transferable to U.S., 223–26
history of, 128–32
problems of, 147–57
Juniors, 147

272

Index

U.S., 7–9, 19, 22, 48, 56–57, 101,
   230, 232
 See also P.T.A.
Parsons, Talcott, 35
Past decisions, as priority, 194–95
Permissive approach. See Child-
   centered philosophy
Pessimistic critique, 41–42, 44
Peters, R. S., 37
Philosophic approach, 37–38, 43
Piaget, Jean, 39, 91, 114–15, 136,
   155, 222
Pike, Geoffrey, 88
Play groups, 84, 85, 123
"Please Sir" (TV series), 204
Plowden Report, 25, 29, 39, 59,
   124, 145, 149, 197, 232
 criticisms of, 30–42
 on infant schools, 96, 97, 100, 122
 on nursery schools, 80, 81, 85
Political interference. See
   Community control of schools
Poverty area schools, 25–26, 83,
   86, 92, 94, 148, 192, 198
 See also Educational Priority
   Areas; Inner London
   Education Authority;
   Working-class children
Practice teaching, 167–71, 226
Precious, Norman, 142
Preschool education. See Nursery
   schools
Pre-School Play Group Association,
   86
Primary schools, English
 aims, 36–37
 criticism of, 42–44
 defined, 3n.
 features, essential, 229–33
 infant schools. See Infant schools
 junior schools. See Junior schools
 nursery schools. See Nursery
   schools
 problems of, 4
 reform in, 12–15
 teacher training. See Colleges of
   Education
 See also English education

Principal, American
 authority, power, and status of,
   54–55, 60
 and English head, compared, 7,
   18–19, 47–49, 215–16
 parents, relationship to, 56–57
 role of, 47–49, 52–53
Privacy, respect for, 135, 224
Private schools
 England, 41, 42, 84, 97–98, 195
 U.S., 4
Process rather than product, concern
   for, 136, 223
Professors. See Colleges of Education
Progressive education, American
   dislike for, 93
Psychological services, 119, 122, 154–
   55
Psychology
 of nursery school children, 90–92,
   94
P.T.A., 9, 54
 See also Parent-school relationship
Punishment, 44, 93, 217
 See also Discipline

R

Racial problems
 England, 25–26, 203
 U.S., 1, 26, 124, 192, 199
Radical critique, 40–41, 43–44
Rank and File, 59
Razzell, Arthur, 147
Reading instruction, 108, 115–16,
   219, 221
Reforms needed in England, listed,
   197–98
Religious education, England,
   149–51
Remedial classes, 119
Research, in England and U.S.,
   compared, 22
Rise of the Meritocracy, The, 34
Robbins Report, 201
Role-playing in nursery school, 92
Russell, Wilma, 139

A 2
B 3
C 4
D 5
E 6
F 7
G 8
H 9
I 0
J 1